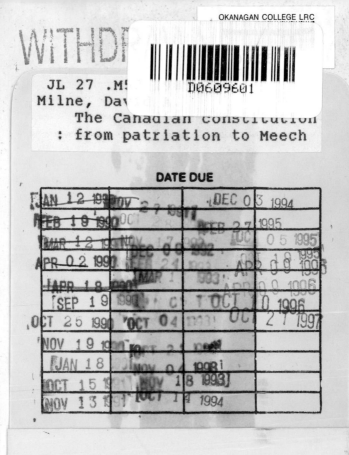

The Canadian Constitution

The Canadian Constitution

From Patriation to Meech Lake

DAVID MILNE

James Lorimer & Company, Publishers
Toronto, 1989

ISBN 1-55028-227-1 paper
1-55028-229-8 cloth

Cover design: Brant Cowie
Cover photo: Brian Willer

Canadian Cataloguing in Publication Data

Milne, David, 1941-
The Canadian constitution
Rev. ed. of: The new Canadian constitution.
Bibliography: p.
ISBN 1-55028-229-8 (bound) ISBN 1-55028-227-1 (pbk.)

1. Canada — Constitutional history. 2. Canada — Constitutional law. 3. Canada — Politics and government — 1980-1984.* 4. Canada — Politics and government — 1984- .* I. Title. II. Title: The new Canadian constitution.

JL27.M55 1989   342.71'02   C89-093552-1

James Lorimer & Company, Publishers
Egerton Ryerson Memorial Building
35 Britain Street
Toronto, Ontario M5A 1R7
Printed and bound in Canada
6 5 4 3 2 1 89 90 91 92 93 94

Contents

To Peter H. Russell

Preface

Only six years have elapsed since the publication of The New Canadian Constitution, and yet, in the wake of Meech Lake and hundreds of charter decisions in the Canadian courts, a revision of the book is clearly necessary. This new edition reviews these and other constitutional matters since 1982, while at the same time providing Canadians with a preview of likely developments in the constitutional field.

I want to thank the Senate Research Committee of the University of Prince Edward Island for a grant to make this revised edition possible. That support gave me the enviable assistance of several research assistants: Courtney Betty, Michelle Gallant and Wanda Wood. Each has contributed generously to this project, and I wish to thank all of them. But I would be derelict in my duty if Wanda were not given special commendation. She has worked tirelessly gathering documents, doing clippings, assembling binders and tracking down leads in the library. Without her help, this book would have been a much heavier task.

I also wish to thank several constitutional scholars who took the time to discuss the subject with me, including Peter Russell, Peter Hogg and Marc Gold. While all were as informative and stimulating as ever, none bears any responsibility for judgements that I have made. I also owe a debt of gratitude to several politicians and officials close to the constitution-making process who have shared their thoughts and impressions with me. I have profited enormously from these conversations. Premier Ghiz of my own province has been especially helpful in this regard and I thank him for his generosity.

I acknowledge with pleasure the strong support which my university has offered me over the years in many research endeavours. My colleagues in the department have also been kind and supportive, and I thank in particular John Crossley and Barry Bartmann for their encouragement during the writing of this edition. As for my secretary, Brenda Young. she has been as diligent, cheerful and unruffled as ever with the pressures of this additional work. What would life be without her?

The bringing out of this revised edition is also a testament to the fine working relationship which I have always enjoyed with my publisher and his staff. I want to thank my editor, Curtis Fahey, and copy editor, Judith Turnbull.

With projects such as this one, undertaken during the short period between university teaching terms, the heaviest burden always seems to fall on one's family. But mine has carried on with patience and good cheer. My love and thanks go to Fran and Kyla.

David Milne
Charlottetown, P.E.I.

Chronology:
Major Events in the
Constitution-Making Process,
1980-88

1980

Feb. 18   Return of the Liberals to power under
            Trudeau's leadership

April 15   Official referendum campaign begins in
            Quebec

May 20   Federalists win the Quebec referendum

June 9   First ministers meet on the constitution
            and set up   agenda of 12 topics

July 7-25   Negotiations between officials and

Aug. 25-29   ministers responsible for
            federal-provincial relations in
            Montreal, Toronto and Vancouver;
            final negotiating session in Ottawa to
            prepare for Conference of First
            Ministers

Sept. 7   Quebec circulates Kirby memorandum

Sept.8-12	First Ministers' Conference in Ottawa; conference failure announced Sept. 13
Oct. 6	Federal government places unilateral resolution before Parliament
Oct. 14	Premiers meet in Toronto and court challenges are announced
Oct.23-24	Closure applied and vote taken to send constitutional resolution to a Special Joint Committee
Nov. 5	Britain's Select Committee on Foreign Affairs studies Britain's role regarding the Canadian Parliament's request

1981

Jan. 12	Justice Minister Chrétien tables the government's amendments to the resolution
Jan. 30	Britain's Select Committee reports that "Westminister cannot act as a mere rubberstamp on all requests coming from the Parliament of Canada"
Feb. 3	Manitoba Court of Appeal supports Ottawa by a vote of 3 to 2
Feb. 13	Special Joint Committee reports to Parliament with proposed amendments; debate begins Feb. 17
March 19	Liberal House Leader Yvon Pinard gives notice of motion to limit debate
March 31	Newfoundland Court unanimously declares Ottawa's unilateral resolution illegal
April 13	Parti Québécois wins Quebec election

April 15	Quebec Court of Appeal supports Ottawa by a vote of 4 to 1
April 16	Premiers in Gang of Eight sign Constitutional Accord in Ottawa
April 23	Final amendments to the resolution adopted in the House of Commons
April 28-May 4	Supreme Court of Canada hearing
Sept. 28	Supreme Court brings down its judgement
Oct. 3	Quebec's assembly passes a resolution denouncing federal unilateralism
Oct. 20	Premiers meet in Montreal
Nov. 2-5	First Ministers' Conference on the Constitution begins
Nov. 5	Announcement of substantial federal-provincial agreements over the constitution; Premier Lévesque dissents
Nov. 9	Quebec declares it will not attend federal-provincial conferences, nor participate in constitutional meetings
Nov. 24	House approves amendment to the Charter of Rights strengthening the section on sexual equality
Nov. 26	House approves amendment restoring "existing" aboriginal treaty rights section
Dec. 2	House of Commons approves final constitutional resolution
Dec. 2	Quebec refers the question of its right of veto to the Quebec Court of Appeal
Dec. 8	Senate approves final constitutional resolution; Governor General Schreyer gives his assent

Dec. 9	Constitutional resolution delivered to Buckingham Palace

1982

Jan. 14	British Prime Minister Margaret Thatcher turns down Premier Lévesque's request to delay proceedings until courts have ruled on Quebec veto
Jan. 28	British Court of Appeal rejects native peoples' claims against patriation package
Feb. 19	Quebec ends boycott of all intergovernmental meetings, though boycott on constitutional meetings remains
March 8	British House of Commons passes the Canada Act
March 25	House of Lords passes Canada Act
March 29	Queen Elizabeth II gives royal assent to Canada Act
April 7	Quebec Court of Appeal unanimously declares that Quebec has no veto
April 17	Queen Elizabeth II proclaims Canada Act
June 23	Quebec enacts Bill 62 to apply the notwithstanding clause to all provincial legislation
Sept. 21	B.C. legislature passes constitutional resolution to include property rights in charter
Nov. 25	Royal Commission on the Economic Union and Development Prospects for Canada, under chairman Donald Macdonald, established

Dec. 6 — Supreme Court rules against Quebec's right to constitutional veto

Dec. 17 Lévesque writes to Trudeau demanding return of veto or full compensation on opting out and exemption from section 23 of the charter

Dec. 22 Joint Senate-Commons Committee struck to study Senate reform

Dec. 22 Special committee established under Keith Penner to examine self-government for native peoples

Dec. 23 — Trudeau responds to Lévesque, giving his continuing support to a veto for Quebec, but indicating that it could only come by convincing all the other provinces

1983

Feb. 2 Joe Clark resigns as leader of the PC opposition party

Feb. 10 Lévesque agrees to attend First Ministers' Conference on aboriginal rights, but not to participate in amendments

March 10 Métis request and receive permission to have separate representation at conference

March 14 Coalition of First Nations breaks away from Assembly of First Nations and boycotts conference

March 15-16 First Ministers' Conference on aboriginal rights

March 16 First amendment to the constitution proposed under Canada's new amending formula

March 17	Office of Aboriginal Constitutional Affairs established in Ottawa
May 18	Native leaders give approval to amendment prepared at the First Ministers' Conference requiring three more conferences on aboriginal questions
May 20	NDP government in Manitoba agrees to introduce constitutional amendment accepting modern bilingual commitments to replace obligations of 1870 Manitoba Act; Ottawa and Manitoban francophones accept agreement and Bilodeau court challenge to English-only laws is adjourned
June 9	Quebec Court of Appeal upholds primacy of charter section 23 over Quebec's Bill 101
June 11	Brian Mulroney wins leadership of PC party
June 29	House of Commons passes first amendment to constitution concerning aboriginal questions
Aug. 29	Brian Mulroney wins seat in Central Nova
Aug. 30	Formation of Parti Nationaliste (PQ federal party) announced
Oct. 6	Commons unanimously passes motion to accept proposed amendments on bilingualism in 1870 Manitoba Act
Oct. 20	Penner Report recommending aboriginal self-government tabled in the Commons

Nov. 30	Saskatchewan becomes last province (excluding Quebec) to give its consent to 1983 amendment

1984

Feb. 27	Manitoba legislative session ends with amendment on French language rights dead
Feb. 29	Trudeau announces his intention to resign
March 9	Second conference on aboriginal rights finds six provinces opposed to aboriginal self-government
April 5	Federal government refers the question of the legality of Manitoba's English-only statutes to the Supreme Court
April 24	Ontario makes French an official language in the court system
May 3	First charter decision from Supreme Court
May 23	Trudeau appeals to Premier Davis to make Ontario officially bilingual; request is refused
June 10	PQ convention determines to fight next election on sovereignty issue
June 16	John Turner wins Liberal leadership race
June 21	First amendment of the new constitution proclaimed
June 28	French made an official language of the Northwest Territories
June 30	Trudeau leaves office and Turner is sworn in as prime minister
July 9	Turner calls an election for September 4

July 26	Supreme Court overturns four sections of Bill 101, including provisions for language rights for anglophones, as violations of the charter
Aug. 3	Davis rejects Mulroney's request to make Ontario officially bilingual
Sept. 4	Tories win federal election, capturing 211 of the 282 seats (and 58 of 75 ridings in Quebec)
Sept. 17	Supreme Court strikes down a section of the Combines Investigation Act, claiming that it allows for "unreasonable search and seizure"
Oct. 8	Davis announces his intention to resign
Oct. 16	Lévesque announces policy of seeking rapprochement with Ottawa and renewed constitutional negotiations
Nov. 19	Lévesque ends debate by announcing that sovereignty will not be an issue for next Quebec election
Dec. 4	Seventh PQ cabinet minister quits over Lévesque's decision
Dec. 6	Mulroney and Lévesque meet regarding future constitutional discussions
Dec. 12	Atlantic Accord with Newfoundland is announced, ceding exclusive federal control of the offshore and promising future constitutional entrenchment of the agreement

1985

Jan. 2	Quebec Superior Court strikes down provisions regarding commercial signs in Bill 101

Jan. 19	PQ special convention endorses Lévesque's call to drop sovereignty from next election; radicals walk out
March 3	Quebec Liberals approve policy program, including five-point constitutional demands that would have to be met for Quebec to sign the 1982 constitutional deal
April 3	Third constitutional conference over aboriginal rights ends in failure
April 17	Charter's section on equality rights, section 15, becomes effective
April 24	Federal Lord's Day Act ruled unconstitutional by Supreme Court
May 7	Resolution of Mulroney government to curtail the powers of the Senate introduced in the House
May 28	Alberta legislature gives unanimous approval to Triple-E Senate proposal
June 6	Two-day talks between native leaders and federal and provincial ministers end unsuccessfully
June 13	Supreme Court rules that all of Manitoba's English-only laws are invalid
June 20	Lévesque announces his retirement
Sept. 5	Macdonald Commission unveils its report
Sept. 29	Pierre Marc Johnson replaces Lévesque as PQ leader and premier
Dec. 2	Liberals win Quebec election under Robert Bourassa
Dec. 13	Bourassa and Mulroney meet

1986

May 9	Rémillard outlines Quebec's constitutional proposals at Mont Gabriel
July 4	Mulroney announces new drive, under leadership of Senator Lowell Murray, for constitutional talks with Quebec
July 21	Mulroney sends letter to premiers urging their cooperation in his attempts to bring Quebec into constitutional fold
Aug. 11-12	Premiers' Conference in Edmonton issues declaration that Quebec's constitutional issues will be focus of constitutional agenda
Sept. 24	Murray and Rémillard meet
Dec. 22	Quebec Court of Appeal upholds decision striking down French-only commercial signs in Bill 101

1987

March 5-6	First full federal-provincial meeting on Quebec's constitutional demands
March 17	PM invites premiers to First Ministers' Conference on Quebec's constitutional agenda at Meech Lake on April 30
March 27	Final required conference on aboriginal rights fails
April 9	Supreme Court declares charter does not guarantee right to strike
April 30	First Ministers' Conference at Meech Lake leads to an agreement (known

	as the Meech Lake Accord) to amend the constitution
May 11	Meech Lake agreement debated in the House of Commons
May 25	Final day of hearings in Quebec City on the Meech Lake agreement
May 27	Trudeau attacks Meech Lake in press
June 3	Second First Ministers' Conference at Langevin Block to study legal draft of the Meech Lake Accord and to approve final changes; unanimous agreement to proceed with the amendments, known as the 1987 Constitutional Accord
June 23	National Assembly of Quebec approves the accord
Aug. 27	Trudeau appears before the Joint Senate-Commons Committee to attack the accord
Aug. 28	Premiers' Conference in Saint John agrees not to reopen the accord
Sept. 21	Joint Senate-Commons Committee recommends endorsement of accord without changes
Sept. 23	Saskatchewan ratifies accord
Oct. 13	Liberals win every seat in New Brunswick election; a known opponent of the Meech Lake agreement, Frank McKenna, becomes premier
Oct. 25	Commons approves accord
Dec. 7	Alberta ratifies accord
Dec. 23	Yukon Court of Appeal rejects argument that the federal government violated rights of Yukoners in signing the accord

1988

Jan. 28	Canada's abortion law is struck down by the Supreme Court
Feb. 25	Supreme Court rules that bilingual requirements in North-West Territories Act of 1886 continue to apply to Saskatchewan (and Alberta)
March 8	NDP government defeated in Manitoba legislature
March 30	Trudeau speaks against the accord in the Senate
April 26	Tory minority elected under Gary Filmon in Manitoba
April 21	Senate amends the accord and returns it to Commons
April 25	Saskatchewan approves bill to override French language rights in the province and to furnish, with federal help, some services in French to francophones
May 2	Commons approves motion for property rights in the charter
May 13	Prince Edward Island ratifies accord
May 25	Nova Scotia ratifies accord
June 22	Commons again ratifies the accord and overrides the Senate
June 22	Alberta introduces bill to overturn North-West Territories Act that had provided for French language rights in province
June 29	British Columbia and Ontario ratify accord

July 7	Newfoundland becomes eighth province to ratify Accord; House of Commons passes Bill C-72, extending official bilingualism in federal offices, tribunals and courts
July 15	Federal Court of Appeal upholds political rights of federal public servants under the charter
July 21	Manitoba announces that it will hold hearings on the Meech Lake Accord and that the minority government will introduce the resolution in the upcoming session
Aug. 19	Annual Premiers' Conference in Saskatoon authorizes Premier Getty of Alberta to send out a task force to consult with other provinces on Senate reform, including his Triple-E Senate proposal
Aug. 31	House of Commons passes legislation implementing the free trade deal with the United States; Ontario reserves the right to challenge the constitutional validity of the legislation
Sept. 5	PM signs land-claims agreement with Dene
Sept. 26	Federal Court quashes a legal challenge to the Meech Lake agreement from the Canadian Coalition on the Constitution
Sept. 29	New Brunswick begins public hearings on Meech Lake
Oct. 1	Prime Minister Mulroney calls an election for November 21

Oct. 26	Lubicons agree to land settlement with Alberta and the federal government concurs
Nov. 21	Conservatives under Brian Mulroney win the federal election
Dec. 15	Supreme Court strikes down French-only sign provisions in Quebec's Bill 101
Dec. 16	Manitoba government introduces Meech Lake resolution into legislature
Dec. 18	Premier Bourassa announces that he will invoke the notwithstanding clause of the Canadian and the Quebec rights charters to override the Supreme Court judgement on French-only signs, while permitting bilingual signs inside commercial premises
Dec. 19	Premier Filmon of Manitoba withdraws the Meech Lake resolution from the provincial legislature, linking it to the question of the treatment of the linguistic minority in Quebec, and calls for a First Ministers' Conference on constitutional reform on "an urgent basis"
Dec. 20	Premier McKenna of New Brunswick calls for amendments to Meech Lake that will protect minority language rights across Canada and for removal of the notwithstanding clause from the charter

Introduction

Patriation; a new charter of rights and freedoms; official bilingualism; an amending formula established and then adjusted; a "distinct society" clause for Quebec; new appointment procedures for senators and Supreme Court justices; action on the spending power, immigration, natural resources — the list goes on and on. This has been a decade when the constitutional logjam broke and amendments spewed forth in record numbers. Never has so much been done in so short a time.

We could just as easily add: never has the country more crucially depended on the constitution-makers. Upon their work, so it seemed, rested the integrity and endurance of the nation. After all, the amendments were not trivial. They touched upon the constituent elements of nationhood — the fundamental building blocks that would either sustain the edifice or bring it down. No people understand that primal function of constitutional politics better than Canadians. They have looked here for more than a quarter of a century to find a way to avoid national defeat and dismemberment.

Sombre brooding over the nation's future had been going on since the late 1960s and culminated in 1980, when a state-backed referendum in Quebec sought to pull the province out of the federation. As analysts ruminated over the future of Quebec separatism, Western separatism, and alienation in the North and East, the country seemed to be pulled apart, not by the class warfare feared by classical liberal thinkers but by deep-seated regional tensions and bitterness. Though some of these divisions found their roots in Canadian capitalist development, Canadians did not typically turn to standard left-right ideological remedies. Instead they looked increasingly toward constitutional solutions to their problems.

The process began first with Quebec. It was natural that a constitutional focus would be given to this struggle. Quebec nationalism had always preoccupied itself with the nature and rights of the local state, which was controlled by French-speaking Canadians, and the state's relations with the larger political community surrounding it. That preoccupation had driven the constitutional debate from the time of the Quebec Act in 1774, and nothing in the modern expressions of Quebec nationalism changed this elemental fact. Whether the question concerned the recognition of Quebec as a distinct society, the conferring of special powers upon that society, or even the issue of outright independence for Quebec, the agenda always suggested some constitutional outcome. When the focus was the other pole — namely, the question of French-speaking Canadians' rights in the larger political community — the result was the same: constitutional remedies of one kind or another suggested themselves. The prominence given to "high politics" of state, complete with all the expected symbolism, is a Quebec legacy to which Canadians have become increasingly attached.

It will become evident in the course of this book how much that Quebec legacy has driven constitutional events in the 1980s. Briefly stated, three powerful and competing francophone leaders, each speaking from a long tradition, asserted themselves on the Canadian constitutional stage. The first and most dramatic was former Quebec premier René Lévesque, who led the battle to transform Quebec into a sovereign state. That enterprise foundered. Former prime minister Pierre Elliott Trudeau is the second protagonist who drew on another part of that Quebec legacy: he led francophones (and other Canadians) in a struggle to reshape and to reform the larger Canadian political community so that Quebec would not have to act out the separation script. In 1982 he won the first major encounter, with constitutional recognition of a French-English partnership in an officially bilingual Canada.

There was yet a third protagonist, Quebec Premier Robert Bourassa, who returned to provincial politics several years after Trudeau's triumph. A resurrected politician from the 1970s, he was the leader of those francophones who, while remaining loyal to Canada, sought to give Quebec more power, not independence. This was the moderate nationalist agenda, attractive not only to provincial politicians but to all who wished to see the Quebec homeland, if not independent, then at least expanded and strengthened. Profiting from the earlier unilateral imposition of Trudeau's terms upon a weakened, separatist-led Quebec, as well as from the more flexible attitude displayed by Brian Mulroney and the Conservative government elected in 1984, Bourassa sought to extract concessions in order to secure Quebec's belated consent to the 1982 constitutional changes. He won much of his agenda at the negotiating table in the second round of talks at Meech Lake in 1987, although he still had to contend with the power and criticism of both the radical nationalists and the Trudeau forces to make that achievement stick.

By late 1988, with the legislated approval of the deal by Parliament and eight provinces, success appeared to be tantalizingly near. And yet, virtually at the eleventh hour, a Supreme Court judgement on December 15, striking down the French-only commercial signs provision of Quebec's Bill 101, forced Bourassa's hand; to overcome that judgement and to impose his own compromise between minority rights and the collective will of the francophone majority, he was forced to invoke the notwithstanding clause of the Charter of Rights and Freedoms. That choice, together with his "outside (unilingual)-inside (bilingual)" compromise, left Bourassa vulnerable to massive criticism from nationalists, minorities, and rights advocates in Quebec; it also directly imperilled the Meech Lake Accord, as the minority Conservative government under Premier Gary Filmon of Manitoba consequently withdrew its support for the resolution. At year's end, with both Manitoba and New Brunswick demanding changes to the accord to protect linguistic minorities in a new round of bargaining between first ministers, it appeared that the constitutional option of the moderate nationalists might also founder.

Even though one set or other of these Quebec personalities and issues dominated the constitutional stage throughout the decade, once the whole drama was set in motion, other players sought to make themselves heard. On the governmental level, the leaders of the regions of East and West would also have their moment to speak and to act both in 1982 and 1987. They would invariably talk of economic and political inequality, of historical injustices and of the promise of a new future. These interventions would usually take at least two forms: one, a demand that Parliament be made more sensitive to their rights and concerns; another, that the provinces in these regions enjoy more authority to chart their own course. Once again, though the underlying causes for their dependency might lie in the complexities of modern political economy, these leaders looked to constitutional change as a remedy for their grievances. Whether the issue was a reformed Senate with stronger representation from the regions or whether it was greater regional control over natural resources, the constitutional preoccupations remained.

The drama became so absorbing that it drew in non-governmental actors: after all, was this not the "people's play"? While political leaders did in fact monopolize the stage, they were sometimes gracious enough to make room for other actors, albeit in minor parts. Occasionally leaders of civil-rights groups would have their moment, as would defenders of linguistic minorities, women or aboriginals. Here, too, the players respected the rules and pitched their claims in constitutional terms. Whether it was liberty secured through a charter, equality under law, or justice won in court-enforced guarantees of aboriginal self-government, the actors poured their energies into their parts. The play was thoroughly entrancing — indeed, the best political spectacle in town.

In short, though the title of this "play" — *The Canadian Constitution* — may at first induce yawns, no member of the audience has reason to be bored. The story, as told in this book, comes in seven parts. There is first a brisk refresher required before the real play can get underway: chapter 1 sets the stage and lays out the essential background needed (aficionados may pass). Chapter 2 takes up the story immediately following the defeat of Lévesque's referendum on Quebec independence and follows the strategy and bargaining until the breakdown of talks in September 1980. Chapter 3 chronicles the exciting days when the federal government decided to act alone to amend the constitution of Canada, without the consent of the provinces, and the chapter ends with the intervention of the courts. The dramatic decision of the Supreme Court and its role in forcing renegotiation constitute the subject of chapter 4. Chapter 5 explains how the final 1982 agreement was reached, follows the painful aftermath, with Quebec left out of the deal, and concludes with the proclamation of the new constitution. The course of constitutional developments over the next several years is the subject of chapter 6. While this chapter touches briefly on the unsuccessful work on aboriginal rights, it is largely concerned with the attempted constitutional rapprochement with Quebec at Meech Lake. Chapter 7 reviews the importance of constitutional change over the whole decade, pointing out strengths and weaknesses, contradictions and anomalies.

Readers familiar with the first edition of this work will quickly note the changes in this new edition: a new introduction and chronology, a new chapter updating development from 1982 to Meech Lake, and a new concluding chapter with commentary on the Meech Lake agreement and on the Supreme Court interpretations of the Charter of Rights and Freedoms. Readers should be warned, however, that the first 160 pages of the first edition have not been touched and, consequently, there remain a few outdated references. The contents of the appendices have changed. The 1983 constitutional amendment respecting aboriginal questions has been added as Appendix 2. The extracts from the Kirby memorandum have been deleted from this edition, and the texts of both the Meech Lake communiqué and the final legal wording of the 1987 Constitutional Accord replace it as appendices 3 and 4. Readers will thus find

...ot simply an expression of collective self-interest;
...ce the constitution represents a fundamental bar-
...in over larger moral purposes, the issue is one of
...inciple and not merely power.

In this chapter, the interrelationships between
...overnmental politics and the constitution are briefly
...xamined. First is an account of the effort to patriate
...he constitution with an amending formula accept-
...ble to the governments of Canada. Then the origins
...and development of the constitutional struggle over
French-English relations, a charter of rights, and the
status of Quebec in Canada are discussed. Finally, the
discussion turns to regionalism in Canada and its role
in the constitution-making process of 1976-82.

Rules for Constitutional Change:
The Price of Legal Independence

In effecting patriation the new Canadian constitution
brought to a close a difficult and protracted struggle
among governments, which began in 1927 with the
first attempts to get agreement on an amending
formula. The problem surfaced that year in the
negotiations which led to Canada's independence as a
self-governing dominion within the British Common-
...ealth, formally recognized by the Statute of West-
...inster in 1931. The issue was straightforward: how
...uld all governments in Canada be brought to agree
...a procedure for altering the constitution so that
...ther legal recourse to Britain would be unnecessary.
...r to 1927, it had seemed perfectly acceptable to
... Britain make the desired changes to the Britis...
... America Act. The convention had al...
...ped that Britain would do so only on the...
...joint address of the House of Com...
..., at that time usually without con...

in the appendices complete documentation on general
constitutional amendments from patriation and the
charter in 1982 to Meech Lake in 1987.

One final word of caution: this play is ongoing —
the last scenes in the Meech Lake story have not been
written. Nor can its outcome be predicted with any
assurance. That should not spoil things but rather add
to the anticipation, whatever the tastes of the reader. I
have, however, for purposes of analysis only, assumed
the finality of Meech Lake. This seemed more sensible
than to interrupt the flow of argument with a string of
"ifs"!

1
Politics and the Constitut
An Overview

Despite the best efforts of constitutional historians
make their subject look dreary and formal, Canadi
constitutional politics is fascinating. It dramati
intergovernmental conflict over questions of po
and philosophy better than any passing policy disp
could possibly do. In a federal state like Canada, c
stitutional politics also permits us to monitor
stresses of federal-provincial and interprovincial r
tions and to see the directions in which the cou
might move.

The constitution in a federal state forms a m
power grid from which all the governmental p
get their authority. Not only does it distribu
power among legislatures, it also limits the ex
these powers, imposes obligations upon gov
and declares and enforces through the cou
principles which thereafter bind all t
Governments therefore are acutely sens
position in the power grid and wary
changes in the distribution of power
governing how changes are made. Th

the provinces. But when Canada was about to end its legal subordination to Britain, a new way of changing the constitution had to be found, and this mechanism would have to respect the federal nature of the country. When no agreement was reached by 1931, Britain retained in section 7 of the statute the legal power to change the written constitution by virtue of Canada's failure to assume it. Over the next half century, the retention of this colonial link offended Canadian legal nationalists who looked to the ritual of finally bringing home the constitution with undisguised enthusiasm.

But even then the symbolic completion of Canadian independence from Britain hid another agenda: the formal structuring of power within Canada. As fondly as any federal or provincial politician might have wished for such symbolic independence, it could not be achieved without settling, through the amending formula, who had the power to determine the constitutional future of the country. Since the actors in the negotiations were all the governments of the country, it is understandable that jockeying to advance or defend sectional interests and jurisdictions was a part of any such discussions.

That made coming to an agreement tough enough. But Canada had additional difficulties. Its history, geography, and economic, cultural and political diversity made a settlement of the power question almost insuperable. First, there was a linguistic division between the French- and English-speaking peoples, principally reflected in the partition of the country into a francophone Catholic Quebec and a predominantly English society everywhere else. Much of Canada's troubled history revolved around the history of these two peoples, especially the treatment of linguistic minorities. Secondly, there were the regional grievances over the unequal benefits and burdens of the union and the wide variations of size, power and wealth among the provinces, which tended to be reflected in demands for special treatment in any amending formula. Because Ontario and Quebec included well over half the Canadian population, it was obvious that amending formulas from federal states with populations less unequally distributed would not easily apply here. Finally, there was antagonism towards the federal government itself on the part of both the "have" and the "have-not" provinces: from the have-nots, the resentment and fear of mere dependents, and from the haves, rivalry for pre-eminence in the state.

Given these divisions, it is not surprising that conference after conference floundered on a sea of distrust and ambition. So great were these forces that amendment proposals were almost invariably complicated, requiring unanimous consent on certain key "entrenched" areas of the constitution and more flexible procedures for others. Even so, the various tortuous formulae outlined in Table 1 failed over the years to win complete agreement. Most often (in 1936, 1964, 1971, 1981), Quebec was the holdout.

The formulae cited in the table reflect delicate governmental balancing of fundamental issues bearing on constitutional amendments in a federal state. All general formulae, for example, declare that basic changes to the Confederation bargain require the consent of not just Parliament but also of a majority of provinces. In proposals forwarded after 1927, the consent of a majority of provincial governments was also required to represent at least 50 per cent of the Canadian population. In all proposed formulae, it has been the consent of *governments* — federal and provincial

—not peoples that has been the historical basis for proposals on constitutional change. Only with Prime Minister Trudeau's unilateral plan of 1980 was the suggestion of change by referenda introduced; even then the new method was advanced as a deadlock-breaking alternative to the "normal" route. Table 1 also shows that until a regionally based proposal was made by Trudeau in 1971, it was always strictly numbers of provinces that would form the basis of constitutional agreements, with no regional quotas. Also, prior to 1971 all formulae gave no single province a veto. Population requirements in formulae since 1936 then entailed the consent of Quebec *or* Ontario; changing demographic conditions might favour diferent provinces, but it is unlikely that shifts in population would ever permit a single province a veto.

In this way, the general formulae sought to provide flexibility for constitutional change and at the same time to enshrine the principle of equality of provinces. This could be accomplished, however, only by giving every province blocking powers on certain key matters. In the column on unanimity, it is striking that every amendment formula except the Victoria proposal set out certain vital areas that could not be changed without every province's consent. Apart from the constant inclusion of language and educational rights, and the usual listing of provincial representation in the federal houses of Parliament and the role of the monarchy, the significant pattern is the consistent demand for protection of provincial legislative powers as outlined in section 92 of the British North America Act. (Federal legislative powers would presumably not need special protection since Ottawa was a required party in any constitutional amendment formula.) At no time except during the Trudeau era

Table 1
CONSTITUTIONAL AMENDMENT PROPOSALS, 1927-81[1]

Year/Formula for General Agreement	Sections Changed by Unanimity Only	Special Features/Comments
1927 House of Commons, Senate, a majority of the provinces (no population requirement)	s.92 h.12[2] (solemnization of marriage) h.13 (property and civil rights) h 14 (administration of justice) s.93 (minority education rights) s.133 (French and English language guarantees)	Of provincial powers listed in section 92, marriage and justice were considered important especially to Quebec, while property and civil rights, as their most general and important source of legislative authority, were vital to all provinces. Minority rights and language guarantees hereafter fall into the "entrenched" category
1936 (near agreement; newly elected Quebec Premier Duplessis dissents) House of Commons, Senate, 6 provinces having 55% of population (i.e., must include Ontario or Quebec)	All sections above s.92 h.4 (establishment of provincial offices and officers) h.5 (management and sale of public lands) h.8 (municipal institutions)	New concern over provincial representation in Parliament and the monarchy reflected in the unanimity column. In section 92 the provinces agree to permit changes in the area of property and civil rights (h.13) and local

	Sections	
	h. 15 (imposition of provincial fines) s.9 (role of the monarchy) s.21 (number of senators) s.22 (provincial representation in the Senate) s.51 (House of Commons representation) s.51A (minimum provincial representation in House of Commons) Amending procedure	matters in the province (h. 16) without unanimity, in return for a right to "opt out." A few other items in s.92 are added to the unanimity list to compensate
1950 not settled	All sections above s.92 s.91 (federal powers)	Entrenchment of whole division of powers pushed by Ont. and Que. but resisted by Sask.
1964 (near agreement; Quebec withdraws) Fulton-Favreau formula: House of Commons, Senate, 7 provinces comprising at least 50% of population	All sections above s.109 (provincial property)	Delegation[3] of powers possible between Parliament and a minimum of 4 provinces except that provinces restricted to transferring only s.92,h.6 (prisons), h.10 (local works), h.13 and 16. Only

Table 1 continued

Year/Formula for General Agreement	Sections Changed by Unanimity Only	Special Features/Comments
		the power to make statutory enactments in these areas could be transferred, not jurisdiction
1971 (near agreement; Quebec withdraws) Victoria formula: House of Commons, Senate, majority of provinces comprising: every province which has or had 25% of Canada's population, at least 2 provinces from both Atlantic and Western Canada (making up at least 50% of population for latter)	None	No categories for unanimity. The largest provinces — Ontario and Quebec — given a veto perpetually. "Regional" formula disguises preferred status for 2 central provinces. A provision for overriding the Senate written in
1979 Alberta formula: House of Commons, Senate, 7 provinces comprising at least 50% of	Amending procedure	Reactivation of "opting out" from 1936 formula, but applying to all provincial powers and rights (s.92). Any province may block an amend-

population

1981
April 16 Constitutional Accord (Gang of Eight's slight reworking of Alberta formula)

s.9
s.51A
s.133

Composition of Supreme Court
Amending procedure

ment in its jurisdiction. Equality of provinces restored. Provision for overriding Senate available

Financial compensation to be made for opting out or delegating powers (latter applies to provinces *and* Parliament)

1981
Parliament's unilateral resolution, April 23: Victoria formula with population requirement for West deleted

None

Amendment by referenda is added wherever a federal proclamation is supported by a majority of voters, both overall and in quota of provinces as set in Victoria formula

Notes

[1] Amendments which strictly concern the constitution of a province may, with the exception of the office of lieutenant governor, be taken unilaterally (s.92[1]). Since 1949 the same right to change the constitution as it affects exclusively federal matters was, with certain exceptions, granted to the Parliament of Canada (s.91[1]). In addition, all earlier proposals had assumed that amendments which concern Parliament and one or some provinces *only* may be achieved by legislative action of the concerned parties. [2] s. = section; h. = subsection. [3] Delegation: the transfer of powers between, and by mutual consent of, two levels of government.

has there been a formula with no protection for each province on at least some parts of the list of provincial powers. Even during the Depression, when the need for national solutions to social and economic distress led to demands for transferring provincial powers to Ottawa, many parts of section 92 required unanimous consent of the provinces for changes. Even constitutional changes in the vital area of property and civil rights (section 92, head 13) and local matters (section 92, head 16), which might be made without unanimity, could still be evaded by a province "opting out."

What is striking in the variation of the pattern is the increase in the areas requiring unanimity during the postwar period of federal pre-eminence. In 1950, to combat centralizing pressures, Ontario and Quebec demanded that the whole division of powers be entrenched; nothing could be changed without unanimous consent. This inflexibility made it highly unlikely that Ottawa would gain any powers from the provinces other than the bare minimum acceptable to all provinces. Despite vigorous opposition from Saskatchewan (where a CCF government placed a high priority on national social security programs), that blanket protection for the provinces continued through part of the 1960s, with the special provisions for delegation offering the only flexibility. Yet in 1964 even so security-conscious a formula as Fulton-Favreau, which gave every province a veto over any changes in the division of powers, was found unacceptable by Quebec premier Jean Lesage. By then, with the "Quiet Revolution" underway, the formula appeared to threaten Quebec's own aspirations.

After it took power in 1960, Lesage's new, confident administration in Quebec reversed the defensive nationalist policies of its predecessors and began to demand more powers for Quebec under a more flexible amendment procedure. In this campaign of national self-awakening, Quebecers found an understanding ally in the province of Ontario. Ontario shared Quebec's concerns over earlier federal intrusions into provincial jurisdictions, and it fully sympathized with that province's determination to develop provincial power. Ontario had already begun to build up administrative power and expertise to rival Ottawa's and it strongly resented federal pretensions to pre-eminence. Since it was axiomatic that Ontario with its vast population could not occupy a status inferior to that of Quebec, Ontario was virtually carried along with Quebec's demands for preferred status. The radical new formula which Prime Minister Trudeau offered in 1971 met these concerns, while at the same time it made changes wanted by the federal government easier to achieve.

In Trudeau's so-called Victoria formula, the protections of unanimity for all provinces were removed in exchange for a permanent veto for Quebec and Ontario. For the first time the inequality of provinces was openly declared as a guiding principle in the formula. Under the new arrangement, Quebec and Ontario could secure their constitutional objectives even with half of the provinces in the Atlantic region and the West in opposition. But provincial authority could be transferred to the federal level in crucial natural resource fields, such as control and ownership of oil and gas, without the agreement of Alberta, for example. Though this formula, so heavily weighted in favour of Central Canada, nearly passed in 1971 (Quebec finally pulled out feeling it had not won enough power over "social policy" in return for its agreement to patriation), by 1976 it was unacceptable to Alberta, British Columbia and others.

The play of political interest and the distrust it generated is evident in all the formulae forged over the years. Three interrelated dimensions of conflict cut across the deliberations: the weaker provinces' hostility toward Central Canada; the central provinces' rivalry with the federal government; and the linguistic division between Quebec and the other provinces. In the end, most players simply preferred the safety of the British connection to the uncertain dangers of a final Canadian constitutional marriage.

But the impasse on procedure did not bring the substance of constitutional change to a standstill. It was still possible to change the legislative division of powers by common agreement of the governments. In fact, during this period there were two major transfers of provincial authority to the federal government: unemployment insurance in 1940 and old age pensions in 1950. In addition, either level of government had the power to change its own constitutional area: section 92(1) of the BNA Act gave the provinces the power to amend matters in their own exclusive jurisdiction except for the office of lieutenant governor, and the British North America Act (Number 2), passed in 1949, enabled Parliament to alter its exclusive areas (section 91[1]). Moreover, the constitution still permitted special changes of particular importance to one or more provinces but not to all. The admission of Newfoundland into the union in 1949 by agreement of that province and Parliament was a good example of the flexibility that existed despite federal-provincial deadlock on a general amending procedure.

The Founding Peoples and a Charter of Rights

Beginning in the 1960s, after the postwar period of federal leadership, an explosive growth of province-building especially in Quebec and Ontario shifted the constitutional balance of power toward the provinces. Ontario was disturbed about being forced into national programs such as medicare and preferred instead to enlarge its own capacity. Quebec demanded a restructuring of the Canadian state so that it reflected the duality of the two peoples of Canada and gave Quebecers plenty of elbow room to be "masters in their own house."

Quebecers demanded that the Quebec state strengthen French language and culture, modernize the educational system, take a more decisive role in the planning and direction of the economy, which traditionally (and especially during the long reactionary rule of Premier Maurice Duplessis) had been left largely to anglophones, and secure a better deal for Quebec either within or if necessary outside the federal system. These demands came from francophones who increasingly saw themselves as Québécois rather than French Canadians, and they reflected a new national awakening in the province. Quebecers demanded a status worthy of a distinct people, a "nation" occupying a "homeland" with as yet an imperfect means to express itself. Quebec francophones rapidly came to accept these values and the resulting need to expand Quebec's constitutional powers. At the same time, many Quebecers sought explicit recognition of the role of the French fact in the Canadian state, which apart from Quebec had for so long been entirely founded on English Canadian supremacy.

Two branches of Quebec's new post-Duplessis elite

expressed these feelings of national awakening in diametrically opposed strategies. One branch, which gravitated toward the "Quebec as homeland" option, was a fusion of separatist and radical nationalist groups that splintered off from the moderate nationalism fostered by Liberal Premier Jean Lesage and moved toward the goal of Quebec independence. This movement emerged as a powerful political force with the founding of the Parti Québécois in 1968 under the leadership of René Lévesque, a former minister in the Lesage cabinet. The other branch of the Quebec elite, under the leadership of Pierre Elliott Trudeau, expressed Quebec's national resurgence in a concerted effort to restructure *Canada as the homeland* for *all* francophones. The options then became renewed federalism versus separatism, Canada or Quebec as homeland. This struggle within Quebec's francophone elite has dominated Canada's constitutional politics for the past two decades.

Quebec's "Quiet Revolution" rocked the Ottawa establishment. In 1965, in part as a response to Quebec's aspirations, Prime Minister Lester Pearson's Liberal government passed the Established Programs Act, permitting provinces to opt out of certain shared-cost national programs and to receive financial compensation. Since the areas in which compensation were provided, such as medical and social assistance plans, were under provincial jurisdiction in any case, it seemed both fair and appropriate to do so. But because only Quebec took advantage of the offer and set up its own programs, the province acquired a *de facto* "special status" which troubled Quebec federalists like Trudeau. In a related gesture of accommodation, Ottawa proceeded to add more Quebecers to the federal civil service, and to commission and then act on the Report on Bilingualism and Biculturalism.

Yet the steady advance of separatist sentiment in Quebec signalled an emerging crisis for Canada. The rise of the Front de Libération du Québec and the increasing political terrorism in the province, which culminated in the October Crisis of 1970, made the legitimate movement for independence seem more menacing. It was natural for federalists in English-speaking Canada and Quebec to see major constitutional reform as an appropriate response to this threat. Prodded by Ontario's Confederation of Tomorrow Conference in 1967, the Pearson government started the first of a series of federal-provincial constitutional conferences in February 1968. The leader of the federal strategy against separatism and nationalism in Quebec was already effectively Pierre Elliott Trudeau, then Pearson's minister of justice. Under his direction, a plan was prepared for enshrining and popularizing the "homeland Canada" option.

The broad thrust of federal political strategy depended on patriating the constitution and entrenching a charter of rights which would symbolize the common political values of all Canadians and which would secure the French fact from coast to coast. This linking of civil liberties with the protection of French language rights was a politically artful response to the rise of separatism. For English Canada, a rights charter defused anglophone backlash against French power such as bedevilled the Official Languages Act, a federal statute enacted in 1968; within Quebec it promised to undercut the notion that Quebec was the only home for francophones. Presented as a question of "rights," this strategy for national unity pitted the rhetorical power of "freedom" against the Sirens' call of Quebec nationalism.

But the nation-building potential of a charter of rights could be expected to go well beyond symbolism and rhetoric. As careful students of American constitutional developments have long recognized, a rights charter as interpreted by a pro-federal Supreme Court can declare and enforce common values and practices in an otherwise diverse federation. In fact, no other national institution might attempt to do so with a surer authority than a court under the venerable mantle of constitutional law. There was therefore more than a hint of covert war against the excesses of Quebec nationalism and regionalism in Trudeau's proposal for unified values under a charter of rights.

Needless to say, the political strategy was disguised with simple talk of "people's rights." In fact, the whole federal plan was sold as a "people's package," which did not directly concern governments or powerfully affect the balance of federal-provincial relations. Although technically an entrenched charter would subtract legislative power from each level of the federation (though not necessarily equally), the power to pronounce on human rights would by the charter be transferred to the federally appointed Supreme Court of Canada. Under these conditions, enforcement of the people's charter might unify the country around individual rights, challenge the moral primacy of Canada's regional communities and resolve some of the chronic historical grievances of the French- and English-speaking peoples.

Naturally, as the chief custodians of regionalism, the provinces were not enthusiastic about an entrenched national charter. But its public appeal was difficult to resist. After a period of inconclusive negotiations, a much reduced charter was agreed to by first ministers at Victoria, in June 1971.

In addition to the amending formula discussed earlier, the Victoria Charter provided for the entrenchment of certain fundamental rights — freedom of thought, conscience and religion; freedom of opinion and expression; freedom of peaceful assembly and association — subject to a broad override. These freedoms could be limited "in the interests of public safety, order, health or morals, of national security, or of the rights and freedoms of others." Political rights were reaffirmed in that there could be no discrimination against a citizen's political rights on grounds of "national origin, colour, religion or sex." In the key area of linguistic rights, the Trudeau government gave way to provincial opposition over the entrenchment of minority language educational rights and legal and equality rights in return for provincial agreement to extend the protection of the French language in political and legal institutions. In the charter, French was declared an official language which could be used in every provincial legislature but Saskatchewan, Alberta and British Columbia; both official languages would prevail in the courts of Quebec, New Brunswick and Newfoundland; all provincial statutes were to be published in both languages; French might be used in communication with provincial governments in Ontario, Quebec, New Brunswick, Prince Edward Island and Newfoundland; and any extensions of these rights by a province could not later be revoked except by constitutional amendment. In terms of the earlier constitution and history of Canada, these initiatives by the English-speaking provinces were a dramatic turnaround, and a logical step from the 1968 Official Languages Act.

In return, Ottawa promised to consult provinces on appointments to the Supreme Court, to provide for a majority of Supreme Court justices trained in civil law, to repeal its power to reserve and disallow legislation passed by the provinces, and to concede provincial supremacy in certain areas of social policy like family, youth and occupational allowances. Since social policy was mostly under provincial jurisdiction, in effect Ottawa had to renounce the right to initiate national programs in these areas without consultation and to leave room for provinces to pursue their own programs. Evidently the concessions were not regarded as sufficient in Quebec, however, for no sooner had Premier Robert Bourassa returned home from Victoria than he was subjected to intense pressure to back out of the provisional agreement. When the Quebec premier caved in, he scuttled the prospects for constitutional talks for the next few years.

Although discussion of the issue continued through public meetings sponsored by the Special Joint Committee of the Senate and House of Commons on the Constitution of Canada, it was not until 1974 that Prime Minister Trudeau again broached the subject of an amending formula. After getting a lukewarm response from the provinces, Trudeau began to drop the first of many hints that Ottawa might act unilaterally if consensus could not be achieved at least on patriation, an amending formula and a charter of rights. As for the provinces, most key players demanded increased provincial powers as part of any overall settlement. Although discussions proceeded in 1975 and 1976, the prospects for agreement were not encouraging.

The 1976 election of the Parti Québécois, which promised good government and a referendum on "sovereignty-association," helped set the stage for a resolution of the constitutional question. For the first time the two hostile francophone elites confronted one another from their respective bunkers in Quebec City and Ottawa. Over the next four years a propaganda war was waged for the hearts and minds of Quebecers with the future of Quebec and Canada in the balance. The debate covered familiar ground: the costs and benefits of federalism and separatism; federalism versus separatism as a protector of Quebec's distinctive language and culture; Trudeau's individual and minority rights versus Lévesque's "tribal" nationalism; Quebec or Canada as homeland. Although Claude Ryan, the former influential newspaper publisher who replaced Bourassa as leader of the Liberal party in Quebec, formally carried the banner of battle within the province, especially as the May 1980 referendum date approached, it was always Trudeau and Lévesque who captured the imagination of Quebecers. Each stood as a powerful symbol of Quebecers' split loyalties toward a new Canada and a new Quebec.

Since maintenance of the status quo was never an option, it was expected that serious constitutional change would result from this struggle, no matter who won. The 1976 separatist victory had shocked English-speaking Canada out of its complacency. Appeals to Quebecers to stay in the union poured in from all parts of Canada. Never before had Canadians been so moved to defend the ideal of a federal union or so ready to admit the shortcomings of their Confederation. This unity movement, blessed and supported by the federal government, reached its high point immediately prior to the May 1980 referendum. Popular expressions of the movement included sentimental vehicles such as the "people-to-people" petition, which pleaded with Quebecers to stay in Canada, while more enterprising groups set to work revamping the British North America Act. Much of this amateur constitution making was naïve, if well motivated. Over the next few years, there were enough constitutional proposals floating about to confound specialists, let alone the general public. But the process of public participation in constitutional renewal mattered more than the product; the groundwork was being laid for public acceptance and expectation of constitutional change.

While the federal government abetted the movement by sending on tour the Pepin-Robarts Task Force on Canadian Unity, many provinces — especially British Columbia and Ontario — and Quebec's Liberal Party under Claude Ryan prepared reports on several aspects of constitutional reform. These initiatives turned up a longer list of grievances, more proposals and even more hope for comprehensive change.

Surprisingly, however, this public celebration of federalism before the dark spectre of a separatist Quebec did not lead the provincial governments of English Canada to rally around Ottawa. Although Trudeau strengthened his bargaining hand over linguistic rights, especially after the passage in 1976 of Quebec's Bill 101, the language bill declaring Quebec unilingual, he could not translate public fears over separatism into federal pre-eminence. Tough bargaining over the constitution went on as usual. Nor did separatism give Quebec more muscle with other governments. Quebecers were later to learn that having installed the separatists in power with no separatist mandate, they had weakened their province's bargaining power in the constitutional talks.

Regionalism and the Rise of the West

The second, but hardly noticed event which prepared

the way for Canada's new constitution was the emergence of a unified constitutional interest in the Western provinces. After the Organization of Petroleum Exporting Countries' cartel brought about a spectacular rise in oil and gas prices beginning in 1973, the politics of energy accentuated Western discontent. Alberta, British Columbia and Saskatchewan, the resource-rich provinces, were thrust into the front ranks of political and constitutional discussions. The premiers of these provinces began to plan joint initiatives, and for the first time since Confederation a regional bloc emerged with the power to rival Ontario and Quebec.

Under Western leadership, the politics of regionalism was given new momentum and legitimacy. The Atlantic and Western regions had always protested the domination of the Canadian state and economy by Central Canada, but their demands for change became pressing as the prospects of wealth from oil and gas appeared to give at least some of the provinces in these regions an equal chance to prosper. But federal policy over these natural resources seemed to threaten the development of these regions. Apart from federal insistence on holding control over offshore resources, the chief struggle took place over the price for oil and gas in Canada, which Ottawa kept at artificially low levels. (Electrical energy from Central Canada was not treated in a similar manner.) An aggravating factor was Ottawa's choice of Sarnia, Ontario, as the location of a major petrochemical refinery, an industry Alberta was trying to foster. In addition, Ottawa consistently lowered the potential revenues for the West from their resources by imposing a variety of tax measures, including export surcharge taxes. When Saskatchewan sought to maximize the benefits it received from its resources by enacting measures to ration potash (to restrict supply and indirectly fix export prices), and to tax excess profits on oil, Ottawa sided with the private companies involved in a successful constitutional challenge to the resource powers of the provinces in 1974. All of these actions pushed the producing provinces into a united regional bloc which demanded that Ottawa stop exploiting Western resoures for the benefit of Central Canada and the Liberals' electoral base there.

Such a political and constitutional challenge was also attractive to the provinces in Eastern Canada. Not only did they share the resentment over Central Canadian dominance, they also anticipated a better economic future. Newfoundland and Nova Scotia sympathized with Western Canadian claims and sought to enlist Western support in their bid for control and development of offshore resources. In this respect, the economics of regionalism were certainly powerful enough to offset any timidity arising from the East's "have-not" status.

But the rise of regionalism was not just a matter of jurisdictional disputes. Canada was already beginning to feel the effects of a powerful shift in economic and political power away from Central Canada. The West was challenging the historic model of Canada with its growing cities and wealth. The state of Western provincial finances and investment funds was healthier than those of Quebec or Ontario, both of which were experiencing a severe weakening of their manufacturing base. Thus when the provinces from the Western and Atlantic regions demanded a new deal from Canada, they did so not primarily out of historic grievances but because contemporary realities demanded that Canada's emerging patterns of power be recognized.

With these pressures, the agenda for constitutional change expanded beyond the federally sponsored "people's package" to include two major provincial concerns. The first was the renegotiation of the division of powers to increase the provinces' powers, especially over offshore and onshore natural resources and communications (telephone and broadcasting systems). Such authority in provincial capitals would strengthen local economic and cultural development and place Canadians' regional loyalties on a stronger footing. In addition, under consideration were proposals to give control over family law matters such as marriage and divorce to the provinces, to give provinces some powers over the fisheries, and to enshrine the principle of equalization payments to have-not provinces in the constitution. The second major concern was to "federalize" the central institutions in Ottawa, especially the Senate and Supreme Court, so that their membership and direction would better reflect distinct provincial interests and needs. The fathers of Confederation had intended the Senate to perform this function, but it had never done so. Instead the Senate had the reputation of a rest home for retired politicians who rarely defied the House of Commons. The Supreme Court, whose members were also exclusively appointed by Ottawa, was similarly suspected of having a pro-federal bias. By permitting a stronger role for provincial governments in shaping these institutions, it was hoped that regional alienation from Ottawa would decline.

With Quebec in the hands of the separatists and regional demands becoming stronger, Trudeau felt that the time for federal action was approaching. Discouraged with the pace of negotiations, he unveiled in 1978 a two-phase process of reform and constitutional change in Bill C-60. Phase one (deadline, July 1, 1979) would complete the updating of the British North America Act in federal areas of jurisdiction; phase two (deadline, July 1, 1981 — the fiftieth anniversary of the Statute of Westminster) would complete the process in the thorny area of federal-provincial powers. Although phase one would be undertaken with as much provincial consultation as possible, the federal government maintained that all the changes fell directly within its own jurisdiction and that they therefore could be implemented unilaterally under section 91 (1). The federal plan for phase one was to entrench a preamble stating the aims of the Canadian federation subscribed to by Parliament, to entrench a Canadian charter of human rights and freedoms in federal areas of jurisdiction only, to entrench the Supreme Court of Canada and change its composition, and to reform the Senate.

That strategy ended in disaster. Not only did Parliament fail to meet its deadline, but, under pressure from the opposition and from provincial premiers, the government referred the question of its unilateral right to amend the Senate to the Supreme Court. It lost. The court found that provincial consent was necessary to such a restructuring. As an essentially federal institution, the Senate could not be considered a subject purely within the concern of a single level of government.

Meanwhile, for Ottawa, life at the bargaining table was getting no easier. The combination of powerful Western provinces and Quebec, together with more aggressive regional pressures from Atlantic Canada, especially Newfoundland, was not easy to resist. The demands on federal powers in many areas, from the fisheries to international relations, had never been greater nor their implications more serious for the federation as a whole. While signalling a willingness to compromise, the federal government attempted to limit the extent of the concessions as much as possible and to secure in return an agreement on linguistic rights. Trudeau was determined to have action "before the electors of Quebec are called upon ... to choose between political independence on the one hand, and on the other, the preservation of a status quo which federal and provincial governments have proved incapable of changing despite 51 years of effort."

By February 1979 the federal government appeared ready to accept the demands of the West over natural resources, even if other issues still remained unresolved. However, the Liberal agenda was put into limbo by the defeat of Trudeau's government on May 22, 1979, and the formation of a Conservative minority government under Joe Clark. The Clark government's idea of Canada as a federal state was much closer to regionalism. Clark's theme of Canada as a "community of communities" was sweet music to the premiers' ears, especially when it promised transfers of powers on offshore jurisdiction to the provinces. It looked as though federal-provincial conflict was about to be toned down and that Trudeau and his plans would become mere footnotes in the history of failure over the constitution. But the Clark government's inexperience turned events around. Not seven months later, its first budget was repudiated in the House of Commons on the eve of Trudeau's would-be political retirement. The country was immediately forced into an election which pre-campaign polls suggested would be won by the Liberal party under Trudeau. He and his lieutenants, especially cabinet veteran Allan MacEachen, reversed the earlier Liberal defeat and on election night, February 18, 1980, a triumphant Trudeau was returned with a majority just in time to take on his old separatist enemies in the May 1980 referendum.

As it turned out, the federal campaign against separatism had to be waged without any constitutional renewal. The only positive alternative which the federalists inside and outside of Quebec offered was the *promise* of significant change. That promise was made by Quebec Liberal leader Claude Ryan, but more particularly by Prime Minister Trudeau and virtually all of the provincial premiers. In the end Quebecers decided to deny Lévesque the mandate to negotiate sovereignty-association for which he had campaigned so hard. The vote was not overwhelming, however, since 40.5 per cent of the electorate were ready to choose the separatist route. It was also not an absolute vote of approval for federalism, but one conditional upon significant reform. If the fight for a federal union — for one and not two Canadas — were to succeed, the onus would now be upon the winners to give form to their rhetoric at the constitutional negotiating table.

2
Option 1: Negotiation with the Provinces

Prime Minister Trudeau lost no time in pressing home his advantage in the wake of the PQ referendum: after sending his constitutional lieutenant and justice minister, Jean Chrétien, on a whirlwind tour of provincial capitals, he summoned the premiers to a First Ministers' Conference in Ottawa on June 9, 1980.

To the federal Liberals, constitutional renewal meant resolving the "Quebec problem" without fanning the flames of regionalism. They were prepared to offer certain concessions to the provinces (though preferably less than what circumstances had forced them to agree to in February 1979) in return for securing linguistic justice for the two founding peoples. As usual, the Liberal conception of such a settlement between English- and French-speaking Canadians was the entrenchment of bilingualism and of the educational rights of official linguistic minorities all across the country. This program for national unity and renewal was contained within the "people's package" of human rights and freedoms, together with patriation of the Canadian constitution. Although events would later show that the federal Liberals were ready to compromise on almost all the general human rights and freedoms in the package — until left with a weak charter of rights that made a mockery of legal protection of civil liberties — they were not willing to give up the linguistic core of their strategy.

The link between this plan for federal renewal and the political revival of Pierre Elliott Trudeau was obvious. After being snatched from would-be retirement, delivered with an election victory and then permitted to preside as prime minister over a federalist win in the Quebec referendum, Trudeau must have found events more than a little fateful. In politics, such a resurrection could not but be portentous. Even before the June meeting, Trudeau had determined that, with or without the premiers, the government would act swiftly to implement *at least* that constitutional package.

But the post-referendum outlook of most provinces was quite different from Trudeau's. The federalist victory reduced concern over national unity as it affected linguistic matters and encouraged a complacent attitude toward the "Quebec problem," especially since the Parti Québécois was now thought to be a lame duck government. The premiers, boasting not a single Liberal among them, mostly looked to constitutional renewal for solutions to their own regional grievances and could not support the political timetable of a national government so heavily dominated by Ontario interests and anti-separatist Quebecers.

In between these two colliding views sat a reluctant player. The PQ government, its sovereignty-association proposal rejected, was in the awkward position of complying with the federalist option against which it had so recently campaigned. Not only was Lévesque's government expected to negotiate *within* the Canadian federation, but to do so gracefully. Under no circumstances, therefore, would Quebec permit itself to be isolated on any item during the negotiation process. Since the regional conception of a federal state suited it far better than Trudeau's idea of Canada, it was easy enough for Quebec to align itself with the discontented blocs of provinces without taking a strong leadership role and then to await the outcome. If the talks failed, it would be vital to show Quebec's ongoing cooperation in the negotiations and to demonstrate that the process necessarily betrayed Quebec's deepest interests. If the federalists were not to play into the hands of the separatists, an accommodation would be required.

But events on June 9 did not suggest that such a bargain would be likely. A statement of constitutional principles that would have affirmed federalism and the status of the French and English languages was proposed by Trudeau and rejected by the premiers. They preferred instead to leave these broad issues to be defined during the summer's negotiations. Moreover, the agreed agenda of twelve items was a pot-pourri of federal and provincial interests with no clear priorities or linkages made to competing conceptions of the country. To resolve all twelve topics — natural resources, communications, the Senate and Supreme Court, family law, fisheries, offshore jurisdiction, equalization, a charter of rights and amending formula, powers over the economy, and a preamble — within the strict three-month timetable (June 9– September 8) imposed by Trudeau was a tall order.

Since there was no grappling with the inherently contradictory agendas advanced by regional and national actors, nor with the relative priorities or possible compromises within them, the struggle to define the shape of Canada would have to be fought out on every agenda item and any concessions left to be settled on an *ad hoc* basis. The three "packages" into which the agenda could be divided were too complicated to become the basis of federal-provincial trade-offs even if the negotiations had been structured to produce such a result.

These packages consisted of the "people's package" desired by Ottawa, which included patriation (with the usual federal-provincial dispute over an amending formula), the Charter of Rights, and a new constitutional preamble; an "institutions package" to include a new Senate and a new Supreme Court, largely supported by both levels of government but of special interest to the provinces; and a "powers package" of agenda items of which all but "powers over the economy" were provincial concerns. The first was essentially the federal nation-building plan which clashed with the ambitions of the PQ and of the regional interests of other actors. As a bloc of constitutional demands it could not be simply exchanged for the powers package since there were too many objectionable features in it. From the point of view of the federal government, the powers package could not be accepted as a bloc since only *some* of the provincial demands were seriously negotiable. Moreover virtually every item in the powers package invited a dispute between the parties over the merits of national and regional perspectives. Even the institutions package was riddled with the same tensions.

Given the unwieldiness of the packages, progress toward an acceptable common ground depended heavily on flexibility by the key players, especially over resource topics and the Charter of Rights. The importance of these issues was reflected in the choice of the co-chairmen of the Continuing Committee of Ministers on the Constitution. Justice Minister Jean Chrétien symbolized the stake the federal Quebec elite put in securing their referendum victory through an entrenched national charter; Roy Romanow, attorney general of Saskatchewan, symbolized the now dominant, resource-conscious Western leadership among the provinces. If an agreement were to emerge, these interests had to come to terms.

But, no such entente developed. Instead, the provinces generally worked toward compromise and consensus *among themselves* on most agenda matters to foil any federal use of "divide and rule" tactics, and they were determined not to give ground over the key federal interest, the charter. In building an interprovincial common front, this strategy worked remarkably well. Despite divergent regional interests, the West and most of the East, including Quebec, joined forces in a common front on most agenda items, thus isolating Ottawa and its most consistent ally, Ontario.

Although Ontario had been one of the first to show the other provinces the rudiments of province building with its own administrative growth and development planning, it did not wish to see its fellow provinces use their new bureaucratic expertise to upset Ontario's comfortable position in Confederation. Hence, Ontario backed Ottawa in its confrontation with the Parti Québécois and generally accepted federal plans for constitutional extension of minority language educational rights and for a charter of rights (provided, of course, that Ontario itself was not legally compelled to bear the financial and political costs of becoming a bilingual province). Ontario took a similarly self-interested stance when it sided with Ottawa in its showdown with Alberta over energy pricing. As the chief beneficiary of the national economy policy for many generations, Ontario was also disturbed at obstructions to the national market which provincial or regional preferential policies for hiring and buying presented. Ontario accordingly backed Ottawa's demands for stronger national control over the economy. Such a record compromised Ontario's ability to play its preferred role as "honest broker" between the contending interests.

The federal government played its hand cagily. On one side, it took a tough negotiating posture, especially over resource topics and the economy; on the other, it refused to commit itself firmly on subjects like communications, the Senate or the Supreme Court. In fact, Ottawa offered the provinces *less* than what it had been prepared to give in the February 1979 talks. On natural resources, it pulled back from its offer to give provinces power over interprovincial trade in natural resources except in situations of "compelling national interest" and it refused to budge from its position that provincial power should not extend to international trade in these resources. In addition to withdrawing some earlier offers, Ottawa brought forward the entirely new "powers over the economy," an item designed to counteract any concessions it might make to the producing provinces. To strengthen federal control over the economy and bar special provincial protectionist measures, such as "locals first" labour policies and restrictive property laws, Ottawa demanded more powers over trade and commerce, a strengthened section 121 which would prohibit protectionist barriers to the economic union and an entrenchment of mobility rights, which would entitle Canadians to move to another province, gain employment and buy property there.

The other side of the federal game plan consisted of offering partial concessions to the provinces and, where convenient, in expressing benign non-commitment. Although federal planners had made provision for further compromises if provinces met their vital demands, there was no question that Ottawa was playing hard ball in anticipation of a break in provincial resistance to the charter. It never came.

In fact the provinces had been brought to near or complete unanimity on the principle of a charter at least twice in the prior decade: first with the Victoria Charter, and recently, in the February 1979 negotiations. By the time of the summer 1980 negotiations, however, the positions of most provinces — especially those in Western Canada — had stiffened considerably. With the separatists defeated in the referendum, the provinces began to listen more and more to Manitoba's arguments that the charter was not compatible with parliamentary democracy and that it would cause a massive shift of power from legislatures to courts. Such a transfer would in their view seriously disrupt provincial ambitions for regional development. Some sections of the proposed charter, especially mobility rights, struck hard at provincial power to foster economic development, as did the federal proposal for a national economic union. There was no question that many parts of the charter would limit the legislative authority of provinces who, after all, had exclusive authority over "property and civil rights." What made the whole question dangerous was that it was impossible to judge just how far the charter might limit provincial powers.

But provincial concerns were not confined to a defence of the provinces' constitutional turf; often they were honest reactions to the administrative headaches, cost or policy implications of a charter. For example, the right of witnesses in criminal and penal proceedings to give evidence either in French or English placed a heavy financial and administrative burden on the provinces. The right to equality appeared to limit the ability of the provinces to apply affirmative action programs, while the right to hold property threatened the land control measures of Prince Edward Island and Saskatchewan. Mobility rights appeared to deprive have-not provinces of the power to defend their residents with job preferences, and all provinces of the power to regulate professional groups within the province.

If the provincial governments were unhappy with many of the specific provisions as well as the principle of a charter, the federal Liberals were most disappointed over the lack of support for their linguistic strategy. Only four provinces supported the entrenchment of minority language educational rights, with most siding with the Parti Québécois on the issue.

By the time the Continuing Committee of Ministers on the Constitution met again in Ottawa in August just prior to the First Ministers' Conference, many of the provinces' objections to the charter had been considered by the federal government and minor adjustments made. The only major changes were the elimination of property rights from the package, the exception of affirmative action programs from the equality rights provision, the promise that courts would not necessarily exclude improperly obtained evidence, and the elimination of the right of witnesses in criminal and penal proceedings to give evidence in either English or French. Most provinces, however, continued to propose more serious changes or deletions in an attempt to gut the charter. After demanding the deletion of many sections, including equality and mobility rights, and the emasculation of most of the legal rights, the provinces proposed that the charter be scrapped in favour of strengthening the 1960 Canadian Bill of Rights. Federal officials brushed off this proposal as inadequate since it would apply only at the federal level, it would ignore language rights, and it would not guarantee basic common rights throughout Canada.

The federal and provincial positions had now become more polarized over the charter than they had ever been. Only New Brunswick, Ontario and Newfoundland even accepted the principle of an entrenched Charter. The Liberal spirit of nation building was being spurned by provincial elites, while federal Liberals came to regard regionalism and province building as but "separatism by another name". And yet, negotiations over many agenda items other than the charter were progressing remarkably well. As Table 2 shows, on family law, equalization, patriation, the Senate and the Supreme Court there was, sometimes in the absence of a clear federal position, substantial agreement on changes. On all other fronts, there were still important differences, though none so great that an acceptable deal could not have been hammered out provided the provinces supported the

Table 2

CONSTITUTIONAL DISCUSSIONS BY AGENDA ITEM, SEPTEMBER 11, 1980

Topics	Agreed Matters[1]	Continuing Differences
Natural Resources	• recognize provincial ownership and management of non-renewable resources, forestry and electrical energy • grant provinces power over interprovincial trade in resources, subject to federal paramountcy[2] • grant provinces power to apply indirect taxes on resources provided they do not discriminate against citizens of other provinces	• federal side refused to do away with declaratory power[3] over natural resources • federal side refused to grant power over international trade in these resources • federal side refused February 1979 best-efforts draft giving provinces paramountcy over trade in resources except when there is "a compelling national interest"
Communications	• grant provinces power over intra-provincial telephone systems • provincial power to license, set rates, and regulate cable intra-provincially	• federal side refused provincial proposal to establish concurrency[4] with provincial paramountcy on everything but frequency allocation and management, networks extending over four or more provinces

Senate	• provinces to be better and directly represented	foreign broadcasting, satellites, aeronautical communications, radio-navigation, defence, or emergencies • number and powers of federal appointees in Senate • provincial representation • status and powers of a possible council of the provinces as part of the new Senate, with veto powers over certain federal decisions affecting the provinces • the future of the Senate as a house of general legislative review
Fisheries	• province to gain right to consultation and administrative input • provinces to gain almost all control over inland fisheries	• seven provinces, led by Newfoundland, wanted concurrent jurisdiction with federal paramountcy only on international fishing, conservation and limits on total allowable catch

Table 2 continued

Topics	Agreed Matters[1]	Continuing Differences
Supreme Court	• entrench the Supreme Court in constitution • direct right of provinces to pose reference questions to Supreme Court • federal appointment of justices on consultation with provinces • alternating civil and common law chief justice • recognition of dualism[5]	• slight differences over number of justices; most wanting eleven, some nine • differences on ratio of common law to civil law justices • majority preferred to avoid Quebec's and Alberta's suggestion of a separate panel on constitutional questions • how to resolve differences if federal and provincial attorneys general disagree on court appointments
Family Law	• concurrency over marriage and divorce with provincial paramountcy	• Manitoba and P.E.I. opposed, wishing national protection on this item, i.e., child custody orders
Offshore Resources	• provinces to get administrative arrangements for revenue sharing	• most provinces wanted offshore resources to be treated the same as

and input into policy planning

onshore resources, i.e., provincial ownership; Ottawa disagreed

Equalization

- entrench principle of equalization payments to have-not provinces
- provide for regular review of equalization mechanism

- slight differences over wording

Charter of Rights

- substantial difference over principle
- some support from Ontario, N.B. and Newfoundland with Saskatchewan supporting only language provisions

Patriation and the Amending Formula

- support for patriation but provinces want agreement on division of powers first

- differences between N.B., Ontario, Saskatchewan, and federal side who wanted the Victoria formula and the others who supported the Alberta formula

Table 2 continued

Topics	Agreed Matters[1]	Continuing Differences
Powers Over the Economy	• all support the principle of economic union	• disagreement over whether union should be protected by court or political mechanism • disagreement over entrenching mobility rights, strengthening federal powers over trade and commerce and over a strengthened section 121 which would ensure the free passage of goods, services and capital within Canada • disagreement over qualifying clause which would permit affirmative action programs
Preamble		• no clear agreement on wording or principle • no agreement on including principle of self-determination for Quebec

• concern over extent of encroachment of preamble on body of constitution

Notes:

[1] In this column are listed the *substantial* areas of agreement between the federal government and most provinces. Dissenters are noted in the right-hand column.

[2] "Paramountcy": Supremacy in the event of conflict in an area of joint jurisdiction.

[3] "Declaratory power": That the federal government can take over any "works" in a province that are declared by Parliament to be for the advantage of the country or of two or more provinces. In effect, this would permit Ottawa to assume ownership and control of any provincial project or industry.

[4] "Concurrency": That both levels of government may legislate in a given area.

[5] "Dualism": In this context, that the distinctiveness of Quebec's civil code required recognition by ensuring a guaranteed number of civil law justices on the Supreme Court.

core of the charter. A clear spirit of accommodation was beginning to develop in the tacit balancing off of resource ownership powers and the federal demand for powers over the economy.

On offshore resources, however, there was a chasm too big to bridge. Newfoundland's vigorous assertion that offshore resources be treated exactly as onshore resources are treated — in short a demand for provincial ownership — was supported by most provinces but got nowhere with the federal government. The federal side tried to placate the coastal provinces by offering them an administrative and revenue-sharing deal, but the item continued to be a stumbling block.

Alberta's new amending formula became a topic of considerable importance since it appeared to be the logical provincial alternative to the federally supported Victoria formula, with its protection for Ontario and Quebec. As outlined in Table 1, this formula for changing the constitution was based on two major principles: equality of provinces on constitutional change and the right of all provinces to "opt out" of certain classes of amendments directly affecting provincial rights and powers. Thus, Quebec and Ontario could still refuse the application of an amendment affecting their powers within their provinces, but there would be no permanent hegemony of *any* province over amendments that might be desired by many other governments. In this manner, Alberta hoped that the obnoxious feature of provincial inequality would begin to be expunged from Canadian federalism, and a general respect for provincial autonomy put in its place. By the end of the third week of meetings in July at Vancouver, a large provincial consensus had begun to develop around the Alberta proposal, which became known as the "Vancouver consensus."

Regional grievances also surfaced over the federal demand for increased powers over the economy. The Atlantic and Western provinces, suspicious of the free-market rhetoric of the federal and Ontario governments, argued that removal of all defensive measures undertaken mostly by have-not regions would not work toward the "equal benefit of all of Canada" but rather would exacerbate Canada's regional inequalities. Justice in the distribution of economic costs and benefits in Canada, they contended, was at least as important as any economist's abstract argument for economic efficiency in a pure economic union. They pointed out that the federal government itself recognized the same principle when it proposed to give job preferences to native peoples in Northern development.

Such were the typical cross-currents of interest and ideology which the negotiations had to bridge. It was clear that genuine renewal of Canadian federalism could not be completed without dealing with both the "Quebec problem" and Central Canadian domination of the federation. The failure of the talks stemmed from the inability of each side to recognize precisely the links between the federal and regional agendas and to make the necessary political sacrifices. Hostile attitudes also limited the chances for success. Provincial leaders and officials doubted federal willingness to negotiate in good faith and were wary of manipulation by Ottawa mandarins like Michael Kirby and Jim Coutts. As secretary of the cabinet for federal-provincial relations, Kirby was deeply involved in masterminding what many premiers thought to be a cynical federal strategy. Coutts' influence as Trudeau's principal secretary was known to be that of a Liberal "backroom boy" par excellence. But the chief suspicion was reserved for Trudeau. His Machiavellian presence haunted the road-show constitutional conference throughout the summer and contributed in no small part to provincial savaging of the charter.

The federal view of the provinces was hardly more flattering. While the Parti Québécois government had long been dismissed as "tribal," Western and Atlantic regionalism was now diagnosed as but a milder form of the same disease. In the 1980 election, Trudeau had lectured the West on the need for sharing and had treated Newfoundland's claims over the offshore as hardly more than parochial greed. Even Premier Davis, who could usually be charitably exempted from the brush of provincialism, was damned for toadying to the prejudices of backwater Ontario on linguistic matters. These attitudes dampened federal interest in the negotiations and they certainly prepared and appeared to justify plans for unilateral action.

The strategic approaches of the players also undermined the negotiations. The provinces' attempt to build up a consensus on agenda issues, with the leadership on each topic usually reserved for the province (or provinces) with the most at stake, was an unfruitful course of action. It tended to blur serious differences between the provinces in order to get at best a tenuous consensus; it encouraged the development of an "all-or-nothing" attitude to the whole package of constitutional reform; it left the provincial consensus on each item to be defined by the provincial "leader" with the most far-reaching demands on federal powers; and it put the whole context of negotiations into a bilateral instead of multilateral framework. Thus Newfound-land defined for most provinces the provincial consensus on offshore jurisdiction, Saskatchewan on natural resources, Alberta on the amending formula, British Columbia on the Senate, and Manitoba on the Charter of Rights. These tacit trade-offs between the provinces were acceptable since they gave each premier his pet project and since the total package strengthened regional and provincial power. But the federal government's priorities were necessarily left out in this strategy, a fact which brought unilateral action closer.

But if the provincial negotiating tactics overlooked the need to give ground on the federal government's central demand for an entrenched charter, the federal strategy, as disclosed in the so-called Kirby memorandum, simply underestimated provincial opposition to the charter. Rather than offering any practical suggestions to get around the fact that seven provinces disagreed with the principle of entrenchment, officials merely recommended concessions on wordings and offers of additional time to comply with the language rights section. This miscalculation was carried over into the total federal bargaining strategy, which assumed that "much of the resistance to the People's Package [the Charter of Rights, patriation, and the amending formula] has been to try to force the federal government to bargain within the Institutions and Powers Package." After mistakenly treating the charter issue as purely a provincial bargaining chip, the federal strategists went on to declare an "easy" strategy of partial concessions within the institutions and powers package which would lead the provinces "at the end of the day...to accept the People's Package."

The memorandum was, in that respect, a facile account of the issues and the flexibility possible over certain key agenda items. The government was led to believe that the separation of the "people's" from the "powers" package, the threats of unilateral action and the force of public opinion in the Gallup polls had "led to closer agreement on a Charter of Rights than there has been before." In fact, virtually all of the evidence pointed in the other direction. Within days of the memo's completion, there was a major struggle between the participants to persuade the public that the charter would alternately perfect or ruin Canada's traditions and future.

What may have made federal officials over-confident was the ever-present option of unilateral action, which had been actively entertained even before the negotiations had started. In the Kirby memorandum, federal officials urged their leaders to prepare the public for such an eventuality and also encouraged them to use unilateral action as a bargaining threat:

> In private, the provinces must be told that there is absolutely no question but that the federal government will proceed very quickly with *at least* all the elements of the People's Package and that it would therefore be to their advantage to bargain in good faith on the other issues so that they too will be relatively satisfied after the Conference. It should be made abundantly clear that on Powers and Institutions, the federal government expects *give* from the provinces as well as *take*.

Although the fallback to unilateral action was thought to be a reassuring alternative to a negotiated agreement, it was in fact a hazardous option. Yet officials returned to it after finally admitting in the last paragraph of the memorandum that "the probability of an agreement is not high."

When the first ministers arrived in Ottawa to open the conference on September 8, the seriousness of the differences over key items and the difficulties created by negotiating strategies were not fully appreciated. The first morning was devoted to an expression of the regional versus the national vision of Canada, despite the federal government's desire to avoid establishing fixed positions. As each province defended the regional theme, it inevitably took a harder line on its central constitutional preoccupations. The federal government then challenged the provincial complaints by maintaining that Canada was already the "most decentralized federation in the world," but argued that the provinces would none the less find the federal government flexible on many issues.

The public statement of positions, topic by topic, did not constitute negotiations. As the press kept a scorecard on who made the strongest public impact from day to day, the business of achieving an agreement slipped by. With television coverage of the talks and behind-the-scenes consultations with officials, the participants were under an enormous strain; "grand-standing" rather than a patient search for common ground was often the result. By the third day of the talks, September 10, when the federal and provincial governments reached a stand-off over the charter, the chances of bridging differences seemed to evaporate. In an eloquent debate over the "principle" of entrenchment, the participants managed to get themselves into hopelessly deadlocked positions.

The debate centred not on rights or linguistic justice but on the nature of the Canadian state, its institutions and its theory of government, and it left the participants further apart than ever. Manitoba's Conservative government had relentlessly fought an entrenched charter all along and Premier Sterling Lyon now set the tone for the debate. He began by charging that "entrenchment was contrary to our traditional and our successful Parliamentary government" and would move our system "towards that of a republican system." Quoting from a paper by G.P. Browne of Carleton University sent to all provincial delegations, Lyon declared that "such a transfer of legislative authority [from Parliaments to courts] would amount to a constitutional revolution entailing the relinquishment of the essential principle of Parliamentary democracy, the principle of Parliamentary supremacy."

By identifying the entrenchment of a charter of rights with the republican model, Lyon also established valuable lines of argument against the charter which were variously taken up by other opponents of the proposal. First, he argued, entrenchment of rights in the United States had not protected Americans any better than citizens in countries like Britain or Canada which had no entrenched rights; second, dubious court judgements on rights had left Americans collectively unable to deal effectively with issues like pornography, crime, the observance of religious and other community norms, and many other matters; third, the wisdom of forcing judges to legislate in the highly political and contentious field of human rights was in doubt; fourth, Canada's political culture and traditions were different from those of the United States and should be respected unless strong grounds could be advanced that revolutionary change would "be beneficial, not harmful"; and finally, rights should be defined and altered by legislatures elected by the public rather than by a few appointed "men, albeit learned in the law, who are not necessarily aware of everyday concerns of Canadians." Lyon finished by urging his colleagues "to retain our own heritage, and reject experiments with concepts foreign to our tradition."

Lyon's classically conservative attack on the charter was followed by that of Saskatchewan NDP Premier Allan Blakeney, which echoed the concern for community rights and democratic decision making over crucial social values such as capital punishment, obscenity and discrimination. "Canadians ought not to have taken away from them the fundamental right to participate in political choices, in particular they ought not to have eroded under the guise of advancing their freedoms their right to make important social choices and to participate in those decisions." To Blakeney, courts were forums giving "an advantage to the rich" and parliaments and legislatures "were less of an advantage to the rich." Therefore, in choosing which instrument was more likely to advance the rights of all, Blakeney wanted Canadians to lobby and not to litigate. Another undesirable consequence of using the courts to protect liberties, he said, was the promotion of "an adversarial society," such as in the United States.

The critics of the charter were advancing important political and philosophical objections, but they were undoubtedly weakest in their defence (explicit or implied) of Canada as a land of freedom where, as Lyon put it, "infringements of basic rights are rare." Trudeau attacked that assumption at the beginning of the discussion, although in a glaring omission he neglected to mention abuses arising from *his* government's invoking of the War Measures Act in 1970:

> It is within certainly our history and the memory of some of us that there have been laws denying basic rights, denying the franchise to Chinese citizens, Canadian citizens of British Columbia, for instance, abolishing the use of French in Manitoba where it had been guaranteed by the constitution or so the French thought. Stripping Japanese-Canadians of their citizenship by the federal government. Suppression of freedom of religion in Quebec. Restricting the rights of citizens to acquire property in some provinces, Prince Edward Island and Saskatchewan. Limiting the rights of citizens to seek employment from one province to another in Quebec and Newfoundland. Limiting the use of English in Quebec. The list is not enormous, but it can go on....

Premier Hatfield of New Brunswick, who with Davis of Ontario was defending the charter, also declared that "all political jurisdictions are guilty of offending rights" and that none of them could therefore be trusted finally to protect and preserve them. He also reminded Premier Blakeney of the costs and difficulty of moving legislatures to undo violations that they may have committed. But Hatfield spoke to the centre of his concerns when he warned that he did not want any future government of New Brunswick to be able to declare the province unilingual, as the province of Quebec had done.

When Jean Chrétien spoke on behalf of the federal government, his central theme was the language provisions of the Charter of Rights. He admitted frankly that rectifying violations of minority education and language rights in both Quebec and English Canada was central to the government's purposes and that the charter was to "cure" these grievances forever. The general question of rights served as good politics for this strategy.

Defending civil rights was politically popular. It diverted Canadians away from their linguistic divisions and prejudices which the charter was to correct. Moreover, the entrenchment issue drew the public into the more abstract questions of parliamentary democracy and federalism. Calling the charter part of the "people's package" contributed to the general impression desired by the federal government. At the same time, its positive role in nation building recommended itself to federal strategists.

Quebec did not take the federal scolding on its treatment of its English-speaking minority lightly. Its premier declared that it had no lessons to learn on that score from any other jurisdiction in Canada and that rights in Quebec were being studiously and carefully protected. Lévesque further claimed that the charter sought to return the province to pre–Bill 101 days with the principle of free choice for French or English schools — a policy "absolutely contrary to the interests of Quebec." This charge drew out a federal rebuttal and yet more posturing by Quebec's political leaders.

It was a curiously muddled debate which pitted the strategy of constitutional entrenchment against separatism and the English tradition of parliamentary democracy in turn. Only the Quebec representatives understood and appreciated the irony of the confusions; most English-speaking federal and provincial politicians largely spoke past one another. Quebec successfully appealed to the other provinces in the language of regionalism against Trudeau's "authoritarian" federalism, while the other provinces interpreted the charter as an assault upon the English parliamentary tradition. It was a paradoxical fate for a federal initiative intended to reconcile Quebec to Canada and to rectify classic Canadian injustices.

After a sophistical attack upon the parliamentary supremacy argument, Trudeau in his concluding remarks came to the heart of the strategy being used to advance justice for linguistic minorities and its relationship to the preservation of the Canadian state. Quoting Lévesque that "one or two generations is all that remains to the [French-speaking] minorities" in English Canada and noting that even the English-speaking minority in Quebec was now lacking self-confidence, he drew out the stark contrasts of two futures for Canada:

> We have one province which is essentially French-speaking and the rest of the country which is essentially English-speaking, and that is almost what we have had for a long, long while. The question is: do we continue to reinforce this kind of Canada and, if so, there is no doubt in my mind, and I don't think in many of our minds, that that will end up in two Canadas. We have certainly the admission of the present government of Quebec, to whom the logic of that demographic reality led them to want to have Quebec opt out of Canada and become an independent political state, speaking French, tolerant to its minorities, with the rest of Canada speaking English. This is one direction in which we have been going and towards which we can continue to go.
>
> The other one, the other conception of Canada is a Canada which respects what Premier Blakeney I think very wisely called the bargain of Confederation .... That bargain of Canada, as we understand it, and I am talking "we," French-speaking Canadians, is that

> anywhere in this country French will be respected and
> accepted as the right of a Canadian citizen.

Bilingualism, Trudeau argued, was important to
Quebec and to the country despite the fears it generated in English-speaking Canada and despite the
contemptuous dismissal of it in Quebec — especially
by separatists who did not wish it to work. Cloaked
under a mantle of human rights, this policy of national
renewal was Trudeau's answer to Quebec nationalism.
Such a program was not likely to be stopped by squabbles over Canada's parliamentary traditions or even
by the niceties of Canada's conventions.

When the premiers gathered together for a breakfast meeting toward the end of the week of negotiations to prepare a list of their final demands, they
ignored the Charter of Rights. Yet their demands on
federal powers were substantial. A tough posture had
been urged by Lévesque who had in fact circulated a
draft for a common stand the night before which, with
some revisions, was adopted by the premiers. Under
the chairmanship of Sterling Lyon, this hard-line
position became the premiers' initial collective bargaining stand, the so-called "Chateau Laurier consensus." It was, in fact, a prescription for a break
down, especially surprising since the premiers knew
the federal game plan as outlined in the Kirby memorandum. When the list was presented to Trudeau,
many items were flatly rejected. There was little
negotiation after that. By Saturday, the premiers were
reading their failure speeches to the nation, assessing
what had gone wrong and uniformly urging continuing discussions. Prominent among the post-
mortem explanations was the ill-will generated by the
Kirby memorandum and the intransigence of the

federal government towards the areas of provincial consensus which had painfully developed over the earlier months of negotiations. There was much talk of the collision between two competing centralized and decentralized definitions of Canada, which neither the provincial nor the federal sides were ready to compromise. But in their statements, virtually every premier but Bill Davis warned the prime minister not to resort to unilateral action, predicting that only a hollow victory could result, won at the price of defying the conventions of Canadian federalism.

With his usual astuteness, Premier Blakeney drew attention in his remarks to the conflating of the Quebec and national questions:

> I don't want to be thought to be abrasive when I say this, but as a result there were two agendas before us, one constitutional renewal for Canada and the other the continuing contest for the hearts and minds of the people of Quebec. In that latter contest, it seemed to some of us that nothing offered was enough and everything being demanded was too much.
>
> Until there is some resolution of this contest I am very much afraid that success will continue to elude us.

When Trudeau responded, it became clearer than ever that the federal government regarded the regional conception of federalism as hardly more than a variant of Quebec separatism: the idea of Canada as a "free association of provinces" was said to be shared by most of the premiers. Noting that "we hear from Premier after Premier that they agree with the concept of Canada put forward by Mr. Lévesque," Trudeau was inclined to see the national interest exclusively served by the central government and its institutions, despite Blakeney's warning that the national voice in a federation like Canada's could only be "the majority of citizens as expressed by the popular will in the House of Commons and the majority however defined of the regional will." With the charter as a tool for constraining these regional forces, Trudeau was now ready to break precedent to see his remedies for national disunity and injustice permanently entrenched in the Canadian constitution. The stage was set for unilateral action.

3
Option 2: Unilateral Action

The September 1980 First Ministers' Conference had ended in failure. It was now time for the federal government to make good on its threat to go it alone. If the provinces had not believed Trudeau's pledge following the referendum victory in Quebec or his warnings afterward, they certainly could not ignore the detailed outline of a unilateral policy option contained in the leaked federal memorandum. It showed that planning for "going it alone" was well advanced, with senior cabinet ministers briefed on the full legal and political ramifications of the policy.

At the outset, the memorandum presented the cabinet with the choice of acting in federal areas of jurisdiction only or binding the provinces without their consent. If the second option were chosen, the memorandum outlined three alternative "packages" of legal intrusions and sweeteners. But the principle of intrusion into provincial areas of jurisdiction had to be faced first, after which political judgement would be required about the scale of that intrusion. If the predominantly tactical preoccupations of the memorandum were a reliable indication of federal thinking, however, debate over the principle of intrusion in a federal state was not likely to be exhaustive and sensitive. Bureaucratic advice was already structuring the policy towards binding the provinces.

Although the memorandum advised ministers that the cautious route would have the advantage of respecting convention, it presented an overwhelming number of arguments against it. Disadvantages outweighed advantages by a margin of at least five paragraphs to one. Unless the charter were binding on the provinces, rights would not be fully and universally protected. The package would be politically "meagre" especially after all the expectations built up with the negotiations and the Quebec referendum. It would "waste a once-in-a-lifetime opportunity to effect comprehensive constitutional change." It would give political advantages to Lévesque and Ryan to push on with their own unacceptable options while criticizing Ottawa, and therefore "it would be unfortunate to have to fight this criticism without in the end having a great deal to show for it." Finally, it would betray public support for the people's package. Against this weight of argument, only a daring minister would do battle with his colleagues on the issue of convention alone.

But the political forces within the cabinet and caucus might also have given a would-be cabinet rebel pause for second thoughts. The Quebec elite in the cabinet and virtually the whole Quebec contingent of 74 MPs were hawkish about putting the Parti Québécois in its place. They had won the referendum campaign and the Lévesque government was thought to be in no position to block the redressing of long-standing grievances over minority language educational rights. With the balance of power in the party so heavily based in Quebec and with virtually no representation from the West, the charter became an instrument for settling scores with the separatists and the Quebec Language Bill, and for barring similar discrimination in the other provinces. At the same time, the charter could provide a constitutional foundation for the traditional federal Liberal strategy on bilingualism and national unity. Quebec federalists enlisted the support of the English-speaking party leaders for entrenching this vision of Canada in the constitution. Such front-benchers as Allan MacEachen, Mark MacGuigan, Robert Kaplan, John Roberts and James Fleming were all reported to have demanded the entrenchment of minority language educational rights in the constitution. But having declared this a condition for Canadian constitutional renewal, they had burned their bridges with the provinces and with constitutional convention.

There was, in short, no way in which traditional Liberal politics of constitutional renewal could be carried out without violating the rights of the provinces. But once begun, the question became one of political calculation. How far must the government go to produce a politically saleable package and how far dare it intrude on provincial powers to do so? For Quebecers, "the question [was] whether ... the protection for French outside of Quebec will fully counterbalance the protection of English within Quebec, and the degree to which the Charter will come into direct conflict with Bill 101." In other provinces, the question was one of avoiding anglophone backlash over the extension of French rights by submerging linguistic rights in a broadly based protection of *human* rights in general.

These objectives had to be balanced against the acceptable political risks with the provinces. Hence, minority language educational rights would be strongly advanced everywhere, but Trudeau himself refused to satisfy the demands of his Quebec colleagues that Ontario be declared officially bilingual. Though he had pressured Ontario privately for this concession, Trudeau knew that he needed Ontario's help and could not compel Premier Davis to give him this important prize. Compromise even on so vital a matter was essential to the success of the measure. Similarly, the cabinet worried over the scale of provincial government opposition that a fully effective Charter of Rights would provoke. They resolved that dilemma by putting in virtually all the rights of the original charter, but with all of the qualifications the provinces had suggested to weaken it. Thus, the *appearance* of an effective Charter of Rights which camouflaged linguistic and bilingual features was advanced, and a signal was relayed to the provinces that the federal government had after all taken their objections into account.

Once the federal cabinet had gone this far, there seemed little reason not to shape the amending formulae in its own favour. The preferred federal option all through the summer negotiations was the Victoria formula, but with the modification that the two Atlantic provinces must, as with the West, include at least 50 per cent of the region's population. Ottawa therefore provided that, unless an agreement was reached between governments or by a special referendum within a two-year period, the modified Victoria formula would be adopted. In addition, on amendments which affected one or more but not all provinces, it permitted change by the consent of those governments. What was far more radical however was a new provision for constitutional amendment by national referenda, an option available only to the federal government. This part of the amendment procedure allowed the federal government, in the event of deadlock with the provinces, to secure changes to the constitution whenever it garnered 51 per cent of the national vote and a specified level of support (though not necessarily a majority) in all four regions of Canada. The referendum prodecure would remain in place after two years whatever the general intergovernmental formula that might be adopted. This action stacked the cards in Ottawa's favour on all future constitutional changes.

The national Parliament was already well protected in any amendment procedure, since every formula required Ottawa's agreement. What was new in the referendum option was that Ottawa could bypass the provinces altogether, and avoid applying the same test of general intergovernmental approval to its objectives that the provinces were required to do for theirs. This referendum playing card was Ottawa's permanent substitute for unilateral recourse to Britain which, once patriation was achieved, would no longer be used. It was a feature that could dramatically centralize Canadian federalism.

By all accounts, the referendum option was pressed upon cabinet by Trudeau himself after it had been advanced by his backroom aides — Michael Kirby, Michael Pitfield and Jim Coutts. If retained as a permanent measure, it would release Ottawa from any constitutional strait-jacket in the next round of constitutional discussions and secure for all future national governments a powerful political weapon. If simply used as a negotiating device, the alternate option would warn the provinces of the dangers of obstruction *or* the measure itself could be used as a bargaining chip on other matters. Either way the government had crafted a device that promised grave dangers for the provinces.

As an initiative against the threats of separatism, linguistic injustice and regionalism, the package for unilateral action was a bolder attack than most had expected. Here, too, the Machiavellian virtue of decisiveness was preferred over any moderate course. The Liberals knew that they were about to enter one of the toughest political fights of the century, but they wished to keep the initiative throughout, be ready to adapt their politics and compromise as circumstances might require. Both the federal plan and its execution certainly confirmed earlier provincial suspicions about their wily adversary.

The Kirby memorandum correctly anticipated that opponents in Parliament and from the provinces "would concentrate their fire on the fact of unilateral action" and that the contents of the package would not engage the public's attention to the same extent. It also predicted a reference to the courts as a necessary complication. The government was advised to deal with both of these challenges with assurances that the resolution was proper and legal, that it was made necessary by fifty-three years of failure and that politically motivated obstruction ought not to be tolerated. It was hoped that the resolution might be pushed through Parliament and receive approval by Westminster before the courts could pronounce on it. That way the risk of an adverse judgement, which might undermine "the political legitimacy, though not the legal validity, of the patriation package," might be avoided. The government also knew that the legal position of the provinces would be much weaker after Westminster had enacted the resolution, and thought that a Canadian court would at best find the process a "violation of established conventions and therefore in one sense ... 'unconstitutional' even though legally valid."

It seems, therefore, that the government knew perfectly well that the process was questionable and possibly unconstitutional (even if technically legal) despite its numerous public statements to the contrary. Its advisers also had even correctly anticipated what the Supreme Court might have to say on the issue. But they hoped to push on brazenly in the hope that the matter could be settled politically in spite of federal-provincial conventions.

Even the management of Parliament had been carefully considered in the planning document. In a section entitled "Strategic Considerations in Parliament," the memorandum outlined a game plan for controlling the legislative process. The government was to table the resolution, permit full debate on it with a view to bringing it to a vote, and then after about two weeks of debate refer it to a joint House-Senate committee for study in apparent deference to the opposition. In this manner, the government could proceed with its budget and the "Canadianizing" National Energy Program (which promised to poison further the Parliamentary atmosphere), while the public was given an opportunity to participate in a review of the resolution. The authors of the memorandum worried about there being more "attackers" than "defenders" in committee and counselled that "careful choice of government members would be essential, and careful orchestration of hearings would be needed to ensure effective presentation of the government's position." They also felt that the matter should be safely "contained" within committee where "easier and more effective relations can be maintained with the press gallery, since relatively few reporters will follow the proceedings."

On the evening of October 2, Trudeau formally opened this phase of the constitutional struggle in a national television address outlining unilateral action. His speech was a well-crafted piece of liberal patriotism:

> It is a long and painstaking process, building a country to match a dream. But as each generation has made the sacrifices so each has reaped the rewards. Every generation of Canadians has given more than it has taken.
>
> Now it is our turn to repay our inheritance. Our duty is clear: it is to complete the foundations of our independence and of our freedoms.

With these words Trudeau fulfilled the dark prediction made by his friend, Paul Gérin-Lajoie in his classic study, *Constitutional Amendment in Canada*, published thirty years earlier. Ironically, Trudeau himself had read and commented on the manuscript and may indeed have been one of the scholars who, according to Gérin-Lajoie, had argued even then "that provincial sovereignty might be abridged .... without the consent of all provinces affected." Gérin-Lajoie thought that position was unwarranted, but openly worried whether events in Canada might not convert this scholarly view into political fact:

> Yet, this contention [federal unilateralism] might result some day — a day which may be not far distant

> — in creating a trend of opinion which would make its
> way openly into the federal Cabinet and would finally
> gain the support of a majority in Parliament ... There
> lies a potential source of friction between the federal
> Government and the provinces which is far more
> serious than the actual frictions of 1943 and 1944.

That day had finally come. Trudeau, the scholar-turned-politician, was about to put an academic dispute to the acid test.

In a remarkable political manoeuvre, Trudeau secured the support of one of the opposition parties even before making his public announcement, and at the same time won himself some badly needed support in the West. He talked NDP leader Ed Broadbent into committing his party, which included twenty-seven Westerners in a caucus of thirty-two. Broadbent gave his endorsement only an hour after he had seen the resolution, before he had consulted with his caucus, and in the face of a resolution to the contrary by his party's federal council. Although he held out for some changes, his praise for Trudeau's proposals — "unquestionably desirable," "sensible," "civilized" — was sweet music to Liberal ears. Although dissension within the NDP ranks followed, Trudeau had success-fully isolated the Conservatives as his only implacable foe in Parliament.

Speaking on television in reply to the prime minister, Clark gave the government a sense of the debate that lay ahead:

> Because a constitution is so basic to a country, it must
> be the product of the broadest possible consensus. It
> cannot be arbitrarily imposed on this nation by only
> one individual or government. Nor can it be achieved
> through threat, ultimatum or artificial deadline. That
> kind of constitution-making does not serve Canada....

Mr. Trudeau tonight offers Canadians the prospect of divisive referenda, prolonged constitutional challenges in the courts, and federal-provincial turmoil. That is betrayal of those Quebeckers who voted "No" in the Quebec referendum, and all other Canadians who seek genuine renewal of our Confederation.

Since both Ontario and New Brunswick had supported a charter during the negotiations, both provinces lined up with the federal government, despite Premier Hatfield's earlier doubts about the wisdom of unilateral action and his opposition to certain features of the current resolution. Ontario's Premier Davis, noting Ottawa's concession to his province on bilingualism, equated the support of Ontario with the "sustaining of [an] effective national consensus for constitutional reform and patriation." (With eight other provinces against the federal plan, only an Ontario premier could possibly have thought that constituted "an effective national consensus.")

The grouping of political forces on the eve of the resolution battle was clear. In Parliament, the only effective opposition to unilateral action itself was that provided by the Progressive Conservatives and later by four dissident NDP MPs from Saskatchewan who broke ranks with the party on the issue. Outside Parliament, the governments in three out of four regions of the country were overwhelmingly opposed to the action: three of the Atlantic provinces, Quebec and all of Western Canada. Most of the dissident provinces began to plan concerted action including court challenges, lobbying in Britain and politicking at home. Saskatchewan's government attempted to continue talking with federal officials in the hope of improving the package, while Ottawa attempted to lure Saskatchewan away from the others with promises of including increased provincial powers over natural resources.

The debate in Parliament after October 6 went much as expected; the Conservatives fought the resolution fiercely and the NDP cemented its alliance with the Liberals in exchange for a government promise to include its earlier offer on natural resources in the package. Broadbent hoped in that way to smooth his strained relations with the NDP government in Saskatchewan and to win some credibility generally in the West; Trudeau won some badly needed support from Western MPs and divided the Parliamentary opposition. In keeping with the plan to restrict House debate to about two weeks, the government invoked closure on October 23 and sent the resolution to the Joint House-Senate Committee on the Constitution.

At this point, the federal government got a break that it had not counted on. The witnesses appearing before the committee represented almost exclusively human rights groups and governments (apart from five expert witnesses chosen by the parties) and were not nearly as critical of unilateral action as the federal memorandum had expected. The government had forgotten to take into account the popular appeal of the Charter of Rights. Although most of the public interest groups were critical of the feeble defence of rights in the resolution, they worried little about conventions or Canadian federalism. For them, the resolution did not go far enough. By catering to these demands, the government was able to strengthen its charter, to give the public the impression of flexibility and to isolate its opposition. The politics of unilateral action were made much more comfortable so long as the public fixed upon its human rights contents and not on the action itself.

This fact underlines the importance of the arena in which constitutional politics are carried out. Conducted as intergovernmental negotiations, talks on constitutional subjects like the Charter of Rights principally focus on their impact on the powers and rights of governments; conducted in a wider public forum, they are instead examined in the light of their contribution to perceived public needs. Such a conclusion seems to justify the view that governmental bargaining subverts the "people's interest," as Trudeau had so often alleged, but the matter is much more complex. The "public interest" on such a question surely must include consideration of both agendas — rights and federalism — a complex balancing act which requires an explicit role for both governmental and other public actors.

Although public participation in the constitutional process was only infrequently permitted by the governmental actors — and then only because it appeared to be politically useful, or otherwise unavoidable — the public input *was* important in shaping the eventual outcome. Hence even if the civil rights groups who appeared before the joint committee found themselves unwitting accomplices in federal political planning, their pressure was indispensable in tightening up and strengthening the Charter of Rights.

The list of groups wishing to appear before the committee was a testament to the federal strategy of grafting people's rights to federal unilateralism. The appearance of human rights' commissions, civil liberties' groups, bar associations, research institutes, and special interest groups supporting the rights of women, the handicapped, the gay community and ethnic minorities all suggested that public participation helped the federal side. Once the government saw that the committee presented no political threat, it permitted it an extension from December 9 to February 6 (later extended to February 17) and rested comfortably with the televised proceedings which had been forced by Conservative and NDP pressure. Only two of the dissenting provincial governments — Nova Scotia and Prince Edward Island — appeared before the committee, and Saskatchewan, which had not yet taken a firm position, also offered useful criticism. In neglecting this opportunity to shape public debate, the other dissenting provinces probably made Liberal management of parliamentary opinion easier.

> On January 12, 1981, the committee's last witness, Justice Minister Chrétien, tabled a long list of amendments to the charter, largely at the expense of provincial arguments and interests. The amendments the government proposed, or which it later accepted from the committee or Commons, fell into four main areas: a strengthening of the Charter of Rights and Freedoms, corrections of some anomalies and unfairness in the amending formulae, recognition of native and aboriginal rights, and enlarging provincial jurisdiction, especially over natural resources. In total, these changes made for a much more saleable patriation package, even if most of the provinces and the official opposition remained against it on principle.

On the Charter of Rights, the government substituted a requirement that any limits on basic freedoms be "reasonable" rather than merely "lawful." It was therefore up to the government to justify in court limits on the citizen's right against unreasonable search or seizure, arbitrary detainment or imprisonment, unjust denial of bail, and so on. New rights were written in: protection against self-incrimination, a right to be informed of the right to counsel, a right to trial by jury for major offences, and improved equality rights, especially for the mentally and physically disabled. Citizens were also given the right to seek remedies from the courts for any violations of their rights, and the courts were given the discretion to exclude evidence where it had been "obtained in a manner that infringed or denied any rights or freedoms guaranteed by this Charter."

Language guarantees were extended to new categories of citizens and better secured. Minority language educational rights were to be provided out of public funds "where numbers warrant" (in the opinion of the courts), and were extended to children of citizens who received their primary school instruction in Canada in English or French. Thus the obligations of governments to pay for minority language services was made more explicit, even if the qualification on numbers worried many advocates of bilingualism. Extending the constitutional protection of minority language education to the children of Canadian citizens who had been educated here in English or French *whatever* their original mother tongue protected the rights of many Canadians who had been overlooked in the resolution. Many other Canadians were protected in the additional provision that if one child in a family was receiving primary or secondary school instruction in English or French, all children in the family could be educated in the same language. Special arrangements were made to permit other provinces to extend language rights without going through the general amendment process. In addition to all of these changes, New Brunswick agreed to make itself a fully bilingual province under the constitution, equally entrenching the rights of citizens in both language groups.

The number of provinces required to put up an alternative amending formula to that of the federal government in a national referendum was changed from eight to seven, but the government gave this power exclusively to the legislatures (not governments) of the provinces. This "reform" was purely cosmetic, however, since the provinces still needed to meet an 80 per cent population requirement to have their alternative amending formula considered by the people; Ottawa's ally, Ontario, could block that option single-handed. A Referendum Rules Commission was established to suggest referendum guidelines for enactment by Parliament. The 50 per cent population provision for the Atlantic provinces was removed so that Prince Edward Island would not be frozen out of the process altogether (the population provision for the Western provinces was dropped in a later House amendment). A time-limit was built into the national referendum option so that Parliament was required to wait twelve months after passage of a special resolution calling for an amendment before a referendum would proceed. That provision underlined the fact that it was to be considered a "deadlock-breaking" mechanism only. Exclusive federal control over the use of referenda remained.

Native rights were specifically protected in section 25 of the charter to avoid their being set aside in order to enforce Canadians' right to equality under section 15. In a new section 33 "the aboriginal and treaty rights of the aboriginal peoples of Canada [were] recognized and affirmed." Section 33 however was capable of being amended in any province by simple agreement of that province and the federal government rather than by the general amending formula and was therefore not on as sound a footing as section

25 in the charter. To emphasize the political protection given aboriginal peoples, the government also allowed a committee amendment that within a year of proclamation the subject of aboriginal rights would be on the agenda of a constitutional conference of first ministers and that the prime minister would invite native representatives to participate in the discussion. Representatives were also required on any agenda item which the prime minister thought "directly affects" the territories. (In a gesture to Canada's policy on multiculturalism, a motherhood section 27 required the charter to be "interpreted in a manner consistent with the preservation and enhancement of the multicultural heritage of Canadians.")

The amendment giving provinces power over indirect taxation of natural resources and over interprovincial trade, with certain reservations, was advanced by NDP members on the committee and accepted by the government. It confirmed the deal offered by the federal government to the provinces in the September First Ministers' Conference. Such a provision, along with the incidental strengthening of the principle of equalization, was intended to win some badly needed support in the West and to solidify the federal NDP-Liberal alliance.

Although this change did not bring any of the Western provinces on side, a concession to the Senate eased any danger to the passage of the resolution there. The original resolution permitted the House of Commons to override the Senate whenever the Commons passed, after a ninety-day interval, a constitutional measure being held up in the second chamber. Since the Senate was threatening to block the resolution unless the offensive section was removed, Liberal members on the joint committee struck it out despite protests by the NDP, which had a longstanding commitment to dismantle the upper house.

Meanwhile, during the joint committee hearings in the fall of 1980 and especially during December, when the cabinet was approving amendments to the patriation package, the federal government was attempting to break the wall of resistance from Western Canada. Its chosen target was Saskatchewan. Blakeney and his affable attorney general, Roy Romanow, were well respected by the federal leaders. Moreover, Saskatchewan had deliberately kept the channels open with Ottawa following the threat of unilateral action in the hope of pressing for an eventual compromise. It seemed natural to use these channels to offer a deal to Saskatchewan in return for its support. Negotiations had gone well until, on February 19, Saskatchewan's distrust of the federal government finally caused it to pull back almost at the eleventh hour. The *Globe and Mail* reported that Saskatchewan had deliberately waited until the committee amendments were forthcoming to see whether the federal government would renege on any of its understandings with Saskatchewan. When the government accepted the motion to permit a Senate veto on constitutional amendments and when it toyed with the Tories by accepting and then retracting a property-rights amendment which threatened Saskatchewan's own land control measures, it destroyed the chances of an accord with that province. Saskatchewan simply feared that it would be double-crossed by the federal Liberals.

Saskatchewan was also feeling the ill will of seven other provinces who had been caucusing over ways of opposing Ottawa. Having begun a series of court challenges in Manitoba, Newfoundland and Quebec, however, they were only too happy to welcome a somewhat chastened Saskatchewan into the legal fray. This group of provinces soon became known as the "Gang of Eight."

The essential lines of the dissident provinces' political strategy had been established in a meeting on October 14 in Toronto. The premiers were determined to resist unilateral federal action. They developed a three-pronged strategy: legal action to defeat or undermine the legitimacy of the resolution, a political campaign to turn public opinion against unilateral action, and a diplomatic offensive to scuttle the chances of passage in Britain. Over the following months of debate in Parliament and the country, these initiatives frustrated the federal attempt to get swift passage. Neither the target date of July 1, 1981, nor the carefully planned national management of the political variables was practical in the face of this opposition. Events confirmed the federal memorandum's warning that "the fight ... will be very, very rough."

The legal option was important in its own right and for its contribution to the other two parts of the strategy. Just as any citizen's intention in going to court is to "win" his or her case, the provincial governments hoped to get a ruling that the resolution was constitutionally improper, if not illegal. If it were found illegal, the federal government would be stopped. If it were found legal but improper, the political odds of forcing a compromise or fighting it successfully at home or in Britain were much more in their favour. In that sense, the provinces always had more than a purely legal purpose in mind. A court judgement carried with it the threat of political defeat or weakening of the federal position.

These political possibilities stemmed from the

provincial and federal courts' duty and power both to uphold the constitution of Canada and to answer what are called "reference" questions. The provinces reasoned that if they framed questions that tested the validity of the proposed federal resolution under the constitution of Canada, they would receive a relatively objective interpretation of the lawfulness and/or constitutional propriety of the federal action. In answering those questions, the courts would be forced to impose a ruling which would in effect either approve or reject the action.

Since the provinces could not themselves refer questions directly to the Supreme Court of Canada, the dissenting provinces decided to put their questions about the validity of the federal action to three provincial appeal courts. Their decisions could then be appealed to the Supreme Court. After agreeing on a set of reference questions asking whether, according to constitutional practice, the federal resolution required the agreement of the provinces, actions were launched over the months of October to January in appeal courts in Manitoba, Newfoundland and Quebec. Six (later eight) provinces participated in the court challenges. The three legal challenges increased the likelihood of a federal defeat or setback, and the timing of the judgements was likely to throw obstacles in the way of the July 1 objective. Finally, any delays caused by the legal questions gave the provinces time to continue the campaign for public support.

The dissenting provinces began their political opposition by threatening to stage referenda (an idea that was later dropped) and by passing resolutions in their legislatures denouncing the federal action. These resolutions gave the dissent a legislative sanction, although only in Alberta and Saskatchewan did the official opposition support the ruling party. Indeed Alberta's Progressive Conservative government found itself embarrassed when one of its members refused to support the resolution and it retaliated by expelling him from the party. To avoid supporting a Parti Québécois resolution in the Quebec National Assembly, Claude Ryan moved an amendment requiring a commitment to federalism; the PQ government rejected the amendment, which allowed Ryan to vote against the PQ motion.

The battle for public opinion was fought out both at home and in Britain. Provincial publicity campaigns were put in place (most notably in Quebec, where Ottawa countered an effective PQ campaign with a million-dollar advertising blitz in October of 1981), and many premiers spoke out on the issue as often as possible. Both Manitoba's Premier Lyon, as chairman of the Gang of Eight, and New Brunswick's Premier Hatfield, a federal ally, travelled to London to warn the British public of the grave consequences that would follow from either acceptance or rejection of the Canadian Parliament's resolution.

The lobbying effort in London began in earnest soon after the opposition strategy was put into place. Quebec took the lead with a furious campaign to warn British MPs and peers of the widespread Canadian opposition to the federal government's proposal. The federal government had already received cautious assurances from the British government concerning the resolution earlier in the summer of 1980, but it remained unclear just how the government would respond to a request from the Canadian Parliament in the face of massive provincial opposition. Britain clearly did not want to get involved in a bitter Canadian dispute nor did it want its own pressing political priorities disturbed. However federal leaders continued to state publicly that Britain would be bound to accede to any request of the Canadian Parliament to avoid "meddling" in Canadian internal affairs. Trudeau's sneering reference to British parliamentarians having "to hold their noses" while passing his measure certainly did not help improve matters in Britain. Ultimately, federal officials counted on the power of the British cabinet to get their measure through, whatever members might think of it privately.

Since the provinces could not approach the British government directly without violating diplomatic conventions, they concentrated their efforts on informing members of the British Houses of Parliament and on shaping British public opinion. They had been preceded by delegations of Canadian native peoples anxious for Britain to protect their treaty rights. In November, the political pressure moved Westminster's Select Committee on Foreign Affairs to inquire into the role which the United Kingdom ought to play on this proposed Canadian constitutional request. It received written submissions from Canadian governments and interest groups, but heard direct submissions only from British witnesses, officials and experts. British civil servants seemed to argue the federal case before the committee whereas the constitutional experts supported the provinces' contention that for the British Parliament to act as a "simple rubber-stamp" would be wrong. Ultimately, when the committee, under the chairmanship of Sir Anthony Kershaw, filed its report on January 30, 1981, it sided with the experts' view that the British Parliament ought not necessarily to act "automatically and unconditionally." Only if a request is seen to convey "the clearly expressed wishes of Canada as a federally structured whole" (either by consent of provincial governments or by regional majorities in a referendum), could the British Parliament rightfully pass any constitutional request of the Parliament of Canada.

The Kershaw report struck a hard blow at the federal government's assertion that Britain must automatically comply with any request from the Canadian Parliament. The report generated a spate of "Britbashing" from the federal side; Trudeau even compared it to a current science-fiction movie, *The Empire Strikes Back*. About the same time, on February 5, 1981, allegations were made in the House of Commons that the British high commissioner, Sir John Ford, had "influenced" two NDP members of Parliament by warning them that the British government was uneasy with the resolution and that it might not be given smooth passage. Leaked cables and memoranda surfaced which showed that the confident front of the federal Liberals was unwarranted. As the Parliament of Canada prepared for a renewed debate on the constitutional resolution, as amended by the joint committee, there was every indication that the fight in Britain was also going to be rough.

On February 3, however, came an important break for the Liberals and their allies which helped reverse the impact of the Kershaw report. The first of the legal decisions was announced from the Manitoba Court of Appeal. The federal side won on every one of the reference questions, although by only a three-to-two majority of the judges. That result buoyed up the federal government's supporters, despite the narrowness of the victory. It appeared to federal ministers more important than ever to push the resolution forward quickly, while the legal and political odds were still in their favour. For the Conservative opposition, the split on the Manitoba court, together with the Kershaw report, signalled the weakness of the government and the need to delay passage of the resolution until the Supreme Court of Canada's decision. In this unprecedented Parliamentary showdown the parties' political tenacity and adeptness in parliamentary procedure would be put to a severe test.

Justice Minister Chrétien moved the adoption of the resolution on February 17, 1981, promising all Canadians "a new foundation on which to build a more united, a more generous and a greater country." In reply, Jake Epp, the articulate Manitoban who was the leading Conservative representative on the joint committee, easily demonstrated the irony of this objective in the face of the "divisiveness" the resolution had already created. He asked instead that the Liberals take the constitutional route which offered the broadest consensus. Patriate the constitution with an amending formula agreeable to the provinces, he said, and leave the Charter of Rights to be added later. At the end of his speech, Epp moved an amendment to the resolution deleting the controversial national referendum option for constitutional change.

The Epp amendment occupied the House completely for more than a month. The Conservatives continued to debate it and thereby prevented either the Liberals or the NDP from putting any other amendments to the resolution. This strategy delayed proceedings and increased with every day the dangers for the Liberals of adverse shifts in public opinion and of legal attack by the courts. As the debate dragged on, the Liberals and NDP found it increasingly difficult to keep their own troops from breaking ranks. By mid-

March, one Quebec MP, Louis Duclos, and four Liberal senators had already indicated that they would not support their party's own resolution, while four NDP members from Saskatchewan (Lorne Nystrom, Simon de Jong, Doug Anguish and Stan Hovdeho) had, as early as February 19, declared that they repudiated the position to which Broadbent had committed the party. Moreover, the entire Quebec Liberal caucus was known to be exceedingly restless with the government's exemption of Ontario from bilingual status.

Challenged to submit its package to the Supreme Court for judgement, badgered for its inflexible attitude to federalism and frustrated in its attempts to proceed, the government decided to move a motion to limit debate to four more days. The motion was put by Liberal House leader Yvon Pinard on March 19. Immediately the Conservatives countered: one by one, Conservative members rose on questions of privilege or points of order to prevent any debate on Pinard's motion. For almost two weeks, the work of the House of Commons was at a standstill. The Liberals and NDP denounced the tactic and waited impatiently for the Conservatives to slip or give up.

On March 31, an appeal court in Newfoundland unlocked the parliamentary deadlock. By a unanimous vote of three, the Newfoundland court found the federal package illegal. There could be no question of proceeding until the Supreme Court had ruled on the resolution. As predicted in the federal memorandum, the Liberal government abruptly agreed to await a ruling of the Supreme Court, and promised to proceed no further with the resolution if it were found illegal by Canada's highest court. In return, the opposition was asked to cooperate in allowing the resolution to proceed through Parliament so that the court might have a finished document to examine. Final vote on the resolution itself would be withheld until the court verdict. If valid, the resolution would be put to a final vote in the House after a maximum of two days debate. The opposition agreed.

On April 23, Conservative amendments were rejected and last-minute Liberal and NDP amendments providing for sexual equality, better protections for aboriginal rights, a short preamble affirming God, and equality of the Western and Eastern provinces in the amending formula were quickly passed. Finally on April 23, 1981, the final resolution was ready, just five days before the Supreme Court was to begin hearing provincial appeals on it.

Although the federal government entered that court more cheerfully after hearing, on April 15, of the Quebec Court of Appeal's four-to-one ruling in its favour, events were certainly not unfolding as the authors of the planning documents had hoped. The political timetable was set back, the legal result was anyone's guess and, worst of all, the Parti Québécois government had decisively shed its lame-duck status. On April 13, 1981, it had won a smashing victory in the provincial elections and undermined the leadership of Liberal Claude Ryan. The result suggested that the PQ under René Lévesque had virtually as much political endurance in Quebec as the federal Liberals under Pierre Trudeau.

What the victory tended to obscure, however, was the paradox of a separatist government with no separatist mandate. As some party insiders recognized, the election results left the party in a difficult philosophical and practical position. It had to go on negotiating the federalist option with its party base committed to separatism, and it could not easily translate its political power into bargaining strength *because* of its separatist leanings. In effect, the results of the referendum lingered on. There was therefore no change in the negotiating strategy of the Quebec government, although the victory deflected its attention from the provincial Liberals and encouraged a more aggressive rhetorical assault upon Trudeau and the federal Liberals.

Only three days after his election win, bristling for a fight with Trudeau, Lévesque made a pact with the other seven dissenting premiers which he hoped would block and ultimately defeat the federal strategy. The premiers' agreement called for patriation, for an amending formula based on the Vancouver consensus and for intensive federal-provincial discussion on the other topics over a three-year period. The most important element was the adoption of the Alberta formula modified to include the possibility of transferring powers by mutual consent, financial compensation for a province opting out of amendments, and, as Table 1 shows, the placement of additional subjects in the unanimity column. Although the press treated the April 16 Constitutional Accord as a last-ditch attempt by the dissenting provinces to show that they could "agree among themselves" on a constitutional package, the deal struck that day signified much more. It demonstrated the premiers' retreat from their long-standing demands for a settlement of the division of powers prior to patriation. It tacitly signalled that bargaining on a smaller package could proceed. It signified that if bargaining were to reopen, their chief interest would be their amending formula. Since satisfaction of that demand would require from them a concession of equal importance to the federal side (patriation having already been conceded), it invited a trade-off with the Charter of Rights. All these developments were the results of federal unilateral action, although the full import of the moves was not clear even to some of the players themselves.

One government which evidently did not foresee that it was structuring the terms of later negotiations was Quebec. In a bold bid to foster a united bargaining position against Trudeau, Lévesque on April 16 signed away Quebec's conventional case for a veto on future constitutional amendments. In return he accepted the protections of an "opting out with compensation" provision along with all the other provinces. Quebec now had formally joined most other provinces in affirming equality of the provinces in Canada. Since this manoeuvre could not be squared with traditional Quebec demands over amending formulae, and since it contradicted *special status* or the PQ's own case for Quebec's uniquely *national* status, this move seems to have been a tactical step on which the PQ never expected to be called to account. The battle between Lévesque and Trudeau had by now begun to take the form of a winner-take-all struggle between separatism and federalism, and Lévesque risked the long-term traditional interests of Quebec as a constituent element in the federation for the chance to defeat the federal unilateral action. The odds for a separatist victory would then be much stronger. But such brinkmanship was all the more daring since it was not needed to preserve the opposition to the federal Liberals and since the federal government had already said earlier that, while it found the Vancouver amending formula "obnoxious," it could live with it. It seemed Lévesque and his minister of intergovernmental affairs, Claude Morin, who as civil servant or politician had taken part in all the constitutional meetings of the previous twenty years, did not consider the prospects of federal compliance with their amending formula. They therefore did not see the necessary quid pro quo — the entrenchment of the Charter of Rights.

But until the verdict was in on unilateral action, it was unlikely there would be any bargaining. Each side struggled for outright victory. It was not until after a Supreme Court ruling some five months later that talk of negotiations based on the April 16 accord was again heard.

4
The Supreme Court Decision

When the Supreme Court assembled on September 28, 1981, to render judgement on the federal patriation package, all participants knew that a milestone in the struggle over the constitution was about to be passed. After almost a year of bitter debate throughout the country, many of the issues were going to be settled. Did the package diminish provincial powers? Was it constitutionally proper to proceed without provincial consent? Were all or indeed any parts of the package legal? Disagreements among experts and the often strident arguments of political elites at the national and regional levels on *both* sides of these questions had left the country unsure about the acceptability and lawfulness of Parliament's resolution. What heightened the uncertainty were the split decisions coming from appeal courts in Manitoba, Newfoundland and Quebec, which had given the federal government a lead of merely two to one. Moreover, appeal court judges who heard the ca. sided with the federal government and arguments of the provinces. There was no think that the Supreme Court decision might not also be a cliffhanger.

The political stakes in this decision were higher than they had been in any constitutional question put before the courts since Confederation. But its gravity and political significance were easy to overlook. With all of the political propaganda and simplistic talk over a Charter of Rights, it was easy to miss the profound nature of the federal package, both for what it said about the constitutional process in Canada and, equally important, for what it contained in political substance.

The question of *process* was raised by unilateral action itself. It pointed to a breakdown in the rules of the game, to the failure of governments to work within the tacit understandings of Canadian federalism to resolve political differences. Although such a departure from the ground rules might be justified by any number of arguments, unilateralism itself suggested that the mutual trust and respect needed to make federalism work in Canada were rapidly disappearing. At the end of the negotiating sessions with the provinces in September 1980, the federal government had already shown a lack of confidence in federalism by labelling so many other governments as separatist or crypto-separatist. Unilateral action was then a foregone conclusion, since according to this view Canada could only be preserved through the national government. Acting on that presumption, Ottawa deliberately polarized public opinion with its charge that federalism did not work and challenged the provinces stop it. The provinces responded to the challenge in part by referring this assault upon federalism to the courts.

Many thought it unwise to refer so highly "political" a matter to judges. But they forgot that Canada and other federal countries had been dropping political hot potatoes onto the courts for a long time. When power is divided by the constitution between two levels of government, the courts always act as umpires, often in delicate political circumstances. For example, the Supreme Court had not long before (in 1976) heard a dispute over federal wage and price controls. If the Supreme Court rules against a government's law, the lower courts simply refuse to enforce it. In general, of course, the court assumes that if any government breaks the constitutional rules it does so accidentally.

In this case, however, the political intent to change the powers of governments especially with the entrenched charter could hardly be ignored. The issue then confronted the court squarely: How was it to discharge its umpiring role? How was it to treat a federal action so apparently inconsistent with the theory and practice of federalism? The matter of *process* raised issues of the highest order in judicial review and invited the court for the first time to define its methods, values and styles of decision making in uncharted legal areas.

On the question of *substance*, the so-called people's package contained political dynamite. It overruled some parts of the Quebec language bill, the cornerstone of the PQ government, and sought to abolish permanently a century of discrimination against minority language educational rights elsewhere in Canada. It also aimed to extend and to entrench bilingualism, to eliminate provincial obstacles to a national labour market, to establish a Charter of Rights which would grant courts the power to "legislate" on moral and social issues, to expose many past and future statutes on provincial and federal books to possible legal challenge, and to impose terms for amending formulae which included, in the event of deadlock, exclusive federal use of referenda to carry out constitutional change over the heads of provincial governments. These were constitutional measures with far-reaching and unpredictable effects. But if American practice was any guide, the charter and other provisions of the resolution would tilt power decisively toward the national capital and begin to reverse the decentralized character of Canadian federalism.

For the Supreme Court, it was an uncomfortable challenge. The questions before it permitted in law either a narrow, technical response, which would evade the broader issues, or a much more expansive answer. If the court chose to address the underlying issues, its answers would define the principles of Canada as a federal state, the status of the unwritten rules which govern the exercise of legal power and, more broadly, the role of the court itself as a guardian of the federal pact. Thus, the reputation of the court itself was at stake at a time when it was a constitutional subject of federal-provincial bargaining. Ironically, the judges were also expected to rule on the validity of a federal action of which *they* were the chief beneficiaries. If, as all the critics were saying, the federal resolution would give the courts much more power, was it not odd that the judiciary would have a decisive say in approving or rejecting it?

Issues and Legal Strategies

The Supreme Court was asked to rule specifically on reference questions put before appeal courts by the provinces of Manitoba, Newfoundland and Quebec — questions designed to test the constitutionality of the proposed federal resolution. Reference cases permit the government using them to draft questions which draw out issues of fact, law and convention on which it desires a ruling. To initiate a reference then gives a government a powerful strategic advantage: it reserves to itself the power to define the issues which the court is expected to answer. That government whose actions are the object of the reference is by the same token placed at a disadvantage, since it must fight its case on terms set by a legal adversary.

Although the questions from each of the provinces were not exactly the same, they were all designed to test three things. Did the federal constitutional resolution affect provincial rights, powers and privileges? Was there a constitutional convention requiring provincial consent for constitutional resolutions affecting provincial powers, rights and privileges? Is the agreement of the provinces "constitutionally required" for such amendments? The reference case was not directed toward settling the question of the *legality* of the federal proposal (the question that would have suited federal interests best), but its *constitutional propriety* or *legitimacy* (the question that suited the provinces best).

From the point of view of the public interest, it is just as well that the broad set of questions was referred to the court. A decision on the narrower ground of legality would not have answered the moral and political concerns about how amendments affecting federal-provincial powers ought to be conducted. That larger matter had by now become a part of the national debate. Canadians were not interested merely in legal mechanisms but in the principles and practices surrounding this kind of change.

Just as the terms of the court battle were set by the provincial reference questions, they also shaped the legal strategies developed by the federal and provincial governments. Ottawa was determined to downplay the significance of the first two questions in the reference and to treat the third as though it were simply a legal question. As it declared in its Supreme Court factum (its written statement on the issues and legal arguments), the essential issue was whether Parliament's resolution had "the force of law in Canada." It argued that since that was the fundamental matter, answers to questions one and two would become unnecessary and irrelevant. In this manner, federal attorneys hoped to influence the judges' disposition of the questions in a way that would be closer to what Ottawa would have put to the court had it initiated the reference. Such a strategy assumed that a forceful argument, which focused the question in the desired direction, would shape the hearing in court and the eventual judgement.

Of course, this plan did not permit the federal government to ignore the first two questions but merely to belittle their significance. This strategy was pursued with great skill and erudition, but counsel was unable to persuade enough appeal court judges to rule decisively in Ottawa's favour. By the time of the Supreme Court hearing, federal attorneys were attributing errors in lower court judgements to judicial confusions over law and convention. There was throughout the federal factum a distinctly confident and instructive tone.

Although the dissenting provinces had caucused over the questions put to the appeal courts, the quality of their factums varied sharply as each of the attorneys general handed the legal assignment to their deputies and staff and/or to local legal notables. No attempt was made to establish a joint research bureau staffed by leading constitutional lawyers and scholars who might match the experience and stature of noted Toronto lawyer J.J. Robinette, one of those advising the federal government. With as many as eight provincial governments participating, the possibilities of a uniform legal strategy were slim. But the disunity made it possible for distinctive approaches to be taken by some provinces, notably Saskatchewan.

In general, the provinces spent their time establishing the effects of the resolution on provincial powers, the existence of conventions and the general implications of the proposed federal action for a federal state like Canada. Although this strategy exposed them many times to criticism about the *political* nature of their submission, it had the virtue of reminding the courts of their special umpiring responsibility in a federal state and of the need to take a larger view of the matter. By underlining the importance of the second question in particular, the provinces could challenge the constitutional legitimacy of unilateral action.

Arguments and Judgement: Question One

If the amendments to the Constitution of Canada sought in the "Proposed Resolution for a Joint Address to Her Majesty the Queen respecting the Constitution of Canada," or any of them, were enacted, would federal-

provincial relationships or the powers, rights or privileges granted or secured by the Constitution of Canada to the provinces, their legislatures or governments be affected and if so, in what respect or respects?

In all the appeal court hearings, federal counsel had insisted, as it did in its factum to the Supreme Court of Canada, that the court ought not to answer this question on the grounds that it was "speculative" and "premature." When, for example, the Manitoba and Newfoundland courts were questioning the matter, the resolution was being amended and revised as a result of parliamentary study. It was premature then to ask a court to pass on whether it affected provincial powers and, if so, in what respects. Manitoba's appeal court by a majority of three to two accepted the federal argument but the appeal court of Newfoundland by a unanimous vote did not. The Newfoundland court thought there was sufficient substance in the resolution as it then stood to answer the first question. Once the resolution was finalized in Parliament and after Quebec's appeal court also rejected the federal contention, the federal position became harder to maintain. Yet even in its factum to the Supreme Court, the attorney general of Canada insisted that the question was "too vague" and "too general" and thus it was "impossible to give a general answer."

The factum went on to assert rather extraneous political points that had come up earlier in debates in Parliament: that the resolution increased the powers of the provinces by giving them a lawful status in future constitutional amendments; that it "will submit the exercise of certain of their legislative powers to objective standards" (presumably a supercilious reference to court reviews of provincial laws as they relate to human rights); and that no "transfer of legis-

lative competence to the prejudice of the provinces"
was involved. This political blustering was to no avail
in the Supreme Court hearing, where the federal
government finally conceded that the answer to question one had to be yes. In its ruling on September 28,
after excusing the Manitoba court for refusing to
answer the question earlier, the Supreme Court voted
yes unanimously, without expounding on which provincial powers were affected.

Arguments and Judgement: Question Two

*Is it a constitutional convention that the House of
Commons and Senate of Canada will not request Her
Majesty the Queen to lay before the Parliament of the
United Kingdom of Great Britain and Northern Ireland
a measure to amend the Constitution of Canada affecting federal-provincial relationships or the powers, rights
or privileges granted or secured by the Constitution of
Canada to the Provinces, their legislatures or governments without first obtaining the agreement of the
provinces?*

The answer to the first question was much simpler
than the answers to either of the other two. Since the
third question asked the court to rule on whether provincial consent was "constitutionally required" for
amendments affecting provincial powers or federal-
provincial relations, the answer to the second question
on the existence of a constitutional convention was
crucial for judgement on the third.

For that reason, the federal government's legal
strategy, which first sought to bracket the second
question as "inappropriate for judicial determination,"
was a shrewd one. But, because of their irrelevant
nature, none of the arguments advanced to shut out
court consideration of the second question were suc-

cessful with *any* members of the Supreme Court. The first argument was that the court ought not to answer because the resolution concerned a matter of "internal parliamentary procedure" over which courts exercised no jurisdiction. In a sweeping claim of immunity reminiscent of arguments advanced for "executive privilege" in the United States, Ottawa's attorneys attempted to shield from court review Parliament's right to pass resolutions on *anything* it liked. Not a single judge accepted this argument since it in effect denied any role for conventions under the smoke-screen of Parliament's internal rights and privileges. The second argument was that because the question concerned matters of "political exigency and not law or convention" the court ought not to answer it. Although the political nature of conventions as defined in reference question two was acknowledged by the Supreme Court, this did not lead *any* of the justices to discard the question on that ground alone. The third and fourth arguments were essentially that, since conventions were themselves hard to define clearly and since they were also imprecise and flexible, they were entirely unsuitable objects for courts. Those arguments, too, did not pose any barrier to the court answering the question.

The second stage of the federal legal strategy was to deny the existence of the alleged convention. In the provincial appeal courts, this part of their strategy had been upheld (with some dissents) in two of the three courts; only Newfoundland's court rejected outright the federal arguments. The lawyers for the attorney general of Canada prepared this part of their case with a massive and well-conceived review of *all* previous Canadian constitutional amendments in any way affecting provincial rights and powers either directly or indirectly. The review showed that no uniform practice of consulting the provinces had ever developed and that therefore no convention or rule to that effect existed. This mode of organizing the material and drawing from it the desired conclusion suited federal purposes perfectly, even though there were important distinctions that could be drawn between different kinds of amendments. For example, an amendment which in 1930 finally granted to the Western provinces control over their lands and natural resources (which other provinces had always enjoyed) was by its nature non-contentious so far as the other provinces were concerned; it did not directly affect all provinces' legislative powers in the same way that ceding jurisdiction over unemployment insurance or old age pensions to the federal level did. By treating all amendments alike and by noting the various procedures that were adopted for amendment in each instance, the federal government appeared to overturn any sense that a working convention requiring provincial consent existed.

The statements of responsible actors such as former federal ministers were frequently used by federal attorneys to show that although it was undoubtedly politically desirable to secure provincial consent to constitutional amendments affecting the provinces, there was no requirement to do so. This position was buttressed by the argument "that in no case has the United Kingdom Parliament refused to enact an amendment to the B.N.A. Act on the ground that provincial consents have not been given." (The argument conveniently ignored the fact that no previous resolution had ever gone forward with massive provincial opposition.) The "non-existence of the alleged convention" was also demonstrated by the fact that it

could not be defined: federal counsel claimed
could not be determined whom such a convention
would bind, when it had come into existence, what
kinds of amendments it covered, or what degree of
provincial consent was required. In the absence of any
certainty and precision on these points, the attorney
general of Canada argued that no convention of the
type raised in question two existed.

Finally, the third stage of the federal strategy was to
argue that even if a convention existed, it was not
legally enforceable. Thus a convention might be
recognized especially as an aid to the interpretation of
a legal issue (in the same sense that "courts 'recognize'
that people usually sleep at night and are awake
during the day"), but it could not lead to court
"declaration" of such a convention; such a task was fit
"for politicians and political scientists, not the courts."
A vast number of constitutional authorities and precedents were marshalled to show that no respectable
constitutional authority (with the exception of W.R.
Lederman, former dean of law at Queen's University),
would support the idea that conventions were rules
which courts could legally impose upon anyone.

All the provinces recognized that success on question two was essential to winning at least a moral and
political victory and possibly a legal victory on the
third question as well. In the appeal courts, the provinces too had busied themselves with scores of statements by cabinet ministers, prime ministers and
British parliamentarians showing that there was a rule
requiring provincial consent to constitutional amendments affecting provincial powers. They brought
together all the constitutional amendments which
showed that this was a consistent practice, especially
since the Statute of Westminster was passed in 1931.

...develop an effective response to
...ment's apparently overwhelming
...ctice of consultation was variable,
e... ...unanimous consent on some amendment... ...consent on others. For that reason, the
provinc... ...case did not fare well on question two in
either Manitoba or Quebec. Even with those justices
who dissented, there was evidence of discomfort with
the counting-up-amendments approach; they chiefly
relied on the contention that after 1931 the provinces
enjoyed a legal status as equal and sovereign partners
with Ottawa in a federal system of government.

The more forceful of the provincial factums attempted to draw out the absurdity of Ottawa's contentions by showing that the central government was
claiming an absolute legal power to do whatever it
might wish to the constitution of Canada. If Ottawa's
arguments were correct, it could unilaterally convert
the country from a federal to a unitary state, strike
down the use of the French language in Quebec or
transfer the control over natural resources to itself.
Such power at the centre could not be squared with
the principles of a federal state.

By the time of the Supreme Court hearing, Saskatchewan had joined the other provinces in the legal
battle and presented through its attorney, Ken Lysyk,
a much more defensible legal argument on question
two than the courts had yet seen. Saskatchewan's
counsel saw with much more clarity the use the federal
government was making of the practice on all the constitutional amendments and at the outset of its submission proceeded to cut the Gordian knot.

> It is submitted that the questions before the Court in
> this Reference in essence, although not in terms,

address a specific class of constitutional amendment, namely, those amendments which change provincial legislative powers under the Canadian constitution. Accordingly, it will be further submitted, the central issue is *whether there is a constitutional convention or constitutional requirement for agreement of the provinces to amendments which change provincial legislative powers*. It is therefore unnecessary to address the broader, and very different question of amendments to the British North American acts, 1867-1975 generally. Indeed, to approach the matter in terms of examining all amendments to the B.N.A. act, as an undifferentiated group, tends to obscure the central issue raised in this Reference.

Saskatchewan then proceeded to sever those amendments that touched federal-provincial relations only indirectly from those that did so directly. Only the latter class of amendment was pertinent. This was an astute counter-attack on the federal government's principal case against the existence of the convention. There was no question that the provinces were chiefly contesting amendments which directly affected their powers and that the federal explanation of the practice on other kinds of amendments was quite deliberately obscuring that issue. Once Saskatchewan had established that point, it went on to show that there was with respect to this class of amendment a clear convention: the precedents allowed for no exceptions, the actors in the precedents treated the convention as binding and the convention itself rested upon a sound rationale. Thus, the usual tests for establishing the existence of a convention were met.

The contribution of the Saskatchewan factum did not end there however. After showing that every amendment since Confederation which touched directly on provincial legislative powers proceeded only with the consent of the affected province or provinces, Saskatchewan pointed out the errors of justices Samuel Freedman and Roy Matas of the Court of Appeal of Manitoba on three points: their failure to distinguish between classes of amendments, their consequent failure to see that uniform practice as well as a 1965 federal government white paper on the subject had sanctioned the convention of provincial consent, and their failure to interpret correctly the section of the federal white paper sanctioning the rule. It was the last oversight which was of tremendous importance not only to the existence of the convention, but also to the unanimity rule to which all dissenting provinces but Saskatchewan were committed.

Justice Freedman had argued that the federal white paper in 1965 entitled *The Amendment of the Constitution of Canada* did not disclose and confirm a convention in the following three-sentence section:

> *The fourth general principle is that the Canadian Parliament will not request an amendment directly affecting federal-provincial relationships without prior consultation and agreement with the provinces.* This principle did not emerge as early as others but since 1907, and particularly since 1930, has gained increasing recognition and acceptance. *The nature and the degree of provincial participation in the amending process, however, have not lent themselves to easy definition.*

In particular, Justice Freedman argued that the third sentence contradicted and negated the first. Saskatchewan countered in the following way:

> It is respectfully submitted that Chief Justice Freedman erred in this analysis. The third sentence

is concerned not with the *existence* of a principle (or convention) but with the *measure of provincial agreement* ("the nature and the degree of provincial participation") that is necessary with respect to this kind of constitutional amendment. The distinction is of considerable importance and it relates to [Saskatchewan's] position that... there is both a constitutional convention and a constitutional requirement that the agreement of the provinces be obtained for a proposed constitutional amendment changing legislative powers, but that it does not follow that the agreement of *all* the provinces must be obtained.

Supporting this conclusion with quotation from Prime Minister William Lyon Mackenzie King on a 1940 amendment, Saskatchewan concluded that there may be "some uncertainty on whether unanimity is necessary, but none on whether substantial provincial support is necessary." This legal argument seriously eroded the federal case.

When the court's answer to question two was revealed on September 28, 1981, a clear split emerged between the judges with six voting yes and three voting no. Justices Ronald Martland, Roland Ritchie, Brian Dickson, Jean Beetz, Julien Chouinard and Antonio Lamer united to give the provinces a "win" by declaring that there *was* a convention or rule which required substantial provincial consent for Ottawa's constitutional resolution. Therefore unilateral action by the federal Parliament would be "unconstitutional in the conventional sense." Chief Justice Bora Laskin and justices Willard Estey and William McIntyre ruled that no such convention existed and therefore that the national government could proceed without any legal *or* constitutional concern for provincial consent. Thus, the decision of the Newfoundland Court of Appeal on the second question was upheld and that of the appeal courts of Manitoba and Quebec rejected. Doubts remained, however. How was the split to be explained? How could the members of the court disagree so sharply on a matter of this importance?

Before the reasons for judgement are assessed, one should recall that divisions within the court are not unusual. Since matters come before the court mostly because they are questions over which reasonable men might differ, they are by their nature non-technical. They call on the judges' reason, experience and philosophy. In addition, judges are human; they necessarily bring their political biases and personal values to their work, even though they are expected to exercise unusual self-restraint in this respect. Therefore two (and sometimes more) quite defensible answers may be given to any question before the court and the values or principles on which such answers are based clearly laid out.

Although it was evident that the majority and the dissenters were at loggerheads over many matters of law and principle, the issues over which they fought were essentially defined by the factums of Saskatchewan and the federal government. Just as these two adversaries, personified in co-chairmen Chrétien and Romanow's friendly "Tuque and Uke" show, tended to dominate the political negotiations of the 1980 summer, the same antagonists took the limelight in court. The majority of the Supreme Court inclined to favour Saskatchewan, while the dissenters, after brushing aside the first part of the federal legal strategy, followed pretty faithfully the federal line of argument concerning the non-existence of conventions.

Saskatchewan had provided the first bone of contention between two factions of the court by refusing to treat the second question as though it were a test of the unanimity rule. Saskatchewan argued that the question merely enquired into the existence of a convention requiring provincial consent for those matters described in the question, without reference to the exact measure of consent required; the federal government had treated the second question as though it were asserting a convention requiring unanimous consent. The issue was an important one. If a convention requiring unanimity was being advanced, it would be easier to show that there was no consistent practice or agreement and therefore no such convention. If the reference question was not asserting unanimity, the case for such a convention was much stronger.

The dissenting judges thought that the reference question clearly asked for a convention requiring the agreement of all the provinces, as every party but Saskatchewan was alleging, and that it was that question and that question only which must be answered. In their reasons, the dissenters bluntly pointed a finger at the majority of their brethren for "editing the questions to develop a meaning not clearly expressed." Declaring that the words "of the provinces" in the reference question "in this context and in general usage mean in plain English all of the Provinces of Canada," it concluded that "the Court may answer only the questions put and may not conjure up questions of its own which, in turn, would lead to uninvited answers."

The majority bloc replied to that scolding by declaring that the question did not and could not be read as though the last part of the question had read "of all the provinces."

It would have been easy to insert the word "all" into the question had it been intended to narrow its meaning. But we do not think it was so intended. The issue raised by the question is essentially whether there is a constitutional convention that the House of Commons and Senate of Canada will not proceed alone.

After pointing out as well that the Quebec reference question clearly pointed to "something less than unanimity," the majority suggested that if there were ambiguity in the question, the court "should not in a constitutional reference be in a worse position than that of a witness in a trial and feel compelled simply to answer Yes or No." There were clear precedents in earlier reference cases to show that the court should not be a victim of any misleading wording or possible misunderstandings.

Striking differences also arose between the two factions over the role and significance of convention in a federal state. Although both sides agreed with Justice Freedman of Manitoba that

- a convention occupies a position somewhere in between a usage or custom on the one hand and a constitutional law on the other,
- [that it is] nearer to law than to usage or custom,
- [that it] "is a rule which is regarded as obligatory by the officials to whom it applies" and
- that the sanction for breach of a convention will be political rather than legal,

they still did not agree to give to conventions the same *constitutional status* in a federal state. This dispute went to the root of their philosophical differences over the Canadian state.

The majority bloc began by describing conventions

as those largely unwritten rules which, for example, compel the government's resignation when the opposition gains a majority at the polls or dictate the queen's or governor general's exercise of legal power only on advice of ministers. Such conventional rules are not enforceable by the courts, since they do not form part of the law of the constitution. But noncompliance with the first convention could "be regarded as tantamount to a coup d'état," while noncompliance with the second would produce a "political crisis." Conventions therefore "ensure that the legal framework of the Constitution will be operated in accordance with the prevailing constitutional values or principles." Thus they "may be more important than some laws. Their importance depends on that of the value or principle which they are meant to safeguard."

Since the majority had agreed with the dissenters that such conventions could not be enforced by the courts, it appeared that conventions could none the less be discarded whenever politicians felt strong enough to do so. To provide a constitutional sanction against such action, the majority proceeded to label any violation of such conventions "unconstitutional." Such a declaration could not make any legal difference, but its moral and political force would be considerable. In this way, the majority of the court went as far as they could in giving conventions in a federal state the maximum defence possible. This part of the majority decision was daring and well-conceived:

> [Conventions] form an integral part of the Constitution and of the constitutional system. They come within the meaning of the word "Constitution" in the preamble of the British North America Act, 1867:

> Whereas the Provinces of Canada, Nova Scotia, and New Brunswick have expressed their Desire to be federally united...with a Constitution similar in principle to that of the United Kingdom;

That is why it is perfectly appropriate to say that to violate a convention is to do something which is unconstitutional although it entails no direct legal consequence. But the words "constitutional" and "unconstitutional" may also be used in a strict legal sense, for instance with respect to a statute which is found *ultra vires* or unconstitutional. The foregoing may perhaps be summarized in an equation: constitutional conventions plus constitutional law equal the total Constitution of the country.

The dissenters were moved by a different spirit. After reiterating what the majority had conceded about the non-legal status of convention, the dissenters went on to remove any constitutional status for conventions. They declared that the "observance" of a convention could not be made a constitutional requirement even in the non-legal sense. "In a federal state where the essential feature of the Constitution must be the distribution of powers between the two levels of government, each supreme in its own legislative sphere, *constitutionality and legality must be synonymous, and conventional rules will be accorded less significance than they may have in a unitary state such as the United Kingdom.*" This conclusion suggested that, even if the dissenters had agreed that a convention requiring provincial support existed, they would have been unwilling to give it constitutional significance. Why legality should exclude a role for conventions in a federal as opposed to unitary state was also not really explained. The dissenters' argument was, on the face of it, a blanket exclusion of a court's role in recognizing the constitutional functions of conventions. This left conventions (even those with legitimate constitutional features) as purely political matters, as the federal government had been contending. If the dissenters were required to put their views "in an equation," it would have amounted to: the *law* is the *constitution*.

Thus the two blocs on the court centred on the views of the Canadian state of the Saskatchewan and federal governments respectively: the importance of constitutional convention and the federal principle versus the strict question of law and an "imperfect" more centralized federalism. Such a division of philosophy was clear over the demands of a convention itself: the majority was able to separate the *principle* of provincial consent from the *measure* of consent required and insisted that to demand that a convention have the precision of a legal rule was "tantamount to denying that this area of the Canadian Constitution is capable of being governed by conventional rules." The minority group argued that lack of precision over "fixing the degree of provincial participation ... robs any supposed convention of that degree of definition which is necessary to allow for its operation." The majority simply replied that if "a consensus had emerged on the measure of provincial agreement, an amending formula would quickly have been enacted and we would no longer be in the realm of conventions."

When the majority offered its reason for the convention, it came quickly to the heart of the matter: unilateral action was inconsistent with the *federal* nature of Canada.

> The federal principle cannot be reconciled with a state of affairs where the modification of provincial legis-

lative powers could be obtained by the unilateral action of the federal authorities. It would indeed offend the federal principle that "a radical change to [the] constitution [be] taken at the request of a bare majority of the members of the Canadian House of Commons and Senate."

The purpose of this conventional rule is to protect the federal character of the Canadian Constitution and prevent the anomaly that the House of Commons and Senate could obtain by simple resolution what they could not validly accomplish by statute.

The dissenting judges rejected this argument on four grounds:
• that a convention providing for partial provincial consent would not protect federalism since "those provinces favouring amendment would be pleased while those refusing consent could claim coercion";
• that unanimous consent, while protecting federalism in theory, would "overlook . . . the [centralized] nature of Canadian federalism which is neither 'perfect' nor 'ideal,'" i.e., Ottawa enjoys legal power to strike down provincial laws ("disallowance") or to seize provincial property ("declaratory power"), etc.
• that unilateral action would protect the "federal state without disturbing the distribution or balance of power and enshrine provincial rights" in a new amending formula;
• that the threat to Canadian federalism (i.e., to convert Canada into a unitary state) was purely hypothetical and not actually before the court and that in any case "it is not for the Court to express views on the wisdom or lack of wisdom of these proposals."

Since the convention required "substantial provincial support," it would seem that the dissenters' first argument that federalism would not be protected was a trifle far-fetched. It confused a province's sense of coercion with the degree of provincial participation needed to pass the "federal" test. All the others were essentially arguments advanced by the federal government, and the majority of the court had this to say about them:

> It is true that Canada would remain a federation if the proposed amendments became law. But it would be a different federation made different at the instance of a majority in the Houses of the federal Parliament acting alone. It is this process itself which offends the federal principle.

From that position, the majority of six answered yes to the second question and declared further that "the agreement of the provinces of Canada, no views being expressed as to its quantification, is *constitutionally required* for the passing of the ... resolution ... and that the passing of this resolution without such agreement would be *unconstitutional in the conventional sense*." (Emphasis added.)

Arguments and Judgement: Question Three

Is the agreement of the provinces of Canada constitutionally required for amendment to the Constitution of Canada where such amendment affects federal-provincial relationships or alters the powers, rights or privileges granted or secured by the Constitution of Canada to the provinces, their legislatures or governments?

It would appear that the last words of the majority on question two also answered question three: yes, the agreement of the provinces was required. This decision however was qualified by the words, "in the conventional sense," and the third question was thought to ask if the agreement of the provinces was also required *by law*. Thus to deal with the distinct elements of law and convention, the court felt that it had to split the question into two parts. The requirement of provincial agreement by constitutional convention was then brought forward from question two to answer the first part of question three.

To answer the *legal* requirement of provincial consent, the court reformed into a new alignment of seven judges who said no and two judges who said yes. Among the no faction of the court were the three dissenters (Laskin, Estey and McIntyre) who had rejected the second question. They were joined by four of the justices who had formed the majority on question two, justices Dickson, Beetz, Chouinard and Lamer. This new majority declared that strictly speaking the law did not require provincial consent. On this issue alone, the federal attorneys had scored a "win."

How was it possible that this "swing" group of four justices could answer question three in a split way: yes, provincial consent is required by convention; no, it is not required by law? It was clear from that group's position on question two that winning on the matter of convention would not mean winning on law, because the courts could not enforce conventions as though they were legal rules. If a convention were improperly violated by those with legal authority, the courts would still "be bound to enforce the law, not the convention." The remedy for violation of convention would have to be a political sanction.

The provinces, especially Manitoba, had attempted to argue that the conventional rule in question two had "crystallized" into a rule of law. Quoting from an extensive series of cases and authorities, they sought to limit Parliament's legal power to draft such a resolution and to limit the Parliament of the United Kingdom from complying with such a resolution if it did not carry provincial consent. The majority rejected these arguments. They declared that to argue otherwise would distort the case law and established opinion and invite the court into the odd position that Canada had always had an amending formula:

> It would be anomalous indeed, overshadowing the anomaly of a Constitution which contains no provision for its amendment, for this Court to say retroactively that in law we have had an amending formula all along, even if we have not hitherto known it; or, to say that we have had in law one amending formula, say from 1867 to 1931, and a second amending formula that has emerged after 1931.

Drawing on the Statute of Westminster and on statements in conferences prior to it, the provinces had argued that Britain had given up legal authority to amend the Canadian constitution in the way in which Ottawa was contending, and that it could do so now only on the advice of the "proper constitutional authorities." If the amendment touched provincial powers or interests, those authorities would be the provincial legislatures or governments. The majority dismissed this argument: "it distorts both history and ordinary principles of statutory or constitutional interpretation." The parliaments of Canada and the United Kingdom retained unlimited legal power to proceed without provincial consent.

Manitoba had advanced an interesting argument that Ottawa "cannot do indirectly what it cannot do directly." Since it could not pass the resolution on its own, "it would be illegal to invoke United Kingdom authority to do for Canada what it cannot do itself."

Although the court majority rejected this argument on the grounds that it "confused the issue of process . . . with the legal competence of the British Parliament," the Manitoba submission drew attention to the colourable or specious nature of the federal position. Similar arguments had frequently formed the basis of Privy Council decisions and they deserved a more thoughtful response than they received from the majority.

The final general contention of the provinces had been that the Parliament of Great Britain must take account of the federal nature of Canada. The provinces were equal and sovereign in their own sphere of legislative authority, and therefore any federal unilateral action which limits provincial powers must be found illegal. The court must "project externally, as a matter of law, the internal distribution of legislative power." The majority refused to do so even though the two dissenters on the court, justices Martland and Ritchie, reminded them that Parliament's treaty-making powers had been limited in precisely that manner by the Privy Council in the 1937 Labour Conventions case. In that decision, the court had ruled that Ottawa could not escape the division of legislative powers merely by signing an international agreement promising to enact certain labour measures which ordinarily fell under provincial jurisdiction; the federal principle limited Ottawa's ability to do what it liked in its external commitments. But the Supreme Court decided that the law, as distinct from convention, provided no shelter for federalism. "The law knows nothing of any requirement of provincial consent, either to a resolution of the federal Houses or as a condition of the exercise of United Kingdom legislative power."

Such a conclusion was more than justices Martland and Ritchie could accept. They insisted that Ottawa's assertion of absolute legal power "to cause the B.N.A. Act to be amended in any way they desire" was inconsistent with the federal character of Canada's constitution. The preservation of the federal nature of the country was a "dominant principle of Canadian constitutional law" which it was the primary duty of the court to address and defend.

> In our opinion, the two Houses lack legal authority, of their own motion, to obtain constitutional amendments which would strike at the very basis of the Canadian Federal system, i.e. the complete division of legislative powers between the Parliament of Canada and the Provincial Legislatures. It is the duty of this Court to consider this assertion of rights with a view to the preservation of the Constitution.

The dissenters showed that the courts had developed principles to defend federalism in unprecedented circumstances even where there were no express provisions for such principles in the BNA Act. In each case, these principles flowed from the federal nature of Canada's constitution and were given "full legal force in the sense of being employed to strike down legislative enactments." There was therefore no excuse for taking a timid position on the legal question any more than on the matter of convention. Whatever statutory authority Parliament had to pass resolutions requesting amendments to the constitution, it "excluded the power to do anything inconsistent with the B.N.A. Act." Although the dissenters also accepted other technical arguments for upholding the provinces, it was essentially the federal principle which they thought required legal recognition and protection.

The Martland-Ritchie dissent, founded on a broader set of concerns arising out of Canadian constitutional law, did not draw a thoughtful response from the court majority. The majority view, its attention distracted by the sharp distinctions between convention and law, did not appear to consider seriously what legal impediments federalism placed upon the doctrine of the unlimited sovereignty of Parliament. In effect, having severed law from convention, they concluded that there was no obstacle to Parliament legally proceeding with a constitutionally improper measure. This is an unusual posture for any court to have adopted in a federal state. The clear implication is that the principle of federalism itself has no legal force even where a government action, to use the majority language on question two, "offends the federal principle." It is difficult to make that conclusion square with the fact that the Privy Council, the British court that served as Canada's final court of appeal on constitutional cases until 1949, had given the federal principle legal force in several landmark decisions. These cases and rationale were produced by Martland and Ritchie, but the best that the majority could do in reply was to say that federalism would remain intact in spite of this measure, and that Canada's federal system was not a standard or perfect model of federalism. While such arguments were consistent for Laskin, Estey and McIntyre, who as dissenters had argued the same points on question two, they were a dramatic reversal for the "swing group" of judges.

Martland's and Ritchie's argument drew out the brazen nature of the double-barrelled federal contentions. The Canadian Parliament may pass *any* constitutional resolutions it likes; the United Kingdom *must* subsequently pass them. The dissenters rejected the first contention as an attack on the legally recognized federal principle and a "perversion" of Parliament's resolution procedures. In addition, they challenged the court majority's view that the absence of a clear prohibition against an action of this kind was sufficient to conclude that "the law knows nothing of any requirement of provincial consent." Instead, the dissenters insisted that the absence of a specific grant of power for such action, together with the express prohibition of any similar action by direct legislative enactment of Parliament under section 91 (1), suggested that the federal government's claims went too far.

With the September 28 judgement, Prime Minister Trudeau finally received an answer to an almost forgotten scholarly debate from the 1940s. In the end, the court had come down with an ingeniously split decision which Trudeau, Paul Gérin-Lajoie and the others in the debate could hardly have anticipated: seven to two that such a resolution was legal; six to three that it was improper and "unconstitutional." But the results were just as puzzling to non-specialists. The decision appeared to move in the direction of both parties and to settle nothing. But even if the decision was a split ruling, giving neither party a decisive win, the view that it settled nothing was quite wrong. It resolved two critical matters vital to everything that came afterward: *the resolution was legal* **and** *the resolution was constitutionally improper*. It would remain for the Canadian people and their legislatures and governments to see what value they placed upon legal power and principle respectively. It also remained to be seen what weight the country would give to national power and purpose on the one hand and regionalism and the federal principle on the other.

Hence, if the split decision is looked at from the perspective of statecraft, it must be acknowledged as artful. By giving each side a victory but neither a decisive win, the result constituted a virtual order to return to the bargaining table. Moreover, the rejection of unanimity had the effect of withdrawing blocking power from provincial hard-liners and of opening the way for a deal based on substantial agreement only. In refusing to define that measure more precisely, the court avoided the pitfalls of pronouncing on what was neither clear nor even required of it. Finally, the split ruling protected the court from the potentially dangerous political assault it would have faced had it decided wholly in favour of either bloc. It was not long before events bore out the political foresightedness of the court judgement.

5
The Strategy of Agreem

The court decision tossed the issue back into the political arena, but not before it had shaped the terms of the ensuing struggle. On the one hand, it legalized federal unilateral action but stripped it of legitimacy; on the other hand, it threatened the provinces by removing any lingering doubts about the need for their unanimous consent to constitutional change affecting provincial powers. The pressure was immense for a return to negotiations and, though the atmosphere was still poisonous, events were forcing the governments towards a compromise deal where no single player could be a spoiler.

Before the implications of the court judgement had sunk in, the two sides began their usual jockeying. Justice Minister Chrétien waited scarcely a couple of hours before appearing before the nation to claim a federal victory on the grounds of legality. Forgetting entirely the broad grounds of justification for unilateral action that the federal government had been using for over a year, Chrétien claimed that the issue was strictly a matter of legality versus political connience. The role of conventions was dismissed and the question of acting unconstitutionally even if legally was side-stepped entirely. It was an odd performance for a Canadian minister of justice. Dubbing Chrétien's posture as "legal trickery," opposition leader Joe Clark promised to fight the Liberals if they pushed on with the resolution in the face of the court's judgement.

The provinces decided to wait to hear Prime Minister Trudeau's reaction before responding to the decision. He did not speak until the evening of September 28 in a special broadcast from Seoul, South Korea, where he was paying a state visit. While Trudeau acknowledged the convention of provincial consent, he noted that after a half century of observance, it had frustrated efforts at patriation and could no longer be blindly followed. Unless there were signs of possible accommodation with the provinces, the message was clear: legal power rested with the federal government and it would "press on."

B.C. Premier William Bennett, who was acting as chairman of the eight provinces opposing the resolution, seized the olive branch reluctantly extended by Trudeau. He declared he would immediately visit all the premiers and would meet with the prime minister on his return to discuss the possibility of a further first ministers' conference. After correctly interpreting the court decision as an invitation to the political actors to resolve their differences, Bennett reiterated the premiers' view that the judgement had fully vindicated their contention that the resolution violated the constitution and the federal principle.

On October 3 the National Assembly of Quebec strengthened the hand of the Parti Québécois government by passing a resolution calling on the federal government to renounce unilateral action and to respect the conventions of the Canadian constitution. Most important, the resolution declared that the assembly "opposes every act which could interfere with its rights and affect its powers without its consent." The resolution passed 111 to 9 with all-party support. Federal leaders were upset that only nine provincial Liberals from predominantly anglophone ridings refused to join forces with the PQ.

Meanwhile, Blakeney and Bennett, the members of the Gang of Eight most inclined to compromise, were already signalling to Trudeau and Premier Davis of Ontario their conciliatory outlook. To them, Quebec's hard-line posture seemed unwise. Blakeney thought the Quebec assembly's action "premature," although Premier Lévesque argued that it did not go against the "essentials" of the dissident provinces' common front. Already members of the gang were beginning to move in opposite directions.

Lévesque's government, ignoring the dangers of isolating itself from the gang after the Supreme Court had appeared to give no province a veto, remained unyielding. There was constant talk of a Quebec referendum on federal unilateralism or even a national referendum to test whether the people supported Ottawa's package. The Quebec government also threatened to turn the PQ political machine onto the federal Liberals in Quebec. And while Lévesque upbraided Quebec MPs for their "incredible treachery" and "servility," the Quebec federal caucus responded with equal truculence and with a publicly paid $1 million advertising campaign to put its views to the Quebec people. The signs of an all-out political war between Quebec separatists and federalists were apparent.

Meanwhile on the broader federal-provincial front, political posturing went on among first ministers continents apart. Petty squabbles arose over who must offer the next compromise, whose timetable would be used, and who had the political muscle in Westminster. Trudeau had hoped to squeeze the Gang of Eight with an exceedingly tight timetable, a demand for compromises within the terms of his package and repeated threats to act unilaterally if the provinces did not comply. An angered Gang of Eight rejected Trudeau's position, demanded that he compromise on their Constitutional Accord of April 16, 1981, and on four separate occasions turned down Trudeau's calls to start talks. Both the preliminary meeting on October 13 between Trudeau and Bennett and later written exchanges between the dissenting premiers and the prime minister were unpleasant. Finally, following a premiers' meeting in Montreal on October 20 (which found premiers Davis and Hatfield asked to leave the meeting early), an invitation to meet was extended to Trudeau for the first week of November. He grudgingly accepted and set November 2 as a time for "one final attempt" to come to an agreement.

The dissident provinces had won the first round over timing. If they were to succeed at the negotiating table, however, they would need to agree on a minimum package acceptable to all sides. Although they publicly declared their April 16 accord to be that minimum, they all knew that they must be prepared to give further. But internal divisions made further movement as a bloc difficult. Thus, in private meetings, the premiers or their ministers failed to address a new "bottom-line position" and instead largely spent their time planning a strategy against any possible unilateral action.

For Lévesque and fellow hard-liner Sterling Lyon, the April accord was the negotiating minimum. Concerned about reports of separate exploratory talks between federal supporters and Saskatchewan and British Columbia, Lévesque hoped to put a stop to it by privately charging the moderates with betraying the group. But every premier knew there was little likelihood that the group could stay together once bargaining started in earnest. The real question was whether Lévesque and Lyon could keep the bloc together long enough to frustrate the prospects of an agreement satisfactory to the federal government. On the other hand, if the moderates could prevent the negotiations from becoming so polarized by offering concessions, the chances were much stronger that the hard-liners would be isolated and an agreement forged. Thus, although the appearance of federal-provincial conflict alone caught the public eye, the politics of inter-provincial conflict was quietly being worked out within the "common front."

The moderates had by now realized that bargaining by a tough first-line "provincial consensus" ultimately played into the hands of the federal government. Although a provincial consensus was a vital part of the bargaining — an indispensable first step — it could not be advanced inflexibly. That was the mistake made in the September 1980 talks. But the Gang of Eight could not compromise beyond their April 16 accord for reasons of basic political incompatibility.

For example, in the bargaining conducted largely through the media before the talks began, most members of the Gang of Eight had indicated a willingness to compromise on the Charter of Rights, as had the federal government. But, although most governments in English-speaking Canada were prepared to compromise to permit the entrenching of minority language educational rights, Quebec would not. And on this issue, as Premier Bennett sensed, the federal government would not move. There was no provincial consensus on this item (except for an entirely toothless "mini charter" allowing for provinces to opt in), despite its obvious importance. In the event of deadlock between the governments, Quebec on October 5 was already on record as favouring a referendum to settle the matter, while almost all the other provinces in the Gang of Eight were not. This difference remained unresolved. On the broader question of rights in the charter, the "common front" betrayed divisions between a premier like Lyon, who was unalterably opposed in principle, and a premier like Brian Peckford, who from the start was ready to support a charter. Even raising these issues would threaten their uneasy alliance.

Of course, at the root of unresolved differences, lay a fundamental incompatibility between the politics of committed federalists and a separatist premier of Quebec. Political differences could be glossed over in a common opposition to Ottawa's unilateral action, but once the business of federal renewal began they made unlikely partners. For Ontario, New Brunswick and the federal government, that was the most startling feature of the gang and they attributed its continuing at all to Lévesque's "duping" of the others. In its contacts with the moderates, Ontario reminded them of this incompatibility and of the fact that the PQ government could not afford to have a genuine compromise deal. It became part of the federal strategy to disengage the moderates from the bloc, to isolate

Quebec and reduce its influence over the others, and to secure a deal even if it had to exclude Quebec.

As the participants gathered in Ottawa on the Sunday evening prior to the First Ministers' Conference, each side prepared its position for the most sophisticated constitutional poker game since Confederation. But unlike September, 1980, there was more hope now for a negotiated solution. Public opinion demanded a settlement. Britain expected a consensus. The players themselves had only three (instead of twelve) items on the table. But most important, the requirement of unanimity was gone. Now, thanks to the Supreme Court, a deal could be concluded with "substantial" provincial consent only. Under these new conditions, the bargaining resembled a zero-sum game: not all players need be satisfied with an outcome and any outcome could advantage some at the expense of others. With the known divisions in the Gang of Eight, no province could be assured of not being odd man out if it proved inflexible.

On Monday, November 2, Trudeau opened the talks before a barrage of television cameras in the National Conference Centre. After citing the three topics to be settled — patriation, an amending formula and a Charter of Rights — he lost no time in seizing the initiative. The federal government was "flexible" on the amending formula though it preferred the Victoria formula and had reservations concerning "opting out" in the provincial accord formula, which it regarded as a form of "incremental separatism." On the Charter of Rights the government was ready to compromise on "timing and substance," but not on the principle. This staking out of the federal position with a generally conciliatory tone was important to assure the public of federal willingness to compromise and to strengthen the moderates' bargaining position within the Gang of Eight.

But the initiatives towards compromise did not end here. The federal government's provincial allies, premiers Davis of Ontario and Hatfield of New Brunswick, each proposed compromises on the two most contentious issues. Davis shifted dramatically toward the principles of the Gang of Eight by offering to give up an Ontario veto in the Victoria amending formula now in the federal resolution. This offer was a major concession. Not only was Ontario signalling its abstention from a claim to primacy on the grounds of population, but it was now virtually guaranteeing that the principle of formal constitutional equality among provinces might finally be adopted.

Hatfield offered an important compromise on the Charter of Rights. His proposal was to entrench most provisions of the charter, including those pertaining to language and education, but to hold in suspension the three sections that were most contentious as far as the provinces were concerned. As was seen in Chapter 2, these were the sections conferring legal and equality rights, together with the clause empowering citizens to get their rights enforced by the courts. Hatfield suggested that if, after a three-year delay, any six provinces continued to oppose these sections, they would become inoperable. This was the first concrete version of a limited charter which might overcome areas of contention and meet each side's minimum objectives. No other premiers spoke to the proposal in the public session, preferring, as one of them put it, "to poke at it with long sticks" before making any commitment. Hatfield's compromise was valuable in showing the kind of trade-off which an ally of the federal government thought necessary for success at the table: acceptance of the federal Liberals' bilingual program in return for a chance to delay and possibly defeat sections of the charter that most provinces found objectionable.

For the public part of the First Ministers' Conference, the Gang of Eight had decided to take a different tack. They used the occasion to lecture Ottawa for having attempted unilateral action and to underline their Supreme Court victory on the constitutional question. Although it dampened public expectations about their willingness to bargain, this strategy had several advantages. It preserved the common front; it signalled that the federal government would not get an agreement without significant concessions; it prepared the public for the complex battle over federalism which would follow if the talks broke down. The strategy permitted the provinces to confront the federal government directly for the first time in over a year and to express in the strongest terms their profound disagreement with the unconstitutional nature of federal actions.

Lévesque termed the federal resolution a "legal and political absurdity" and demanded that Trudeau seek an electoral mandate for unilateral action. Alberta Premier Peter Lougheed declared that the resolution "violates the spirit and intent of Confederation" and "flagrantly disregards our nation's history, traditions, and its principles." Lyon scolded Trudeau for sowing discord so deep that the federal system was prevented from tackling other urgent problems. And so it went. Although most moderates were less aggressive, they too reproached the government for violating federalism. Saskatchewan and British Columbia, however, went out of their way to declare themselves ready to compromise. And with unanimity "a ghost of conferences past," as Allan Blakeney pointed out, they had now from the Supreme Court "a whole new set of rules" and an "unparalleled opportunity to succeed."

The first afternoon of private bargaining was largely spent discussing the question of the amendment formula, with neither side giving any indication of what compromise might be acceptable. The Charter of Rights was not discussed until late afternoon, and the issue failed to isolate any members of the Gang of Eight in separate positions.

Tuesday, November 3, proved to be more fruitful, not because any agreements were actually reached, but because the way was prepared for an agreement. In the morning, the hard-liners Lévesque and Lyon tackled Trudeau in a bitter exchange that threatened chances of a deal. They appeared to be tempting a conference breakdown by drawing the players into personal antagonisms. At this point, Davis appealed to the other premiers to bargain in good faith, as they had promised in the public session, and offered to make the first move towards compromise. Provided compensation for opting out were dropped, Ontario would support the Gang of Eight's amending formula in return for its support for a modified Charter of Rights. This trading offer made explicit for the first time the linkage between the proposals of Davis and Hatfield the day before.

This deliberate swap had the desired effect. It permitted the players to put aside their differences over an amendment formula to see whether an accommodation over the charter could be worked out. This put pressure on the Gang of Eight at precisely the point where it was weakest. Premier Davis was deliberately vague on what kind of charter he had in mind, but Trudeau made clear that the charter on the table was contained in the current resolution as recently amended by Parliament.

In the afternoon, the Gang of Eight met with Premier Davis at the Chateau Laurier to discuss his compromise proposal and sent him to Prime Minister Trudeau across the street at the National Conference Centre to see whether he would entertain a proposal from the eight on the Charter of Rights. Trudeau agreed and premiers John Buchanan of Nova Scotia, Lougheed and Bennett were sent off bearing the group's "mini charter" proposal. Their offer was to defer most sections of the charter pending further study and to permit a provincial opting-in clause on minority language educational rights. This was the Gang of Eight's only united bargaining position on the charter, but it was unacceptable to the federal government. Trudeau lashed out at the premiers for bringing such a proposal, and suggested that they were being "duped" in their bargaining strategy by Quebec. Under no circumstances would the federal government give way on minority language educational rights.

When the Gang of Eight reassembled shortly afterward, it was clear that they were without a further common position on this critical matter. Premiers Blakeney and Bennett indicated that they had proposals of their own to make at the talks on the following morning. For Quebec, the long-feared break-up of the Gang of Eight seemed imminent, even though the premiers were still scrupulously abiding by the group's rules by giving "notice" of offering their own positions. Unless the group could coalesce around a new more substantial concession on the

Charter of Rights, the most moderate members would undo the alliance. All the earlier talk of secret bargaining among Saskatchewan, British Columbia and Ontario before the conference began to assume a more threatening form. A "chance" meeting of Ontario and Saskatchewan delegations at an Italian restaurant that evening did nothing to allay suspicions.

On Tuesday evening, the federal cabinet met in emergency session to consider its response to the Gang of Eight's amending formula and to consider final concessions over the charter. It was becoming clear that if a deal were to be struck, some give would be necessary on both items. At the same time, however, the federal side needed to examine its next strategic step carefully. If the momentum were to be retained and Ontario prevented from making a premature move towards the Gang of Eight, the referendum card on the Charter of Rights had to be played soon. By offering to put the Charter of Rights as well as the amending formula to a referendum if faced with deadlock in two years' time, the federal government knew that it could overcome any obstacles to its package in Britain and that it would force the provinces into a difficult political fight. But most important, it knew that the referendum proposal would split the Gang of Eight and isolate Quebec. Quebec was on record as supporting a referendum, while the English-speaking premiers regarded referenda as divisive. To federal strategists, these differences between Lévesque and the other premiers in the Gang of Eight could be exploited.

The following morning Saskatchewan tabled its compromise proposal for immediate entrenchment of all sections of the charter except for provincial "opting in" on legal and equality rights and for a non-enforceable declaration on minority language educational rights. Because this proposal did not fully protect minority language educational rights, the federal government could not accept it, nor were the other governments particularly enamoured with the compromise. None the less, Saskatchewan had started negotiations outside the terms of the provincial bloc of eight. For that reason, Quebec's minister of inter-governmental affairs, Claude Morin, in what he later described as a state of "consternation," angrily denounced Saskatchewan for departing from the "common front" principles. British Columbia meanwhile had that morning declared itself ready to accept the entrenchment of minority language educational rights.

In the presence of these divisions Trudeau introduced again his referendum card. Lévesque, losing confidence in the Gang of Eight's ability to stick to its principles, accepted Trudeau's challenge. After only the most general discussion of the referendum proposal on the Wednesday morning's closed-door session, Lévesque and Trudeau appeared before the television cameras. These arch-rivals had now apparently agreed on a referendum to settle their differences if a negotiated settlement proved impossible. Lévesque was confident that he could defeat a referendum on a Charter of Rights and, in any event, he was willing to let the decision be made by the people after extensive debate. If the April accord were to be abandoned, a referendum seemed a surer defence of Quebec's interests.

Premier Lougheed and virtually all the other English-speaking premiers were offended by the idea of a referendum and were shaken by Quebec's violation of the gang's principles. While Saskatchewan had given advance notice of its compromise proposal, Quebec had given the other premiers no notice of its lining up with Trudeau on a referendum. This move presented them with a clear threat if they could not come up with a negotiated settlement. Premier Lévesque in this respect misjudged the extent to which most premiers in the group wanted a settlement to avoid public wrath at home, ongoing national divisiveness and the embarrassment of a public brawl in Britain.

The referendum option was seen to be a trap by Lévesque only after he belatedly learned the implementation details of the federal proposal. In a paper tabled in the afternoon session, Trudeau offered him a referendum only if, after enactment by Westminster, all provinces agreed to have one. Without such agreement, Trudeau's proposals would apply as law. Lévesque began to pull back, complaining to the other premiers and the public that the federal referendum details were unacceptable. But it was too late. The damage to his earlier alliance was already done and Quebec's ability to contain events severely circumscribed.

From Trudeau's perspective, the referendum idea worked either as a bargaining lever or as an acceptable method, after two further years of talks, of breaking federal-provincial deadlock. The irony of the situation was that his tactic enjoyed the support of his archrivals in Quebec, even though it threatened them above all others. Closing Wednesday's full meeting with a promise to work on the referendum details over which Quebec took exception, Trudeau kept pressure on the players. Unless there was some change, all of them would face a fractious referendum debate and public contempt for yet another failure to compromise.

Faced with those conditions and only one more day of talks, a deal was put together that night giving the dissenting provinces their amending formula (minus the section providing for intergovernmental delegating of powers and Quebec's demand for financial compensation for "opting out"), and the federal government a limited Charter of Rights. The essential strength of the bloc trading strategy was therefore borne out, even though massive public pressure for a compromise including the Charter of Rights played a crucial role in getting an agreement.

The six moderates among the Gang of Eight, this time led by Premier Peckford of Newfoundland, decided to accept the entrenchment of minority language rights for each of their provinces. In return they demanded a "notwithstanding clause" — the right to legislate so as to expressly override certain sections of the charter whenever their legislatures might think it necessary to do so. This was the essential bargain struck. In many respects, it was the compromise towards which the parties had been painstakingly moving all week, if not for a month before the talks had started: acceptance of the key federal interest in the charter in return for accommodating the opposition of the English-speaking provinces to entrenchment as a method of protecting rights. As fortune would have it, the deal was accomplished without the attendance of the two hard-liners among the Gang of Eight. Manitoba's Sterling Lyon was forced to depart from the conference early to resume electioneering in an unsuccessful bid to retain power. Quebec's René Lévesque, who was now thought to prefer a referendum to any such compromise, was not invited to participate.

The negotiations had been conducted between two groups: premiers and representatives from six provinces meeting in Saskatchewan's suite on the Peckford proposal and a group of key ministers and aides — Jean Chrétien, Michael Kirby, Roy Romanow, and Ontario attorney general Roy McMurtry (and later Premier Davis himself) — meeting on their own to see what kind of compromise might save the conference. Among other matters, they agreed to qualify the mobility rights section to allow for affirmative action programs in provinces with low employment and to drop aboriginal treaty rights, reportedly on the insistence of Alberta and British Columbia. After the main lines had been settled, spokesmen from both Prince Edward Island and Alberta conferred with Manitoba's ministers to bring that province into the accord. Premier Lyon agreed on condition that Manitoba's legislature later approve the minority language education provision. Ontario used its influence with the federal government to convince it to go along. Premier Hatfield could be expected to agree especially since entrenched minority language rights were part of the package. Only Quebec's participation was in doubt as the final parts of the deal were concluded around 4:00 Thursday morning. It was not until the regular breakfast meeting of the old Gang of Eight that Premier Lévesque learned of the full compromise which had been worked out without him.

Confronted with a *fait accompli*, Lévesque felt black-mailed. He was happy neither with the deletion of the fiscal compensation feature of the original provinces' accord, nor with the wording of the mobility rights section.

When the full meeting reconvened later in the morning, Trudeau asked Peckford to summarize the new proposal and then heard every premier speak on it. All but Quebec assented. Trudeau then finally showed his hand by declaring that he felt there was "common ground." He asked however for three important changes to the agreement.

● He requested that the last sentence in section 3 (c) be struck. The section read as follows:

> We have agreed that the provisions of Section 23 in respect of Minority Language Education Rights will apply to our Provinces. Any Province not agreeing to be bound by this Section continues to have the right to accept the application of the Section to their Province at any future time.

By securing the deletion of the last sentence, Trudeau removed any suggestion of Quebec retaining the right to opt out of the minority language educational guarantees.

● He asked that a sunset provision be put on the use of "notwithstanding clauses." Thus, if any government made use of the right to legislate against fundamental freedoms or legal and equality rights, the limitations would lapse after a five-year period unless re-enacted by that legislature. This change was designed to put the responsibility for acting against the charter on each government and to make it face regularly the political consequences of continuing to act against it.

● Finally, he asked that the subject of aboriginal rights be put on the agenda of a future first ministers' constitutional conference and that representatives of the aboriginal peoples of Canada be invited to participate in that discussion. This suggestion, which reconfirmed one of the promises made to native peoples in the earlier resolution, was accepted. In this way, Trudeau tried to soften the impact of the ignoble deletion of aboriginal treaty rights.

As for Quebec, Trudeau did not agree to consider its demands that financial compensation be provided a province which opted out of amendments to the constitution or that the mobility rights section be re-written. To guarantee compensation to any province, Trudeau asserted, would invite the wealthier provinces to opt out of all amendments that imposed a heavy financial burden on the central government. Even though Lévesque hinted that he might go along with the minority language educational guarantees if these two demands were met, Trudeau did not take up either suggestion. He only promised to consider Quebec's case later. Perhaps fearful that the package would unravel if Quebec's demands again were entertained at the eleventh hour, and conscious that a firm deal was in hand, Trudeau decided not to risk all in an effort to bring Quebec in. Besides, by forcing Lévesque to go before the people with limited objections to the deal, Trudeau deprived the Quebec premier of the broadest grounds of political opposition which might otherwise have been effective in Quebec. Trudeau knew too that he could later offer substantial concessions to Lévesque and hence politically box him in. As the first ministers returned to face the cameras, it was clear who had suffered most by the court's rejection of the unanimity rule. Once again alone, once again odd man out, Quebec, Lévesque declared, stood abandoned by its anglophone partners in the Gang of Eight, an unwilling victim of an apparently correct constitutional procedure. As the others celebrated, a bitter Lévesque warned that the consequences would be "incalculable."

The conference bargaining was over. An agreement had been forged between nine provinces and the federal government. But the debate over the subject was just beginning. With Quebec out of the deal it was clear that the acrimony between the Quebec government and Ottawa would go on. Moreover, the settlement could be presented in Quebec as a defeat of the province's interests, creating yet further instability in the relationship between that province and the rest of Canada. This time the dispute was not confined to a PQ-Ottawa feud, but had escalated into a fundamental collision between the PQ government and all other governments in Canada. Now the bonds of "friendliness and understanding" which had, according to Claude Morin, developed between the Quebec government and the other provincial governments appeared to be severed. It was, from the point of view of the Quebec government, a "deplorable and painful" conclusion to a unique interprovincial enterprise.

At the same time, from the perspective of the other participants the conference had to be reckoned a success, even if the exclusion of Quebec made it a less than complete one. The other governments had finally agreed on a package of constitutional changes which, even if it did not fully satisfy each, achieved what none before them had been able to secure: patriation, an amending formula, a Charter of Rights and several other important changes. Most of them did not accept the Parti Québécois charge that the other governments had "misled" and "abandoned" Quebec.

The PQ government subsequently declared that it was betrayed when, during the negotiations on the

Wednesday, the other members in the Gang of Eight began to leave the interprovincial common front and put forth alternative propositions, developed without Quebec, and when Quebec's delegation was left out of the crucial compromise discussions that night. According to Claude Morin, the April 16 accord was "a real contract" which could not be unilaterally modified in order to find a negotiated solution with Ottawa. Yet if a negotiated settlement with Ottawa was to be achieved, further movement from the premiers' April 16 accord was unavoidable, as Quebec's government well knew. Indeed, Quebec had received notice from Saskatchewan about its readiness to propose a separate compromise, and it had known for at least a month before the talks began that several members of the gang were publicly indicating their willingness to compromise beyond the accord.

If a negotiated settlement were to be pursued then, the April 16 provincial accord would be on the table for discussion just as would the Charter of Rights and other proposals of the federal government, Ontario and New Brunswick. Since the gang had no coherent collective compromises to put into play in the negotiations, it was obvious that members who wanted a settlement would eventually have to float their own proposals or face a breakdown in the talks. Once the federal side had virtually conceded to the gang's amending formula, the pressure was intense on the dissenting premiers to come up with a compromise over the charter. Yet no sooner had they begun to do so, than the Quebec government broke ranks and accepted the federal government's referendum offer. This action freed the hands of those premiers who were ready to compromise.

Thus it might be more reasonable to see Quebec's dilemma at the bargaining table as stemming not from "betrayal" but from the impossibly difficult situation in which the PQ government was placed. Its deepest commitment lay not in renewing federalism but in dismantling it; yet Quebecers had empowered the government to pursue federalism only. Success at the bargaining table would undermine the Parti Québécois's argument that federalism does not work, set back the independence movement and imperil the government's position with its party base. Therefore its fundamental political interest lay in continuing federal-provincial conflict, in goading the federal government into more arrogant displays of unilateralism and in preserving a bloc of provincial opposition. To advance such objectives, the PQ government had signed the April 1981 accord, tactically conceding its veto in return for a right to opt out with compensation; when faced with negotiations in which members of the gang began to show signs of compromising with the federal government, Lévesque seized the first opportunity which Trudeau extended to him to avert that danger by preserving on-going conflict in a final referendum battle over the Charter of Rights. Yet nothing could have been better calculated to push the other premiers into a final negotiated compromise with Ottawa.

The Return of Public Participation: Women's and Native Rights

It took less than two weeks for Parliament to debate the new constitutional resolution. It was passed with all-party agreement on December 2, 1981. Though amendments to give Quebec full compensation for opting out, to strengthen the rights of Quebec's anglophone minority and to protect the rights of the unborn were attempted, none were successful. The Senate, after turning back similar amendments, including one which would have restored the Senate veto over constitutional changes, confirmed the package on December 8 and the resolution was immediately dispatched to Great Britain. That rapid turnaround after more than a year of wrangling was possible chiefly because the resolution, whatever its merit, now appeared to carry constitutional legitimacy. Nine provinces and the federal government had sanctioned it — probably enough intergovernmental agreement to meet the Supreme Court's test for "substantial [not unanimous] provincial consent." This political achievement also stemmed from the relative open-mindedness and flexibility which the federal government showed to most criticism of the new constitution. Since the deal was not entirely of its making, it was easy to agree with public and opposition criticism that it did not go far enough and to blame that result on the hazards of negotiations. The government had preferred a stronger charter but had been pressured into bargaining over clauses in exchange for federal-provincial consensus; if the results were not to everyone's liking, that was manifestly *not* the government's fault. The accord would be honoured, unless nine provincial premiers could be persuaded to amend its terms to meet public disappointments.

The notwithstanding clause permitting provinces to override certain sections of the Charter of Rights came in for the most general criticism; women's groups in particular decided to do battle to have the clause removed from section 28 of the resolution, which enshrined equality between men and women. Even though such a result ironically might threaten the effectiveness of affirmative action programs for women by making it easier for *men* to use section 28 against such legislation, strengthening section 28 became a cause célèbre for women's rights. The federal government declared itself ready to make that change, if provincial consent could be obtained. A national lobby campaign began to influence provincial governments. One by one premiers caved in to public pressure until only Premier Blakeney of Saskatchewan remained opposed. He declared Saskatchewan ready to comply only if native treaty rights were also restored.

This linkage between the grievances of both groups was a timely suggestion. Ever since the accord had been announced, native peoples had expressed disgust at the deletion of their treaty rights from the constitutional package. They too had begun a campaign to see their treaty rights restored. The federal government was ready to do so, although it reminded native peoples that some native groups had actively opposed the earlier resolution. Pressure in Parliament, especially from the New Democratic Party, and the steady pressure of native groups and public opinion brought the premiers around, particularly after Blakeney had stated his position. By November 26, Parliament had unanimously restored both sections, although the word "existing" was attached to the definition of aboriginal treaty rights, an addition that left native peoples uneasy.

This second entry of public interest groups into the constitutional struggle was fully as interesting and important as the first. Two of the same interest groups (particularly the women's associations) that had pressed for changes in the federal resolution in the fall of 1980 now converted themselves into a national lobby to make the governmental players respect the rights they had won earlier. Since Ottawa had already been convinced, the new targets were the provincial governments. To bring pressure to bear in all the provincial capitals required the combination of active local associations, a vigorous national campaign and relentless media exposure. It was too much for the premiers to withstand.

Apart from the commitment of the organizations' many supporters, the success of the campaign owed a good deal to the broad popularity of the federal charter and the strategic support which the federal government gave its "allies." At this critical point the government extended assistance through Mines Minister Judy Erola (who was responsible for women's issues in cabinet) and it joined with opposition spokesmen in promoting the idea of limited changes. While promising to stick to the terms of the agreement unless changes were consented to by the premiers, Ottawa quietly relished the discomfort which the provincial governments faced from an outraged public. It was no secret that the greatest glee was reserved for Allan Blakeney's government which, in the view of the federal government, had played a crafty and self-satisfied role through the whole constitutional struggle.

Hence, federally sponsored public participation took the lines which planners expected. There was no serious assault upon the essentials of the intergovernmental bargain; though disappointment surfaced over the notwithstanding clause in the charter, there was no concerted attempt to have it removed. In that sense, the public groups focused on more limited matters and tacitly bowed to the outcome of the governmental bargaining.

The role of public participation throughout the constitutional struggle, therefore, was not a one-dimensional "people versus governments" conflict. Although it often flattered public interest groups to think so, and it suited the federal government to paint the struggle in that way, in fact public participation almost always had the stamp of federal management on it. That fact was obvious in the Kirby memorandum's plan for orchestrating public opinion around the clashing themes of "people's rights versus provincial powers"; it was evident in the careful selection, management and wooing of public interest groups in the Joint Parliamentary Committee; and it was apparent in the unleashing of these groups upon the premiers after intergovernmental agreement on the constitution had been achieved. Of course, the strategy did depend on genuine public enthusiasm for a Charter of Rights, but there is no doubt that public participation was carefully channelled into the federal battle against provincial claims and powers. Whenever public participation did not comply with federal requirements — such as with the ill-fated opposition of aboriginal peoples to patriation itself — it was firmly blocked with the full political and legal powers of the central government.

The reason for the selective federal cultivation of the public in its constitutional plans went well beyond the political needs of the moment. The federal argument for amendment by referenda and for the charter had reflected carefully prepared efforts to block growing provincial power by working out a direct alliance between the federal government/Parliament/courts and the Canadian people. The referendum proposals

in particular sought to build a new constitutional alignment between the national government and the
"people" as the prime constituents of Canadian
federalism; the charter sought to tie the people both
practically and symbolically to a new constitutional
system enshrining rights from coast to coast. Such a
sophisticated strategy, reinforced by aggressive federal
unilateralism in many areas of public policy, was
designed to undercut what Ottawa considered a
dangerous advance of provincial power under the
mantle of regionalism.

Patriation without Quebec

This plan was particularly designed for Quebec. Out-
manoeuvring the Parti Québécois government and
securing a package of constitutional reform which
would win over Quebecers to Canada was always the
chief objective of the federal government. Since it was
considered axiomatic that Lévesque's government
could not be a party to any such deal, it was the aim of
federal strategists to win over the people of Quebec and
hence to isolate the separatists. For its part, the PQ
government was determined to identify its case with
that of the Quebec people so that, if it could not accede
to a deal, it would be said that Quebec as a whole had
been betrayed. Hence, the irony that without separatist
endorsement of federal renewal, the province of
Quebec was outside the deal — a stain upon the historic
accord of November 5. It was in this strange setting that
Quebec's federal and provincial leaders — diehard
federalists and separatists alike — sought to voice
Quebecers' split political loyalties. Where Quebecers
actually stood was unclear.

Lévesque, outside the agreement, tried to give full vent to what he hoped would be his people's sense of isolation and anger. Quebec, he declared, would not accept federal overtures to talk over remaining differences and would not participate in future federal-provincial conferences except when they concerned its vital financial interests. Lévesque spurned Trudeau's belated offers to consider compensation for opting out in education and cultural matters in the amending formula, to rewrite the mobility rights section provided other provinces agreed, and to refrain from imposing on Quebec minority language educational guarantees for immigrants. In the end, Trudeau put most of these protections into the resolution on his own (with support from the other premiers) and took upon himself the mantle of Quebec's protector.

Rarely had the rhetoric of Quebec politicians become as vituperative as it then did. Federal leaders were branded as "whores" and "traitors," while Quebec itself was pictured as the innocent victim of rapists. On the subject of Quebec's loss of veto, Trudeau in turn acidly remarked that the province lost out at the April '81 Premiers' Conference when Lévesque "left [the veto] at the door with his galoshes."

There was no disguising that Lévesque was politically boxed in. Polls suggested that he could not win the support of the Quebec people either in a referendum or snap election. Nor could he win all-party support for a resolution in the Quebec assembly; even Claude Ryan, unhappy with the deal, could not support the Parti Québécois further. In vain, Lévesque demanded recognition of a Quebec veto and acceptance of the principle of "national self-determination." The Quebec government finally decided to issue a formal veto against the constitutional resolution, an action which the Supreme

Court appeared to have rendered legally redundant; it also referred the question of the alleged violation of Quebec's veto to its Court of Appeal. But neither of these initiatives could now block the way to patriation.

It appeared that Ottawa had won at the bargaining table and in the immediate battle for public opinion. Indeed, Lévesque became so enraged over the federal manoeuvres that he threatened to run on an outright separatist plank in the next Quebec election, a sudden shift from his government's formal sovereignty-association platform and one he later recanted. But his invective stirred up the hard-liners, which contributed to a collision between the government and party delegates over the strategy for Quebec independence at a convention in Montreal on the weekend of December 5. Despite the pleas of the premier and most ministers, the delegates vented their anger with English Canada by voting to drop "association" from the party's platform and to push for unqualified sovereignty. The cabinet only retrieved itself from the embarrassing spectacle by demanding a vote of the full party with Lévesque's own resignation hanging in the balance if the vote went against him. And even before the results of the mail ballot supporting Lévesque had come in, Claude Morin, the PQ's experienced minister of intergovernmental affairs and architect of Quebec's ill-fated negotiating policy, had tendered his resignation. His departure alone signalled that the Quebec government's position was weakening.

Meanwhile, with only Quebec isolated from the deal and largely preoccupied with the painful aftereffects of the constitutional bargaining, the last steps toward patriation were quietly proceeding in Britain. With the achievement of substantial federal-provincial agreement over the new Canadian constitution, the political turbulence which the Canada Act had generated in Britain largely passed away. The central battle over unilateral action was over. As the formerly dissenting premiers mothballed their meticulous battle plans for a propaganda war in Britain, Westminster looked forward to a relatively easy passage. Although the opposition of the government of Quebec and of Canadian native peoples certainly was a matter of regret, it did not present Britain with anything like the serious political and constitutional difficulties it would have faced from federal unilateral action. The news of an agreement was therefore received at Westminster with relief.

Although Quebec's lobbying in Britain continued and on December 19, 1981, an appeal was made to the British government to delay action until Canadian courts had finally pronounced on the matter of a Quebec veto, Westminster saw little reason for further delay. The legal and conventional requirements set out by the Canadian Supreme Court for requesting patriation and other changes appeared to have been fully met. Even Sir Anthony Kershaw, who had chaired the committee studying Britain's responsibility on the question, now agreed that Westminster should act swiftly in accordance with the request.

Native peoples also continued their opposition in Great Britain. They won sympathy for their cause, but since the issue of native rights was regarded as an internal Canadian matter, Westminster could not change the resolution without trespassing on Canadian sovereignty. Native leaders challenged the proposition that jurisdiction over native peoples had been totally transferred to the Parliament of Canada by arguing before the British Court of Appeal that the British crown retained responsibility for Canada's native peoples, but the court on January 28 unanimously rejected the contention. A request to appeal the matter to the House of Lords was denied.

As the Canada Act proceeded through the required legislative stages, some members of the Commons and House of Lords continued to voice concern over Quebec's dissent and over the opposition of native peoples, but at no time did these objections seriously threaten passage. On March 8 the Canada Act received final approval in the British House of Commons; on March 25 the endorsement of the House of Lords. Four days later the queen assented to the Canada Act. The only remaining formality was the proclamation or bringing into force of the act; at the request of the Canadian government, the queen agreed to come to Canada to proclaim the new constitution on April 17.

If the process of approval at Westminster was quicker and smoother than participants could have thought possible only a year before, many Canadians still had doubts about the advisability of proceeding with the Canada Act prior to court judgements over Quebec's right of veto. Though the Supreme Court decision appeared to have weakened *any* province's case for a veto, it was still unclear whether Quebec might not constitute a special case. Many constitutional specialists were by no means certain that Quebec did not have a powerful argument. But on April 7 the Quebec Court of Appeal delivered a unanimous decision rejecting Quebec's claim to a veto. It ruled that the constitutional agreement reached on November 5 by Ottawa and nine provinces satisfied the Supreme Court's requirement of "substantial provincial consent," and that all provinces were on an equal footing under the constitution. Both the force of the strongly worded legal opinion and the fact that it was unanimous appeared to sanction the position that the British and Canadian governments had taken. Planning for the proclamation on April 17 continued, undeterred by Premier Lévesque's announcement that he would appeal to the Supreme Court of Canada.

After two days of celebration in Ottawa following the queen's arrival on April 15, proclamation day arrived. The signing was carried out on a special platform on Parliament Hill before a nation-wide television audience. Three prominent Quebecers affixed their signatures to the proclamation signed by the queen — Trudeau, Chrétien, and André Ouellet, minister of consumer and corporate affairs and registrar-general — while thousands of dissenters in Quebec gathered in Montreal to hear the constitution denounced by Premier Lévesque. Federal leaders from Quebec could take comfort from polls showing that most Quebecers who had an opinion wanted the province to sign the agreement, but the protests in Montreal, as well as those quietly staged by native peoples, were still unpleasant reminders of opposition to this form of national renewal.

Patriation then was not to be achieved without resistance. Yet the protests did not disguise the fact that the country was undergoing an important transformation. While Britain's ceding of legal power over Canada's constitution was on one level a purely ceremonial act confirming an independence spanning at least a half century, on another level, it symbolized a certain spiritual coming of age for Canadians. With Britain no longer a trustee, no longer able to provide a final outside check against Canadians having to live together under their own rules, the country was now alone and freer to become what it would be. And although historical grievances from Quebec or from the Western and Atlantic provinces did appear to legitimize suspicions and the need for an outside umpire, patriation challenged

Canadians to go beyond past injuries and to structure an independent future.

6
The Road to Meech Lake

The act of patriation, together with the other 1982 constitutional provisions, represented by far the most important constitutional change since Confederation. Canada now had an entrenched charter of rights and freedoms, encompassing not only individual rights but new collective rights for the two dominant linguistic communities. The charter had a new domestic amending formula enshrining provincial equality and extending provincial powers over natural resources. Moreover, aboriginal rights were recognized for the first time; governments had agreed to constitutional discussions with native leaders aimed at defining aboriginal rights more precisely in the constitution.

Yet it is easy to exaggerate the extent of change. These measures did not repeal the substance of Canada's constitution; they merely added to it. The whole corpus of Canada's older written and unwritten constitution, including those parts relating to the division of powers between Ottawa and the provinces, remained intact. So, too, did the country's larger pattern of political economy, political culture and history. Indeed, to the degree that the formal constitutional changes had not yet established firm foundations in the thought and practices of the country, it remained unclear how enduring the new legal architecture would be.

There was also the whole nexus of constitutional grievances that had simply been left behind when Ottawa decided to take unilateral action on the constitution. From the perspective of the twelve-point agenda of 1980, the actual changes in 1982 were modest in scope. There was no sign of Senate reform in the 1982 amendments, nor of progress on the subjects of the Supreme Court, offshore jurisdiction, the fisheries, communications, a new preamble and the like. Ottawa's own interest in expanding its powers over the economy was also left untouched. If, then, 1982 was widely regarded as something of a constitutional revolution, it was also an incomplete one.

That said, the politics required for this scale of constitutional change was brutal and unprecedented. The rupture with Quebec was one sign of the price paid to secure patriation and the charter; the other was public distaste for the whole enterprise. Certainly, with the onset of recession in that year, Canadians turned away from these non-material subjects. Indeed, the whole question of the powers and role of federal and provincial governments became passé — a preoccupation that presumably could be afforded only during better economic times. Thus, much of Trudeau's broader political program for the 1980s, aimed at restoring the balance of power between the different levels of government in Canada, became untenable. Not only was there little will for pursuing constitutional renewal, but the other elements of his liberal nationalism — including the National Energy Program, the hoped-for national industrial strategy, and new fiscal and social measures — were all under threat. Besides being increasingly doubtful about the merits of this program in the midst of a severe economic downturn, Canadians were listening more attentively to the rhetoric of cooperative federalism from the federal Tories.

Under these circumstances, the Trudeau government turned more of its attention toward economic recovery and sought to find other ways of carrying forward its remaining constitutional plans. Essentially, the strategy was now to take constitutional matters outside the realm of immediate governmental action and to put them instead under active study. At the centre of the new approach was the decision on November 25, 1982, to establish a major royal commission headed by former finance minister Donald Macdonald. The new commission was to look into the Canadian economic union, federalism and the broader functioning of Canada's political institutions and policies. It was hoped that in this way some of Ottawa's objectives, such as increased federal power over the economy, could continue to be assessed, and political energy later injected into the old debate. Another element of Ottawa's strategy was the decision in the same month to establish a joint parliamentary task force to study Senate reform.

Faced with an angry Quebec government intent on boycotting all federal-provincial conferences except those concerned with the economic interests of the province, Ottawa thought that this was no time for contemplating broad constitutional discussions. Moreover, since Trudeau had already secured in the charter the substance of his constitutional goals, what value was there now in seeking further conferences — even if Quebec were agreeable? The old constitutional agenda was filled with provincialist demands on federal powers — hardly attractive from Ottawa's point of view. While Trudeau indicated a willingness to entertain some compromises to win over Quebec's consent to the 1982 changes, he was under no illusions about Lévesque's eagerness to do constitutional business with him again. Only the formal constitutional requirement to discuss aboriginal rights gave life to the ongoing process from 1982. Although not in itself a critical priority for any government, the aboriginal question, almost by default, occupied constitutional centre stage.

Aboriginals and the Constitution

Native peoples were, of course, among the groups most bruised in the constitutional melee of the 1980s. They had been strongly attracted to the idea of seeking constitutional redress for their grievances, and they had put unusual energy into trying to get their full rights recognized "prior" to Britain's ceding its remaining legal links to Canada. For the native peoples, patriation was hardly a stirring exercise when, in their view, Canada had long refused to live up to treaty obligations and other legal undertakings assumed in Britain's name. Viewing the ending of legal ties under these circumstances as the mother country's abdication of her duty toward them, they took cold comfort from flag-waving Canadian nationalism.

Moreover, they were even less impressed than were women's groups with the results of the first ministers' bargaining in November 1981. They alone had found their hard-won rights in the charter suddenly deleted at the insistence of premiers such as Lougheed and Bennett. While women were incensed over the merely hypothetical application of the notwithstanding clause to their rights, native peoples discovered on the morning of November 5 that their rights had been outrightly excised. When their rights were later restored, they understood it was only because of the leverage of women's groups on the premiers and the accidental politics that linked their two causes together. In the end, even the native groups' vain attempts to stop patriation by appealing to the mother country led to nothing more than polite and embarrassed sympathy. They were, after all, peoples who could call only upon justice, not power, to assist them.

Yet, despite these inauspicious signs, there was the reality of a promised constitutional conference, this time with their own leaders present, where the question of native rights would be discussed. Should they bow to the fact of patriation and make the best of defeat, or should they go on in stubborn symbolic protest? By early 1983 most native leaders had accepted the first option, but others split over the issue. On March 15 the promised constitutional conference was held, and after two days of initial discussion the government leaders, using the new domestic amending formula, were able to agree on Canada's first constitutional amendment. The amendment granted the native peoples' request for a constitutional guarantee of ongoing discussion on their full agenda of issues at no fewer than three further conferences in a four-year period. The 1983 Constitutional Accord also guaranteed equality in treaty rights between male and female persons and made provision for constitutional recognition of existing and future land-claims agreements. On May 18 the accord was subsequently approved by native leaders and was thereafter rapidly adopted by all legislatures except Quebec's, which, while sympathetic to native groups' concerns, continued to register its opposition to the imposition of the Canada Act by refusing to play a formal role in constitutional amendments.

Although native persons did not wish to acknowledge the Canada Act any more than did the government of Quebec, and though they continued to regard the federal government rather than the provinces as the government they must deal with, the legal facts indicated otherwise. Constitutional change affecting aboriginal peoples was now increasingly a federal-provincial matter, with multilateral bargaining from the level of officials all the way to the First Ministers' Conference itself. As native leaders learned, this would be a complicated playing field where winning over the governmental players would not be easy.

While many issues preoccupied native peoples, the conferences quickly focused on the heart of the aboriginal concerns, namely, aboriginal self-government. This was a novel idea that raised serious questions of definition. What was meant by the term? Was aboriginal self-government an ethnic or more inclusive public concept? How far did it extend — was it local, regional or national in scope? How could it be incorporated into a federal system? Was the idea to grant native people the equivalent of municipal powers or some more substantial grant of sovereignty? Since so many of the native leaders themselves were divided on its meaning and since government leaders varied sharply in what they were prepared to grant, the initial plan was to entrench the principle of aboriginal self-government only and to make a commitment to work out the details in subsequent negotiations. This idea was unacceptable to the governments of Alberta and British Columbia, which insisted on an understanding of the principle prior to entrenchment. Other provinces, such as Saskatchewan and Newfoundland, objected to the binding constitutional requirement to negotiate a plan for self-government. Compromises over the latter issue in the crucial 1985 conference failed to win native support.

In broad terms, more governments were beginning to address the idea of self-government for aboriginal peoples than ever before, but there was still considerable resistance. Some politicians and officials were apprehensive about the kind of devolution of power being sought and about what the courts might do in interpreting the idea of self-government; native peoples increasingly saw the issue in symbolic terms — self-determination would wipe out the indignity of hundreds of years of being treated as a subject people.

These dynamics continued under two prime ministers, Pierre Trudeau and Brian Mulroney, the new Conservative leader elected with a landslide majority on September 4, 1984. With the disappointment of the 1985 conference, both government and native peoples started to look elsewhere for a solution, to turn away from the constitutional "top-down" approach to the question and seek instead a more practical "bottom-up" approach by negotiating separate agreements outside of the constitutional framework. That process, however, did not move matters quickly and appeared by 1987 to be a poor substitute for an overall strategy. In the end, all three conferences failed to overcome the difficulties, leaving native persons, at the end of the March 1987 conference, without an agreement and without further promises to continue discussions.

While the conferences' failure to address the aboriginal peoples' demand for self-government had been ostensibly because of doubt over what the concept might mean, native leaders were soon to point out that the same logic did not extend to the constitutional provisions secured by Quebec at Meech Lake on April 30, 1987. Here, the entrenchment of such vague declarations as the "distinct society" of Quebec gave first ministers apparently little pause. But then native peoples and the government of Quebec were decidedly unequal "losers" in the constitutional changes of 1982, a bitter reflection of the cruel dynamic between political power and success at the first ministers' table.

The Reconciliation with Quebec

On the face of it, the 1982 constitutional settlement left the province of Quebec in a very weak position. After all, not only was the legal deed done, but the PQ government was itself in complete disarray. For a time it appeared as though the "enemies within" had been scattered, the separatist movement spiked, and even the Quebec-based nationalist movement successfully rechannelled outward toward Canada. On the other hand, there was no denying that the constitution had been imposed on Quebec without its government's consent. While Quebec remained in legal terms entirely subject to the new constitution, it nevertheless remained politically outside it. This was, to say the least, an uncomfortable anomaly.

Even if the courts had declared that there was no requirement for Quebec's consent to constitutional changes either by law or by convention, there still remained an obvious disquiet in the country over the legitimacy of both process and product. In the immediate bitterness of the constitutional aftermath, prominent analysts both inside and outside Quebec were inclined to brood darkly on this "dangerous deed" and to wonder whether it might prove to be another Pyrrhic victory purchased at the expense of future national unity. The precipitous decline in Quebec nationalism after 1982 appeared to mock these hasty judgements, but no one doubted that eventually an accommodation would have to be struck with Quebec; only with the consent of its government or people would the constitution enjoy legitimacy.

Yet the conditions for an eventual reconciliation were hardly propitious. On the one hand, in the poisonous post-November 1981 climate, Lévesque was in no mood to talk again about the constitution with the federal government or, for that matter, with the other nine provincial governments. Quebec spurned all offers to discuss eleventh-hour adjustments to the patriation package and responded coolly to the changes unilaterally made in Quebec's interest by Trudeau and the other premiers. Besides refusing to participate in any future constitutional amendments, including the ongoing consideration of aboriginal self-government, the province proceeded to take full advantage of the notwithstanding clause to exempt Quebec in wholesale fashion from all those sections of the new charter covering fundamental legal and equality rights. These were desperate measures, weak if not ineffectual, but they conveyed Quebec's profound sense of isolation. Renegotiation, if not with the PQ then with a moderate successor government in Quebec, was a foregone conclusion.

It was not until the retirement of Trudeau in June 1984 and the subsequent defeat of the federal Liberals in the September election that the Quebec government again turned its face toward Ottawa. In the election campaign, Brian Mulroney had promised reconciliation with Quebec within the framework of cooperative federalism. René Lévesque, for his part, having already forced the PQ to drop its sovereignty plank for the next provincial election, wanted to seek an accommodation. However, there was little inclination on the part of the federal Tories to begin serious negotiations with the PQ government, at least until after the next provincial election. With polls indicating that the PQ was in serious trouble, the Mulroney government could look forward to carrying out its promise to negotiate Quebec's endorsement of the 1982 changes with a provincial Liberal party that was at least openly in support of Canadian federalism. With the election of Robert Bourassa's Liberals on December 2, 1985, the way was open for a serious renewal of constitutional discussions with the province of Quebec.

It was clear from the Liberals' election campaign, and particularly from the February 1985 party policy program entitled *Mastering Our Future,* what the ingredients of a Liberal constitutional program would be. Their terms of reconciliation were

- an explicit recognition in the preamble of the constitution of Quebec as a distinct society, "homeland of the francophone element of Canada's duality";

- guarantees for Quebec's cultural security by entrenching a constitutional right to an equal say with Ottawa on the selection and number of immigrants settling in Quebec, so that the existing linguistic balance within the province and Quebec's political power within the federation would both be maintained;

- acknowledgment of Quebec's right to participate in the selection of judges from Quebec for the Supreme Court;

- limiting the federal spending power by requiring that any new federal conditional grants (federal offers of money to the provinces with "strings attached," such as medicare) in areas of provincial jurisdiction be approved by the provinces under the rules of the general amending formula, and that the conditional grant programs set out only broad norms and not dictate the regulation and administration of programs; and

- provision for a general Quebec veto in the amending formula *or* full compensation on opting out of amendments transferring provincial powers to Ottawa, together with a veto over changes to national institutions or the creation of new provinces.

Over the past quarter century, Quebec had rarely defined so precise and short a list of demands. At the same time, however, fulfilling them would not be easy. Some of the issues were politically sensitive, and the whole climate for constitutional change was much less pressing and urgent than it had been a few years before. No longer were Quebecers threatening to pull out of Canada; indeed, Quebecers themselves had become much less enamoured with constitutional issues and were instead preoccupied with economic issues like free trade. Moreover, Quebec's continuing non-participation in constitutional matters was not even the real obstacle in settling the question of aboriginal rights. In short, there seemed to be very little public concern about the constitutional impasse with Quebec.

This relative calm, however, masked but did not remove the continuing problem of Quebec's dissent from the 1982 constitutional changes; nor could the apparent public acquiescence really answer the obvious desire of most Quebecers to become full and willing partners in the country's constitution and especially in the new Charter of Rights and Freedoms. While the Bourassa government removed the application of the notwithstanding clause against the charter shortly after taking office, Quebecers had still not collectively endorsed this important part of the Canadian constitution. The 1982 humiliation of Premier Lévesque, whether deserved or otherwise, remained a bitter and embarrass-

ing memory of the constitutional struggle in the minds
of Quebecers; the question remained how best to convert this negative public image into an honourable
peace with history.

Prime Minister Mulroney proceeded cautiously. He
gave Senator Lowell Murray the daunting task of
developing the federal strategy, and Murray was assisted later by his new deputy minister of federal-
provincial relations, Norman Spector. Since the
government wanted at all costs to avoid another public
failure in constitutional talks with Quebec, stress was
placed on finding out in a series of careful informal
meetings with all the provinces whether there existed
minimal conditions for success. Only if reasonable
chances existed for a successful outcome would a full-
scale constitutional conference go forward. Besides, the
failures in the constitutional talks with aboriginal
peoples had served to underline the need for seeking out
a common ground prior to public posturing at a First
Ministers' Conference. Although constantly prodded by
Quebec governments to move forward more swiftly,
Ottawa took an exceedingly modest pace.

In fact, Ottawa left a good deal of the work of making
the case to the Quebec government itself. This task was
taken up with determination by the new Quebec Liberal
minister of justice, Gil Rémillard, himself a leading
constitutional scholar. Taking advantage of the opportunity of a conference called by academics to discuss
Quebec's accommodation to the constitution, held at
Mont Gabriel on May 9, 1986, Rémillard decided to
move the process forward decisively by publicly staking out his government's position. Although this was a
surprise for many of the other government and
academic participants, the actual list of Quebec
demands was not; it merely restated the five known

conditions from the earlier Liberal party policy on the
constitution. There was, however, an additional
negotiating goal outlined in Rémillard's speech: a commitment to further the interests of the francophone
minorities in the other provinces. In this way, Quebec
tried to balance its traditional concern for the rights and
powers of the province with its broader role as protector
of French-speaking communities elsewhere in Canada.
The speech was distinctly conciliatory in tone toward
many of the provisions of the 1982 constitution, particularly the Charter of Rights and Freedoms, and indicated an earnest desire to end the province's isolation
from both the constitutional process and the 1982 constitutional amendments.

This gesture underlined the importance the Quebec
government attached to the constitutional agenda and
its impatience with further delay. In the summer of 1986
a series of informal bilateral discussions took place
between Quebec and Ottawa. These meetings were
followed by a Premiers' Conference in Edmonton on
August 10-12, where the matter was again discussed
and an important declaration issued. The premiers
agreed

- to embark immediately upon federal-provincial
  negotiations "to bring about Quebec's full and active
  participation in the Canadian federation" — this was
  "their top constitutional priority";
- to use the Quebec government's five proposals as a
  basis for discussion; and
- to leave negotiations over other elements of the
  constitutional agenda, such as Senate reform, the
  fisheries, property rights and so on, to a subsequent
  round.

This was a critical stage in the process of negotiations. Quebec had succeeded in isolating its own con-

cerns from the constitutional demands of the other provincial governments, thus ensuring its own goals would not be subject to assorted linkages and trade-offs. Since some of Quebec's five conditions for signing the 1982 constitution, particularly a veto for Quebec on constitutional amendments, could well threaten the success of the constitutional objectives of other provinces, it was no mean achievement to have its own agenda considered separately. After that mandate had been won, Ottawa and Quebec each began to schedule a series of bilateral meetings with the provinces. The process was given an additional impetus when the Vancouver First Ministers' Conference in November agreed that discussions should be intensified and expanded in order to determine the chance of success of formal negotiating sessions. Following a multilateral meeting of officials on March 5-6, 1987, the prime minister took the decision to call a constitutional conference of first ministers at Meech Lake in Quebec on April 30 of that year.

It was clear even before the conference that some of Quebec's five conditions presented very little difficulty: the recognition of Quebec as a distinct society; the provision for a Quebec government role in the appointment of Supreme Court justices from Quebec; and the entrenchment of an improved version of the Canada-Quebec immigration agreement signed in the 1970s. The major problems were a Quebec veto and the demand for prior provincial approval for any new federal shared-cost programs in provincial areas of jurisdiction. These difficulties would need to be ironed out in the negotiations.

After an examination of the options available on the question of the amending formula — an outright Quebec veto, an indirect veto (that is, the requirement that consenting provinces represent 80 per cent instead of the current 50 per cent of the Canadian population), or unanimity — it quickly became clear that the first and second options were non-starters. "The breaking point," claimed Premier Howard Pawley of Manitoba, "was the recognition that all provinces, all Canadians, ought to be treated with the principle of equality." Hence, the logic of "equality of provinces" that had been built into the 1982 constitutional amending formula was, in effect, reinforced. To accommodate Quebec, more inflexibility had to be added to the formula. Unanimous provincial consent would be required for all changes in subjects listed in section 42 of the 1982 agreement — those dealing with federal institutions and the creation of new provinces.

Such a result should have given Premier Don Getty of Alberta, clutching his Triple-E Senate proposal, some pause. How could all provinces ever agree to his three "E's" — equality of representation for each province, election of senators, and effective powers for the second chamber? He had gone to the conference insisting on some action on Senate reform before his province could deal with Quebec's agenda items. But when he pushed this issue, he found Premier Brian Peckford just as intransigent over the fishery. The other first ministers quickly recognized that there would be no action unless the agenda was limited to Quebec's concerns. They gave Getty and Peckford only the concession that Senate reform and the fishery would be listed on the agenda of future constitutional conferences. These would be called every year with no sunset clause. That still left Premier Getty with nothing but a commitment to discuss the Senate issue. Even more troubling, any action on his preferred Triple-E Senate would then take place under the terms of a tougher amending formula than at present. This could not be described as a great bargaining victory.

The province of Manitoba firmly opposed Quebec's suggested limits to the federal spending power and instead proposed, and won acceptance for, the compromise permitting dissenting provinces to opt out of new shared-cost programs with compensation, provided they initiate programs "compatible with national objectives." This was, once again, building on the logic of the 1982 amending formula: no province could block the initiation of programs, yet no province would be bound to accept the application of the federal program in its own jurisdiction. The "opt out" gave each province the defensive right to protect itself, without the inflexibility of an outright veto.

The first ministers agreed to release the Meech Lake communiqué and to reassemble a few weeks later to sign a final legal text, after which changes would be acceptable only in the event of "egregious errors." At the second meeting, in the Langevin Block on June 2-3, attention was directed almost exclusively to two clauses in the agreement: the distinct society and spending-power clauses. At the suggestion of Premier Peterson of Ontario, the ministers agreed to change the disturbing language in section 1(a) of the distinct society clause. The explicit notion of two Canadas was scotched when the words "French-speaking Canada" and "English-speaking Canada" of the communiqué were changed to read "French-speaking Canadians" and "English-speaking Canadians." The first ministers questioned constitutional specialists such as Peter Hogg, Roger Tassé and Frank Iacobucci at length, and received assurances that the distinct society clause would not materially affect the division of powers or the charter. To secure themselves an additional safeguard, the ministers approved the addition of non-derogation clause 2(4) to ensure that there would be no derogation from the "powers, rights or privileges" of any government or legislature.

The discussion on the spending power was difficult, since provinces were under heavy political pressures at home to take quite different courses of action. In Quebec, Premier Robert Bourassa was being attacked not only for having ceded his requirement for a provincial role in approving any new federal spending programs in provincial areas of jurisdiction, but for having granted Ottawa the long-disputed legal power to use the spending power to influence provincial priorities. He sought and received from the other first ministers a non-derogation clause to answer his critics: it declared that no extension of federal (or provincial) powers resulted from this section. In Manitoba and elsewhere in English-speaking Canada, other premiers were under pressure to ensure that the federal authority to initiate new social policy and to ensure reasonable national standards was not undermined by the language in the Meech Lake communiqué. Premier Pawley sought to strengthen the spending-power section with the stipulation that it would be the federal Parliament, in legislation setting out the terms of any new shared-cost program, that would establish the "national objectives" all provinces must meet. After considering many legal versions to give effect to that principle, the first ministers accepted the suggestion of Premier Joe Ghiz of Prince Edward Island to add the words "that is established by the government of Canada" to the section. This addition permitted premiers in English-speaking Canada (and Prime Minister Mulroney) to say that they had not, in fact, weakened the federal role in social policy in the negotiations.

Meanwhile, on the question of Senate reform, Premier Getty appeared content to leave this item for later negotiation under the terms of a new amending formula requiring unanimity. Despite widespread criticism that such a procedure would cripple his efforts at securing agreement on his Triple-E proposal, he thought it preferablethat Alberta itself continue to exercise a veto over any proposed reform rather than have another version of Senate reform approved over the province's objections. Whether the new unanimity requirement would actually hamstring the negotiations at the next round was a much-debated topic, particularly in Western Canada, where the Triple-E Senate was so widely regarded as a panacea for the region's ills. Yet however much Getty's judgement was questioned in this regard, there was general satisfaction with his winning an explicit declaration of provincial equality in the final accord.

In the early-morning hours of June 3, after opportunities to meet with their officials, the first ministers were finally asked to indicate whether they would approve the legal text as amended. The prime minister looked to Premier Pawley first and received his reluctant consent; he then turned to Premier Peterson. The Ontario premier was not enthusiastic and remained concerned about the impact of the agreement on the charter, but, in the end, he too consented. One by one, the approval of all first ministers was secured. The quiet process of prior consultations, the absence of countervailing constitutional demands, the careful federal preparation, together with the prime minister's tact and ability to foster trust and cooperation, had finally borne fruit. Yet there lay a long road ahead to secure legislative ratification of the agreement in every legislature in the country. It was time to unveil the legal text and to await the public's verdict on their handiwork.

Within weeks of the release of the communiqué, the general battle lines over Meech Lake were drawn. There was first the immediate euphoria and surprise that the first ministers had managed to sign an agreement at all; for most Canadians there was special pleasure in a settlement that finally appeared to heal the constitutional rupture with Quebec. That was, of course, the strongest political virtue of Meech Lake, and it contributed mightily to silencing doubts and dampening criticisms that might otherwise have been expected. Indeed, virtually every critic of the Meech Lake agreement was at pains to stress support for reconciliation with Quebec, even if the price was so often said to be too high. The same dilemma was faced by the opposition parties as they tried, on the one hand, to expose weaknesses in the agreement and, on the other, to welcome Quebec back into the constitutional fold. This painful struggle of conscience was exacerbated by political and electoral realities: critics who demanded corrections prior to approval were very easily and none too subtly branded as enemies of Quebec, while acceptance of the flaws in the name of securing a settlement with Quebec seemed an electorally safe, even statesmanlike, position.

But there were critics ready to buck the anti-Quebec charge who insisted that these constitutional provisions must respect the same strict standards of soundness, precision and care as would be expected in any other set of amendments. If found wanting, the provisions must be changed even if that should mean reopening negotiations and facing the possibility of failure. As Table 3 indicates, there was a bewildering range of reactions outside of Quebec to each of the elements of the Meech Lake agreement. Under appropriate section headings are the typical lines of argument used by both supporters and critics of the accord. What is striking is how the same provisions could produce such diametrically opposite conclusions.

The debate in Quebec often contrasted sharply with that held in the rest of the country, reminding Canadians once again of the reality of the "two solitudes." While former prime minister Trudeau and his close Liberal associates took strong issue with Meech Lake along lines similar to those heard elsewhere in the country, and the radical nationalists denounced it as a sellout of Quebec's interests, there was broad support for the agreement precisely for reasons that would not have gone down well in other parts of the country. The distinct society clause was welcomed in Quebec, not just as an exercise in symbolism, but as a substantial enlargement of the province's legislative powers. Moderate nationalists were, on the whole, well disposed to the agreement because it was said to grant Quebec significant new authority to promote the French fact in the province. Both Rémillard and Bourassa were quick to point out that once the accord was approved, the charter itself must henceforth be read and interpreted in the light of the principles accepted at Meech Lake.

Such declarations caused no alarm among most Quebecers; even Quebec women's groups remained strong supporters of the accord, despite the appeals of their sister organizations in English-speaking Canada. The Meech Lake principles were popular because they appeared to enshrine the collective rights of Quebecers acting through their own elected assembly. Against this value, charter advocates would battle in vain. In fact, it was chiefly the vocal linguistic minorities in Quebec who worried most incessantly about the conflict between Meech and the charter. Not least of their worries was how the Supreme Court would balance their newly recognized charter rights against laws restricting use of their language if Meech were approved. They recognized, as did the Quebec government, that such legislation might then be successfully defended as a necessary measure to promote the distinct society of Quebec. If successful, that would mean that the Quebec legislature need not resort to the notwithstanding clause of the charter.

Even some of the former PQ leadership were ready to back Meech Lake as an attractive "backdoor route to separatism," although most regarded it as an exceedingly modest victory. The success in retrieving a Quebec veto over constitutional changes, in guaranteeing new powers over immigrants settling in the province, in nominating senators and Supreme Court justices from Quebec, and in winning the constitutional right to opt out of new shared-cost programs with compensation was welcomed. It was chiefly the concession to accept the federal spending power that drew the most criticism in the province. Even here, however, the argument was the reverse of that heard through much of English-speaking Canada. In Quebec there was more concern for protecting provincial rights, not for shielding a federal role in social policy. In short, Meech Lake was not denounced as an abject federal concession to provincialism, but accepted as the bare minimum required for Quebec to sign the 1982 constitution with honour.

In fact, for many Quebecers, this constitutional settlement was merely a start in the restructuring of the federation according to a Quebec-based nationalist agenda. Rémillard later made it quite clear in his speech to the National Assembly in Quebec that the Meech

Table 3

MEECH LAKE REACTIONS

Topics	Accord Defenders	Accord Critics
General	Quebec is brought "into the constitution" by securing its consent to the 1982 changes.	Quebec was always legally "in" the constitution. Only a separatist government, not the people, rejected 1982 changes.
	National unity is furthered.	National unity set back, particularly with aboriginal peoples and Northerners.
	Intergovernmental peace and cooperation are assured.	Peace is temporary. Ongoing constitutional conferences will provide provinces with forum for demanding more and more powers.
	Division of powers is not affected.	Shifts power from Ottawa to provinces as rival centres of authority.
	Strengthens the voice of the provinces at the national level.	Parliament and legislatures become redundant. Premiers and PM make the decisions.
	Practical document achieved	Limited public input. Hastily

	through compromise. Flaws can be easily corrected in future.	drafted at the elite level. Flaws may become permanent burden in the future.
Distinct Society Clause	Recognizes "sociological reality" of Quebec's distinctiveness within Canada.	No need to give *constitutional* significance to this reality. Special status for one province is entrenched.
	Guarantees Quebec "the security it needs to develop within the federation" (Premier Bourassa).	Quebec already has sufficient power to guarantee its security.
	Balances recognition of Quebec as distinct society with duty to preserve linguistic minorities. Respects spirit of bilingualism.	Attacks bilingualism by promoting separate dualist linguistic communities. Linguistic minorities are merely to be "preserved." Distinct identity of Quebec is to be "promoted."
	Distinct society "includes" anglophones.	Essential meaning is "francophone" society and character. Can lead to justifiable discrimination against non-francophone minorities.

Table 3 continued

MEECH LAKE REACTIONS

Topics	Accord Defenders	Accord Critics
	Confers no additional powers on Quebec. An interpretative principle only. Will not override the charter.	Will expand Quebec's powers and take precedence over the charter.
Amending Formula	Least rigid of options if Quebec is to be protected and equality of all provinces respected.	Unanimity requirement for changes to national institutions such as the Senate will make reform difficult.
	Fundamental changes to the federation should not be made unless all parties agree.	Admission of new provinces is made very difficult. Northerners will suffer discrimination.
Senate and Supreme Court	Both institutions acquire renewed legitimacy and are more responsive to regional needs.	Federal institutions are put under "remote control" of provinces.
	Federal patronage over both is removed, but federal control	Provincial patronage replaces federal, while ability of federal government to

	over appointments remains. Federal government can reject provincial nominations.	refuse provincial nominations is weak, particularly in the event of election.
	Senate will protect regions by challenging the Commons more readily. Election of senators can still take place prior to provincial nomination.	Unelected Senate would still be no match for the Commons. It could be an obstacle, however, to parliamentary government. The whole process leaves out Northerners either as the nominators or nominated. This region is not protected.
Immigration	Quebec is guaranteed right to select immigrants to promote its distinct identity and demographic weight in the federation. Other provinces also can have that right.	Converts Canada into a mere "community of communities". Provincial integration of immigrants fosters provincial patriotism rather than national patriotism.
Spending Power	Provinces are protected from federal control of their jurisdiction through use of "strings-attached" dollars.	Provincial opting out with compensation undercuts Ottawa's ability to develop new social programs and to foster "a sense of nationhood" thereby.
	Federal right to spend in areas of exclusive provincial jurisdiction	That legal right is secure in any case, while legitimacy is achieved now under

Table 3 continued

MEECH LAKE REACTIONS

Topics	*Accord Defenders*	*Accord Critics*
	is finally recognized legally. Political legitimacy follows.	reality of modern welfare state structure.
	Intergovernmental cooperation is furthered, with rights of provincial variation in social programs protected.	Fragmentation and unevenness in programs will follow. The demands of the poor and disadvantaged will receive less recognition.
	Federal power to spend directly on individuals and institutions is preserved.	There will be more pressure on Ottawa not to depart from norm of intergovernmental consensus in its spending in the provinces.
Required Conferences	Will ensure intergovernmental cooperation and coordination.	Platform for provincial encroachment on federal policy and powers.
	Regularity of conferences establishes legal basis for interstate federalism.	Requirements of conferences without sunset clause ensures endless pressure on Ottawa. Mixes constitutional with ordinary politics.

Lake Accord was a first but indispensable step toward that restructuring; Quebec had every reason to look forward to more important future changes, especially from the required annual constitutional conferences that would follow in the wake of this settlement. As Bourassa also argued, adoption of Meech would "enable us to consolidate what we already have and to make even further gains."

It now appeared that the Quebec nationalists, whether moderate or radical in stripe, were winning constitutional recognition for their goals after struggling against the vision of former prime minister Trudeau for almost a quarter century. Only a few years had passed since the constitutional debacles of 1982 and the defeat of the radical nationalists in the 1980 referendum, and yet those setbacks had ironically prepared the way for this victory. It was not surprising then that critics such as Donald Johnston would wonder bitterly what the value of winning the 1980 referendum had really been.

Quebec opinion was, however, not monolithic. The differences between the nationalists were still very substantial. In fact, many of the more militant Quebecers opposed Meech Lake for the usual reasons. There were charges that too much had been given to Ottawa and too little to Quebec. There was also strong opposition from Quebec's English-speaking minority, from immigrant groups and from native peoples.

But perhaps most significant of all, there was a deep rumbling of discontent within the Quebec wing of the federal Liberal party about the federal Liberals' failure, under new leader John Turner, to fight Meech Lake in the name and vision of the Trudeau legacy. That shortcoming was never more apparent than when Trudeau himself took Meech Lake and its architects (and, in effect, his own party) to task in blistering and scornful public statements in late May. That opener was followed up by his special appearances before the Joint Committee of the House of Commons and Senate on August 27 and before the full Senate on March 30, 1988. While Trudeau's arguments were dismissed by many as sour grapes or as outdated, there was in fact a serious question over whether Meech Lake was steering the country away from its foundations and toward a newer and more dangerous definition of the French-English relationship.

Indeed, as noted earlier, in the subsequent legal draft of the Meech Lake agreement approved by the first ministers on June 3, corrections had to be made to ensure that the constitution would not in fact officially enshrine two Canadas, one French and the other English, in the constitution. The draft statement of principles at Meech Lake had referred to the "existence of a French-speaking Canada, centred in but not limited to Quebec" and an "English-speaking Canada, concentrated outside Quebec but also present in Quebec." Such language appeared to hark back to the old two-nations theory and to invite a fundamental restructuring of the Canadian state along the lines of this imagery; it carried the disturbing implication that Canada consisted of two unilingual collectivities, rather than suggesting a single federal country, officially bilingual, with rights for multicultural communities and aboriginals. While section 16 of the accord, reaffirming the role of multiculturalism and aboriginal rights, tended to qualify this simplistic bifurcated theory of Canada, the two-nations rhetoric in a section that was to appear at the very outset of the constitution was hardly encouraging. In the end, the language was changed to make "the existence of French-speaking Canadians and English-speaking

Canadians" — that is, individuals not communities — the focus of the section. This change removed some of the more obvious dangers in the first draft, but there was little doubt that the politicians were playing with fire, since the idea of two linguistically defined Canadas still lurked conspicuously in the background.

To be sure, the recognition of Quebec's character as "a distinct society within Canada," together with the provision affirming the role of its government and legislature "to preserve and promote the distinct identity of Quebec," encourages a radically different conception of dualism than that which was enshrined in the 1982 constitutional amendments. In the accord, the focus was redirected away from the linguistic rights of individual Canadians in an officially bilingual Canada toward a territorial and state-based idea of dualism. As the official provincial Liberal party program had made clear, the idea of recognizing Quebec as a distinct society was not merely to recognize "a sociological reality" but to recognize Quebec as "homeland of the francophone element of Canada's duality" and to grant it "the accompanying political rights and responsibilities." That shift, as Trudeau recognized in his submission to the Joint Committee, was "contrary to what the whole Charter of Rights, including linguistic rights, tried to achieve" — namely, to accept bilingualism and to give linguistic rights to individual Canadians on the basis of tolerance and respect for both the French and English languages within a common Canadian homeland. Trudeau put it this way:

> If you do that, if you give the rights to individuals, then we do not need any more special protection in Quebec. Quebeckers will have the same rights and privileges as

any other Canadians.... anglos [will] respect our language and accept it in the law and in the Constitution.

What astonished Trudeau was that after his bilingualism policy had begun to work, after "anglos [were beginning to] accept it," a contrary vision of the accommodation of the French and English in the country was being enshrined in the Meech Lake agreement. That amounted to bad faith and an abdication of a working, successful strategy.

> After it is working, suddenly you turn around and say, okay, now that we have all of you to accept the French as an official language, as equal, we have a little something more to ask; we want to have more powers for Quebec because it is defending the French language here.
>
> I say that is really welshing on a deal.
>
> [Such an approach is really] a fast track towards sovereignty association. I really mean that. When a province becomes distinct, when it says it is a society different from the rest of the society and it seeks more powers to maintain that difference, it is really saying that in a measure sovereignty is being transferred from the national government to the provincial government.

At the same time, Trudeau complained, the Meech Lake agreement was doing nothing to advance the interests of linguistic minorities or of bilingualism as a national strategy. Was it not after all easier, he pointedly asked, for premiers like Bill Vander Zalm of British Columbia to acknowledge Quebec as a distinct society speaking French and leave their own provinces largely unilingual, rather than to assume the burden of bilingualism by doing more to promote the French fact or to advance the interests of the francophone minority in the province? Was there not also something in it for them, in this provincializing trend whereby all provinces would claim the same powers flowing to Quebec by virtue of the new approach? Ultimately, this route led logically to the philosophy of René Lévesque and to separatism:

> I am asking you whether it has ever struck you that a lot of Canadians prefer the kind of Canada that some Quebec politicians prefer, in which Quebec will be French, Canada will be English and we will all be friends. This is what Mr. Lévesque used to be preaching; you speak English in your provinces, and we will speak French in ours — this stuff of bilingualism was a noble dream. It was a bit of poetry, but it is not realistic.

It is doubtful that many Canadians were aware of the deeper implications of the new definition of the French-English relationship in the Meech Lake Accord or that they troubled themselves to think through its possible compatibility with the strategy of bilingualism. The Meech Lake drafters had hoped to balance the acceptance of Quebec as a distinct society with a compensating clause (2[1][a]) that recognized the presence across the country of French- and English-speaking Canadians as a "fundamental characteristic of Canada." Yet even here the clause implied that this linguistic picture should be frozen as a normative standard for the country, committing both Parliament and provincial legislatures "to preserve" it. Since the state of the linguistic minorities, particularly the French-speaking communities but also, increasingly, the anglophone community in Quebec, was anything but healthy, this was not an encouraging constitutional interpretative principle. It might at best be used to commit governments to do what they might to halt further assimilation or weakening of the linguistic minorities, but it certainly would not assist in arguments for change and improvement. Indeed, since it enshrined the linguistic status quo, it could prove a handy weapon in resisting fundamental demographic linguistic change or even the advance of bilingualism itself.

On the other hand, as critics were quick to note, the role of the legislature and government of Quebec was subject to no such limitation in respect to the distinct society clause of section 2. Here the interpretative standard was "to preserve *and promote* the distinct identity of Quebec" (author's italics). This mandate would certainly encourage and empower Quebec to do more than hitherto had been done to *advance* the distinctive French character of the province, while at the same time to shield these measures far more effectively from challenges under the charter. While the governments had written in a non-derogation clause (2[4]) to ensure that their own powers, rights and privileges were not diminished by section 2, the same was not true for citizens' rights. Thus, the powers of governments and legislatures might well be *enlarged* by the section at the expense of the charter rights of individual Canadians.

What is more, the new provisions reinforced the case for a defensive unilingual nationalism in Quebec — potentially hostile to the spirit of bilingualism. That fact became obvious when Rémillard, on June 7, objected to the application to Quebec of Bill C-72, the new expanded Official Languages Act, without the consent of the Quebec government. He insisted that Ottawa's promotion of English in education, trade, the workplace, communications, voluntary organizations and health organizations within Quebec would be "unacceptable" and would threaten Quebec's "distinct society." He went on: "We consider that our position is in complete conformity with the constitutional accord which we just concluded." Even more worrisome, he received assurances from Secretary of State Lucien Bouchard that the act was aimed at the protection of francophone minorities elsewhere, and that a negotiated approval would indeed be sought from Quebec to ensure that the "distinct society must be protected in priority." In that sense, Bouchard argued, the simple "legal symmetry between the rights of the anglophone minority in Quebec and those of francophone minorities in the other provinces will be broken." The report of Quebec's Language Advisory Board on June 15, in its recommendations to "legislate rapidly, systemically, and visibly" under the "distinct society" clause to make Quebec as French as possible, was yet another sign of the conflict with the bilingual strategy.

The Struggle for Ratification

This process of constitution making had been, from the beginning, an exclusive and elitist affair. Except for the general five-point constitutional program of the Quebec Liberals in the 1985 provincial election, a program itself largely incidental to the major election issues, the public had had no role to play in shaping or commenting upon the elements of the Meech Lake deal. First ministers outside Quebec had no mandate from their publics to engage in this process of constitution making, nor had they shared the principles they were discussing with their publics. Such drafts as were exchanged by governments were always kept secret, as was the actual bargaining session that produced the agreement at Meech Lake. In contrast to the 1982 constitutional changes, the public was not invited inside the process this time.

There were no meaningful legislative outlets where public groups could influence the nature of the constitutional product. Instead, quiet diplomacy, secret bargaining and an outright reluctance to involve publics seemed to be the preference of many first ministers and their governments.

The provinces of Saskatchewan and Alberta, for example, approved the accord on September 23 and December 7 respectively, each without providing for public hearings. While the House of Commons and Senate did strike a joint committee on the 1987 accord that heard from groups and individuals from August 4 to September 1, Ottawa had already declared that the accord would not be reopened to correct flaws for fear of endangering the whole agreement. The same argument was put to opposition parties when they tried to move changes to the accord to protect charter rights, to address the plight of Northern peoples or to correct other deficiencies. This posture, together with the fear of being seen as anti-Quebec and of losing votes in that province, was enough to bring the opposition parties into final acceptance of the Meech Lake Accord in a vote in the House of Commons on October 25. Only sixteen members voted against the deal, breaking party ranks in doing so.

The premiers, in their annual meeting on August 28 in Saint John, New Brunswick, took up a similar posture toward criticism of the agreement. They indicated collectively that they would not reopen the accord to answer the concerns of disaffected groups. Women's groups in English-speaking Canada this time sought in vain to have their charter rights exempted from the scope of the 1987 Constitutional Accord; native persons and other residents of the North shared a similar fate. The contrast with their successful public campaigns to protect their rights in the negotiated 1981 settlement could not have been sharper. This time there was no overt intergovernmental rivalry and therefore no opportunity to exploit divisions to push for their own objectives. Instead, they met a wall of resistance at both the federal and provincial levels.

Indeed, the anti-democratic and arbitrary character of Canadian executive federalism went much further in this round than it ever had before, according to Bryan Schwartz in his book-length study *Fathoming Meech Lake*. First ministers did not adequately involve attorneys-general in the process, nor did they give cabinets, caucuses and legislatures any meaningful role in considering the accord prior to its inclusion in the supreme law of the land. He writes:

> Those who believe in responsible government and participatory democracy have every reason to be outraged by the autocratic approach to constitutional reform adopted by first ministers. It is an affront to cabinet democracy for first ministers to agree to anything as significant as constitutional reform without consulting their cabinets. It is demeaning to the role of the legislature for elected members to have no opportunity to debate the merits of an accord until after the first minister has presented them with a fait accompli. It is contemptuous of the right of the people to be consulted for most first ministers to eschew public hearings for all but the Premier of Quebec, to postpone public input until after the formulation of a practically final draft.

While much of this criticism might also be directed at the style of Canadian constitution making throughout the 1980s, and indeed was so directed by critics after the 1982 changes, there was little doubt that, with Meech Lake, a high-water mark had been reached in the domination of constitution making by the politics of executive federalism. "The 'process,'" says Schwartz, "amounted to a cabal of first ministers" and not surprisingly "the real winners of the process were ... the premiers."

Yet a mere rubber-stamping of the accord was certainly not foreordained. This venture was, after all, the first serious test of the new amending formula approved in the 1982 changes. There was a three-year time limit for approval, with the clock starting to tick after the ratification of the accord by the Quebec legislature on June 23, 1987. Since some of the proposed constitutional changes required unanimous consent, every provincial legislature had to act before June 23, 1990, if the whole project was not to collapse. As events were soon to show in the provinces of New Brunswick and Manitoba, the normal hazards of political life could limit even a premier's power to close a deal within the prescribed period. New political developments could also influence the state of public opinion on the accord, as could the growing body of criticism directed at its deficiencies.

By year's end, the 1987 Constitutional Accord had cleared only four of the required eleven hurdles. It had been passed by the Quebec, Saskatchewan and Alberta legislatures, and the House of Commons had approved the resolution and sent it on to the Senate. It had cleared one legal hurdle, too, when the Yukon Court of Appeal had ruled on December 23 that the federal government had not violated the rights of Yukoners when it signed the accord; thus, this part of the Northerners' program of resistance to Meech Lake had not borne fruit. Even so, for those who wished to see the deal done, the legislative wheels were turning excruciatingly slowly.

Critics of the deal were growing in number, and governments were being put increasingly on the defensive. Women's associations continued to demand changes to protect women's charter rights; native persons kept attacking Meech Lake for shutting out their concerns and objectives; Northerners denounced the inequities of the deal with particular vehemence. A national coalition comprised of many concerned citizens, legal experts and civil libertarians was formed to fight for changes in the accord shortly after its announcement. This coalition, named the Canadian Coalition on the Constitution, spoke and wrote against Meech Lake and announced that it would launch a legal challenge against it.

While there still existed strong support for the accord, much of it from the academic establishment, there were many experts ranged against it. Indeed, in the submissions to the Joint Committee, the experts in constitutional law and federalism often found themselves arraigned against one another, offering completely different views on how the accord would affect federalism and the Charter of Rights. Certainly, the influence of Pierre Elliott Trudeau was not an inconsequential part of the growing opposition, since he took full advantage of a meeting with the Joint Committee on August 27 to label Meech Lake an open power grab by the premiers, whose work was made the easier by a weak-willed prime minister.

But the most damaging event was surely the sudden subsequent change in the roster of first ministers. The first to disappear was Richard Hatfield of New Brunswick following a massive electoral defeat on October 13, 1987, which saw the provincial Liberals sweep every seat in the province. The arrival of the new Liberal premier, Frank McKenna, exposed a gaping hole in the intergovernmental phalanx. Not only was McKenna not bound by negotiations in which he had taken no part, but he had also openly criticized the accord before the Joint Committee while opposition leader and had taken the same critical stance in the provincial election. Here was a first minister who clearly did not like the Meech Lake deal and was openly calling for improvements to it. While the newly elected premier refused to declare that he would veto the accord unless changes were made, he indicated that hearings would be held and that he would be duty bound to offer his reservations. Thus, New Brunswick was a province to which critics of the accord could turn with some confidence. Despite pressure from other first ministers, McKenna seemed to be determined to take his good time in studying the accord and certainly was not interested in taking any action prior to the federal election on November 21, 1988.

The second premier's fall from power was almost as fast and pitiless. A frustrated renegade backbencher in the Manitoba legislature unexpectedly turned out his own party barely two years into its mandate. Casting his vote on the provincial budget with the opposition on March 8, 1988, he forced Pawley to call an election for April 26. The NDP government was defeated and a minority Conservative government under Gary Filmon was installed in power. While Filmon personally supported the agreement, he faced a hostile Liberal official opposition, headed by popular leader Sharon Carstairs, and an increasingly critical NDP, some of whose members would join the Liberals in voting against the accord. Filmon even had to watch his own party, since many Conservative rural members were not happy with the agreement. Only days after the election results, Carstairs pronounced Meech Lake "dead," and the premier conceded he was in no hurry to proceed with the resolution supporting the deal. Even though the premier later reversed himself under pressure from Ottawa and his government promised to introduce the constitutional resolution into the legislature following hearings in the fall of 1988, it was by no means clear whether the Manitoba legislature would pass it.

Meech Lake was also unexpectedly battered in political storms that sprang up in provinces that had already approved the accord. The first was in Saskatchewan, which had its Meech Lake commitment to its linguistic minority severely tested by the Supreme Court's ruling on February 25 that an 1886 statute requiring laws in the Northwest Territories to be in French and English was still valid. That left the province facing a dilemma: either comply with the law by translating all of its statutes into French, as the province of Manitoba was now doing, or pass a new law repealing the 1886 legislation and making all its English-only laws retroactively valid. Once again, a Western province was made to confront its past and had to decide whether it wished to make amends for imposing an illegal unilingual regime upon its people.

Unlike in Manitoba, the bilingual guarantee in Saskatchewan was only a statutory, not a constitutional, obligation: the province retained an entirely free hand to decide what course it ought to take. In the end, the Conservative government of Grant Devine, over the protests of the linguistic minority and of national public opinion, chose to have the Saskatchewan legislature pass a new law on April 25 to repeal the 1886 statute providing for French language rights. The new Bill 2 left the Saskatchewan cabinet entirely free to decide what "key statutes" to translate into French; French could be spoken in the Saskatchewan legislature and courts, but the official records of the legislature did not have to be in both languages. Although the premier vaguely promised a bilingual Saskatchewan within ten to fifteen years and asked for more patience and time to deal with a recalcitrant caucus and public, there were no commitments as to targets and deadlines.

Alberta soon followed Saskatchewan's lead in June by striking down minority language rights in the province. In doing so, it offered its minority even fewer concessions: no translation of statutes, only the right to speak in the legislature in French without the permission of the Speaker and the right to use French (with interpreters) in court proceedings. Both provincial decisions were widely endorsed by residents of the provinces.

These incidents indicated how far the country had yet to go on the road to bilingualism. It underlined once again the difficulties that linguistic minorities would have in securing their rights in the political arena. Just as in Manitoba, public dissent with bilingualism in Saskatchewan and Alberta was fuelling a bitter national debate over the fate of linguistic minorities. Despite his appeals to these provinces, Mulroney was eventually forced to accept the meagre explanations for these policies and to put the best face he could on the provinces' actions.

For the critics, however, the actions of Saskatchewan and Alberta symbolized the true spirit of Meech Lake: its implicit acceptance of French- and English-speaking unilingual communities, its reluctance to assume the burdens of bilingualism and its paltry support for the linguistic minorities. That impression was, if anything, reinforced when Premier Bourassa, after meeting with representatives of the protesting francophone community on a visit to Saskatchewan, refused to criticize the Saskatchewan government. For that betrayal of francophone minorities outside Quebec, he was roundly denounced as a "traitor." As Frances Russell of the *Winnipeg Free Press* put it, this was really all part and parcel of a "provincialism which makes a cruel joke of minority language rights in Canada." In Russell's view, "what Meech Lake creates — and what is becoming more visible each day of the Alberta-Saskatchewan language imbroglio — is not a nation, but a collection of feudal states whose lords have made a pact of non-intervention in one another's treatment of vassals and serfs."

This was strong language. But commentators were already interpreting Premier Bourassa's relatively mild response vis-à-vis the Saskatchewan situation as his way of guaranteeing Saskatchewan's non-intervention should Quebec later find it necessary to override the charter rights of its anglophone minority, especially as they related to language questions under Bill 101. These forecasts turned out to be prescient indeed.

Meanwhile, in Ottawa the Senate received in late February a damning report from its commissioned task force on the consequences of the accord for the Yukon and the Northwest Territories. The report called for changes in several sections of the accord to protect the rights of the peoples of the North. The Senate itself decided to hold public hearings throughout the month of February and invited Trudeau to speak against the accord once again on March 30. After the hearings and subsequent debate, the Senate voted nine amendments to the accord and sent it back once again to the House of Commons. Since the 1982 changes to the constitution had provided for a Commons override of a Senate vote on a constitutional amendment if it were again approved within 180 days, the resolution was finally ratified at the federal level when the House again passed the Meech Lake Accord in a second vote on June 22. Indeed, by July 7, all provinces whose premiers were signatories to the deal had given their legislative assent to the resolution.

But there was still no sign of a break in the powerful opposition in New Brunswick and Manitoba, even though the pressure to conform had become intense. Premier Frank McKenna reacted to this pressure with annoyance, resenting the assumption of so many of the other participants that in the end he would not stand in the way of ratification. "Quebec," he said, "had no difficulty in twice blocking constitutional accords and Canada had no difficulty in allowing that to happen. Yet there seems to be some kind of uneasiness when New Brunswick looks like they may be the real spoilers."

It is noteworthy, however, that at no time did Premier McKenna indicate that he would in fact veto Meech Lake. On the contrary, he publicly called for improvements to it and rejected the notion that to open up the accord would be to kill it. New Brunswick began a series of public hearings on September 29 (subsequently adjourned for the duration of the federal election) with over 200 groups and individuals wishing to speak to the special legislative committee on the subject. The premier had promised not to take any action until the people of New Brunswick had had an opportunity to make known their views on the accord. Therefore, whatever direction the province would ultimately take, it appeared unlikely that the New Brunswick legislature would take any action prior to the fall of 1989.

The evident delay caused no small worry among accord supporters. They argued not only that the need to heal the rupture with Quebec was paramount and that corrections could be made in a second round, but also that defeat of the accord would guarantee a return of Quebec separatism. Nothing was more important than promptly acting on the agreement, whatever its flaws. As Senator Murray put it:

> Jacques Parizeau [PQ leader] has said that "if this comes a cropper, this is a great opportunity for us."
> I can assure you that if Meech Lake fails, it will be determined by many in Quebec, many federalists in Quebec, as meaning Canada has said "no" to Quebec.
> And I think it will be a long, long time before you recreate the combination of circumstances that produced Meech Lake.

Yet demands to reopen the accord continued. The Ontario Liberal party, for example, very nearly voted against the pro-Meech position of the premier in a convention on May 7, 1988. As it turned out, Ontario voted for the resolution, but there was little doubt over the extent of public dissatifaction. Indeed, the legislative committee that had held hearings on the agreement acknowledged as much, recommending that flaws be corrected in a second round and that ways be found in future for the public to become more actively involved in constitutional questions prior to agreements being struck by first ministers. This was a needed, if unduly gentle, critique of Canada's exclusive elite system of constitution making.

Hence, there was considerable political turbulence evident during the ratification process in many provinces. Although all of the signatories still in office had been able to put the resolution through their respective legislatures despite these disturbing political currents, they were in no position to control the flow of events in the two provinces that had undergone electoral change since the signing of Meech Lake. The consent of both Manitoba and New Brunswick was crucial to success, and yet there was growing evidence of an opposition strong enough to block ratification of the amendments. Time was also ticking away. Although the return of a Conservative majority government under Prime Minister Mulroney in the election of November 21, 1988, certainly provided further momentum toward ratification of the agreement, success was by no means assured.

It was not until shortly after the Supreme Court judgement striking down sections of Quebec's Bill 101 that the public finally learned that approval of the Meech Lake agreement in its original unamended form would prove most unlikely. Oddly enough, it was Premier Bourassa of Quebec whose actions accomplished this result. Refusing to accept the court's permitted option of *marked prominence* for the French language on signs in the province, Bourassa chose instead a policy of French-only unilingual signs *outside* of shops and commercial establishments, while permitting an option for other languages *inside*. This compromise not only failed politically to satisfy both nationalists and minorities, it also forced Bourassa to use the notwithstanding clause to override the Canadian charter for a five-year period in order to protect the new language law from legal challenge. It also forced him to exempt the law from the Quebec Charter of Human Rights and Freedoms. This setting aside of constitutional rights confirmed the worst fears of critics respecting the legislative loopholes in Canadian protection for citizens.

The price for this course of action became clear only a day after Bourassa announced his new language policy on December 18. Premier Gary Filmon formally withdrew the Meech Lake resolution from the Manitoba legislature and called for a First Ministers' Conference to deal with "a constitutional crisis" flowing from Quebec's actions. Such treatment of the linguistic minority appeared, in his view, to be contrary to the spirit of Meech Lake, even though Bourassa continued to argue that the distinct society clause in the Meech Lake agreement was designed precisely to deal with questions of this kind. Indeed, Bourassa publicly indicated that had Meech Lake been approved, he would have found it unnecessary to override the charter: the distinct society clause would, in his view, have supported his policy of unilingual signs well enough. These remarks confirmed the accuracy of those who had attacked the Meech Lake agreement as a sellout of the linguistic minorities and a backtracking on bilingualism.

It is important to note that the Supreme Court recognized the unique position of Quebec and the legitimacy of promoting and affirming the French fact in the province. It concluded, however, that prosecution of that goal neither required nor justified the total exclusion of other languages from the public face of the province. In that sense, even this worthy goal did not in itself warrant such a blanket violation of the fundamental freedom of expression guaranteed to every Canadian citizen.

In the end, Quebec's action, together with the expunging of French language rights in Saskatchewan and Alberta earlier in 1988, showed that linguistic minorities, whether English or French speaking, remained easy prey for majoritarian attack anywhere in Canada. That, of course, has always been our history. What is discouraging to see is how destined we are to relive it.

7
The Meaning of Constitutional Renewal

The 1980s have proved to be decisive for constitutional change: more has been accomplished over these several years than in all the time since Confederation. The political momentum behind modern Quebec nationalism has sustained and supported the work of restructuring the federation, while regionalism has also made its mark on the constitution. But the changes have neither conformed to a simple and coherent vision nor pointed in the same direction.

The amendments themselves came in stages, each with its own political dynamic, compromises and consequences. Those which brought patriation and a charter of rights during the prime ministership of Pierre Trudeau were products of a different agenda than the amendments developed under Brian Mulroney. The cast of leaders was different; the play of political forces was different; the philosophy of federalism behind the two federal regimes was profoundly different. Even the comprehensive amendments negotiated in 1981 did not by any means reflect a single-minded approach to the issues dividing the country — not in Ottawa, much less in the provinces.

So, even if leaders and officials in the later stages of constitutional reform often spoke of "building upon" the uncompleted work of their predecessors, their effort was certainly not according to the same blueprints. Given the divergence of objectives, the question of the compatibility of the different constitutional elements with each other and with the earlier elements of the Canadian constitution remains pertinent.

Francophone Nationalism and the Constitution

If there has been a central preoccupation in the constitutional work of the 1980s, it surely has been francophone nationalism in Quebec. From the terrorist post-box bombings and kidnappings of the 1960s, to the election of an avowedly separatist government in Quebec City in 1976, to a referendum on "sovereignty-association" in 1980, that nationalism has fully occupied the attention of a generation of Canadians. For federalists such as Trudeau, the constitutional talks have been concerned with finding peaceful ways to rechannel and discharge francophone nationalism while keeping Canada united and strong; for *indépendantistes*, the talks have been at worst a waste of time, at best a way of advancing in piecemeal fashion toward their long-term objective of an independent Quebec state; for the moderate nationalists, the talks have offered opportunity, as at Meech Lake, for renewing the province's terms of association with the country through the granting of additional rights and powers.

Leaders representing each of these different options have been in power either in Quebec or in Ottawa in the 1980s and have helped to shape the different constitutional packages. While the separatists lost most of their capacity to effect constitutional change after losing the Quebec referendum in 1980, it is nonetheless true that Lévesque, by virtue of his membership in the Gang of Eight, had a hand in defining the terms of the 1981 deal, which in the end he refused to sign. As for the Quebec federalists and moderate nationalists, they enjoyed an unusual opportunity to mould the constitution according to their own nationalist inclinations. Both exercised that option — the francophone federalists under Trudeau in 1981 and the moderate nationalists under Quebec Premier Robert Bourassa in 1987. Certainly, these are *not* historically compatible options, but rather competing alternative expressions of francophone nationalism — one looking outward toward a bilingual "one-Canada" federal state, the other looking inward toward a stronger and increasingly unilingual Quebec state. How could Canadians have decided to entrench *both* of these concepts in the constitution within a mere few years of each other?

The federalist case used as its centrepiece the Charter of Rights and Freedoms: here was a cornerstone representing common values upon which the French- and English-speaking peoples could build a single country. These values comprised not only the popular, liberal individual rights and freedoms, but also what we might call social or collective rights. Indeed, the charter, as Canada's version of the social contract, blended the Lockean tradition of individual rights (notably, however, excluding property rights) with a collective agreement between two founding peoples, the French and the English. Bilingualism — the official equality of the two languages for Canada — was at the heart of the agreement between these two peoples, and it led, logically enough, to demands for constitutional entrenchment of certain rights to services in both languages in public institutions wherever practical throughout Canada. These collective rights, particularly minority language educational rights, could be exercised only by individuals by virtue of their membership in minority groups or communities; they were not broad "universal" liberal rights enjoyed by all individuals in the country. The point, however, is this: if Canada could make space for both peoples within the framework of a single state, there would be no need for Quebec to assert itself as a competing homeland.

The Quebec nationalist option leaned toward the idea of Quebec as the state to which French Canadians would principally turn for the defence of their language and identity. Carried through to its logical conclusion, this option meant an independent Quebec state. In attenuated form, the argument could lead at least to special status for Quebec as the homeland for the francophone element of the Canadian population. There would be explicit recognition of Quebec's distinctiveness and a corresponding increase in its powers to express that distinctiveness. Bilingualism would be attractive for its symbolic value in the establishment of the French fact in the country, but it could never be allowed to compete with the primacy of the French fact within Quebec itself. Both *indépendantistes* and moderate nationalists were inclined toward this way of thinking, with the difference merely questions of degree. Neither the radicals nor the moderates could really make peace with a single bilingual Canada that made no special arrangements for the Quebec state itself.

This much was surely clear enough to the antagonists themselves. But instead of backing one or the other of these strategies, Canada's first ministers decided to support both: first, in 1981, the notion of a bilingual "one Canada"; then, in 1987, the vision of special status espoused by moderate Quebec nationalists. As noted in the last chapter, Trudeau has characterized the latter as "welshing on a deal" made in 1981 — giving up in spirit if not in substance the ideal of a bilingual country in favour of separate dualist arrangements. Instead of one Canadian nationalism inclusive enough to contain both French and English in one common homeland, Canada will have different nationalisms supporting different homelands. "In vain we shall have dreamt the dream of one Canada," Trudeau declared, as the logic of the francophone homeland in Quebec pushed inexorably toward two Canadas: one French and one English.

As if in a sleepwalk or a dialogue of the deaf, anglophone leaders refused to see any contradiction in their actions. For them, their affirmation of both bilingualism across Canada and the distinct society in Quebec was simply proof of their generosity in responding to the aspirations of Quebecers. Had not Quebecers themselves wanted both of these dreams simultaneously? Had they not felt thwarted in their idea of constitutional renewal by receiving only Trudeau's idea in 1981? Why could Canada not accept both of these conceptions without necessarily playing roulette with the country?

There was, of course, a powerful political logic behind these plaintive questions. Most important, action on an exclusive Quebec-based constitutional agenda promised to heal a wound dealt the system of executive federalism when Premier Lévesque was unceremoniously dumped in the making of the 1982 constitutional agreement. First ministers would by this act banish any lingering doubts about their bad faith in dealing with Quebec and restore the *status quo ante*. Moreover, normalization of relations would not only ease premiers' consciences but also bring them more power, since all provinces would profit from the devolution of authority which Quebec was seeking from Ottawa. As for Brian Mulroney, accepting Bourassa's vision offered proof of his generous accommodation of Quebec's concerns, a partisan advantage and a chance to legitimize the 1982 constitution. In short, there were reasons to cut a deal. But when the politicians' work was done, how was the more enduring constitution to give simultaneous expression to divergent brands of nationalism?

Oddly enough, that was exactly the crux of the Meech Lake debate around the distinct society and the charter. Would the courts read the distinct society as a powerful principle to give Quebec, in effect, a special status — to permit it to override the charter? Could bilingualism itself be seen as a possible threat to Quebec's distinct identity by arguably undermining its predominantly French-speaking character? As Ottawa proceeded with an expansion of its legislation to promote bilingualism in Bill C-72 in 1988, Quebec politicians were already insisting that the application of any such programs in Quebec must first be cleared with the Quebec government lest the province's distinct society be undermined. Similarly, charter guarantees that might protect the rights of Quebec's anglophones in the use of their language were expected to be among the first casualties of the new legal instruments provided by Meech Lake.

Furthermore, these new legal ententes between the French and English peoples are merely threshold agreements which require ongoing political will to make them work. The bilingual provisions in the charter, for example, while important, still must be seen as a mere first step toward a new definition of the French-English relationship in the country. True, bilingualism has been accorded far more protection than that offered by the 1968 Official Languages Act and has been constitutionally extended to the province of New Brunswick, while minority language education rights have been enshrined for the official linguistic minorities everywhere "where numbers warrant." Yet the gaps are not hard to point out, and they are already giving rise to demands for completing the strategy. In contrast to the full and generous arrangements in the blocked 1971 Victoria agreement for bilingual government services from provinces, the Canada Act 1982 offers such services only in New Brunswick. Bilingual services in the courts are still very uneven and inadequate. The qualification "where numbers warrant" on minority language rights may turn out to be more restrictive than intended; minority control of minority language educational facilities has not been clearly enshrined in the constitution, though a lower court ruling has found a footing for that control in a generous interpretation of "educational facilities" in section 23(3)(b). There continues to be disappointment that, despite their inadequacy in protecting the minority language, mixed or bilingual schools have so far been viewed as meeting the test of providing "minority language educational facilities."

Clearly, the scope and level of political will in the provinces is of critical significance in making a national strategy of bilingualism work. Ontario is still outside the bloc of bilingual provinces despite the fact that, by geography and numbers of francophones, it ought to have accepted bilingual status. Trudeau's appeals to Premier William Davis to that effect in 1981 and on his retirement in 1984 failed, as did a similar appeal by Mulroney. Moreover, Premier David Peterson has followed his predecessor by moving steadily, but only incrementally, in that direction. While the improvements in rights and services for the francophone minority are substantial and important — indeed, virtually creating *de facto* bilingualism — Peterson's hesitation to declare these rights in the constitution and to accept the symbol of bilingualism for fear of backlash is not encouraging.

It is apparent from the experience of other provinces that backlash is not something that can be lightly dismissed. Even in New Brunswick, where bilingualism has been in place for some time and where there is a large francophone population, a government task force proposing to expand bilingual services in 1984 faced ugly opposition in many public meetings. Elsewhere in the Atlantic provinces, francophones have won occasional improvements but their concerns exist precariously at the margins of public policy.

The state of affairs in the West is even less encouraging. Here, despite the fact that legal guarantees for the French language existed both in the constitutional terms of the Manitoba Act, which brought that province into the union, and in territorial statutes prior to the creation of Saskatchewan and Alberta, the intolerant politics of unilingualism hold full sway. Not until 1979, when Georges Forest contested a parking ticket issued in English only, did the Supreme Court have an opportunity to decide the validity of English-only laws, such as the 1890 Official Language Act of Manitoba. It ruled, some 90 years too late, that the legislature did not have the power to expunge French language rights contained in the constitution and that under section 23 of the Manitoba Act of 1870 the following rights applied:

- either French or English may be used in the debates of the legislature and in any of the courts in the province;
- the records and journals of the legislature and all statutes must be published in both languages.

The Progressive Conservative government under Sterling Lyon repealed the offending 1890 act and began to translate all future provincial statutes in both languages. Later, after some period of confusion about what to do with the thousands of earlier illegal English-only statutes and faced with another legal challenge to them by Roger Bilodeau, the new NDP government under Premier Pawley, with federal assistance and cooperation, attempted to strike a compromise with the francophone minority on May 20, 1983. That agreement called for a constitutional amendment of the Manitoba Act as follows:

- English and French would be official languages of Manitoba;
- statutes and regulations enacted prior to 1985 in English only would be valid;
- laws and regulations after 1985 would have to be published in both official languages;
- existing public statutes would be published in both official languages by 1993; and
- Franco-Manitobans would have the constitutional right to communicate with and receive services in French from all head or central offices of provincial departments, certain provincial agencies, and other offices where a significant demand for bilingual services existed.

Ottawa, for its part, agreed to provide financial help for the translation of statutes and for the provision of bilingual assistance to municipalities with substantial French-speaking populations.

Yet opposition to bilingualism in Manitoba was deep and visceral. Despite support from all parties in the House of Commons and relaxation by the provincial government of some of the agreement's terms, the Conservative opposition wouldn't budge. By refusing to return to the House on the ringing of the bells, it brought the work of the provincial legislature to a halt and the initiative died at the closing of the session on February 27, 1984.

Bilodeau's appeal, however, proceeded. In response to a federal reference on the case, Manitoba was ordered by the Supreme Court on June 13, 1985, to translate all its English-only statutes; by November 4 the province was granted five years — until December 31, 1990 — to complete that undertaking. This result left the province with a much heavier job of translating statutes than had been provided for in the agreement and, ironically, with a less useful program of services for the francophone minority. It was a bitter but instructive lesson.

Events in Saskatchewan in 1988 once again suggested that the old forces of unilingualism were alive and well in the West. As noted earlier, on February 25, 1988, Saskatchewan (and, by implication, Alberta) was declared by the Supreme Court to be a bilingual province by virtue of a still valid 1886 territorial statute. When given the option either to accept the legal status quo or to override it retroactively, both Saskatchewan and Alberta chose the latter route. Compensation to the linguistic minorities was meagre and modest. These decisions were variously justified: in Saskatchewan, on the grounds that the political climate in the province would tolerate no more; in Alberta, that its English-only regime was part of its own self-definition as a "distinct society"!

Meanwhile, Quebec continues to refuse to grant protection of minority language educational rights to anglophone immigrants under section 59, and holds fast to its officially unilingual status. Thus, despite the fact that anglophone numbers are dropping in the province and that the French language and culture are secure, the Quebec government is not notably more generous to its linguistic minority. More and more, the respective fates of the linguistic minorities across Canada are becoming intertwined. Quebecers increasingly question why they should offer better terms to the English minority than the English offer to the French in other provinces. Hence, despite Bourassa's promise in the 1985 election that he would adopt a more flexible and tolerant stance on the issue of English language signs, when given a chance to do so in keeping with a Supreme Court judgement protecting these freedoms of expression under both the Quebec and Canadian charters in 1988, he reneged. The politics around language was so intense that even a court-sanctioned *requirement* of French on all signs and of *marked prominence* for French on all signs in the province was not enough. In the end, he chose to override both the Quebec and the Canadian charters to preserve at least a facade of unilingualism.

It would be difficult to treat this outcome as merely a prudent and sober defence of a perceived demographic or economic threat to francophones; given the government's lawful right to require marked prominence for the French language on all signs throughout the province, it is equally unconvincing to accept Bourassa's measure as a necessary response to a genuine cultural threat. Certainly, the Supreme Court in a unanimous decision found such arguments unjustifiable, bearing in mind the scale of interference with civil rights that an official policy of unilingualism for the public face of the province entailed. While there has been steady evidence from polls for over a decade to indicate that most French-speaking Quebecers accept the practical logic of permitting expression of English on signs, the link between the status of the French language and Quebec nationalism makes the issue exceedingly delicate. The matter is essentially symbolic and, consequently, potentially explosive. Canada's commissioner of official languages, D'Iberville Fortier, discovered precisely that fact when he found himself an object of censure in Quebec's National Assembly for daring to register even a fairly mild criticism of Quebec's language law in his 1988 report.

It is plain that carrying the burden of bilingualism is a heavy assignment in this country. It is much easier to placate majoritarian sentiments in the provinces than to fight for liberal restrictions upon them. This is particularly so if Quebec itself accepts a policy of non-intervention respecting attacks on the linguistic minority in other provinces and implicitly accepts a linguistically and geographically segmented Canada.

This direction, of course, reflects the tendency of one brand of French Canadian nationalism — to look to Quebec as the exclusive home of French Canada, the "distinct society" where the expression of the francophone fact can be given full sway. The unspoken corollary of this theory is that English Canada represents the "other society," where the French can live at best a fragile existence as linguistic outsiders. Only Premier Getty in his truculent notion of "Alberta as a distinct society" is unwitting enough to state that fact so brazenly. But demographics are underlining the reality of that portrait of Canada: assimilation of francophones in anglophone Canada is rising sharply, while the exodus of anglophones from Quebec is leaving that minority in Quebec very much weakened. The 1987 decision to entrench Quebec as a "distinct society" accommodates an inward-looking form of nationalism, as does the subsequent grant of additional powers required to give substance to that theory. Yet the moderate nationalists know that this phase brings only the first of those powers that will be needed to make Quebec a secure homeland for francophones. Even while introducing the Meech Lake Accord into the provincial legislature, Bourassa and his minister of justice, Gil Rémillard, were promising additional powers later to round out their program. Meech Lake is a threshold agreement — the most important in 200 years of Quebec history according to its Quebec authors — but it really brings a whole train of consequences in its path.

These realities have not been fully acknowledged in the initial debate around Meech Lake. So much has been said of the legal implications of the distinct society clause — much of it mere shadow-boxing before the unknown — that little thought has been given to the ongoing political implications of this policy. After all, constitutions are not meant to be read only by judges; they also serve as credos for politicians and publics. Not only will the distinct society clause provide a strong defence for French-first policies, but it will also serve equally well as a call for new legislative action. We can fully expect new constitutional demands in keeping with this new principle, whether or not it turns out to be of limited legal significance. We can expect that the existing clause will add immeasurably to the moral weight of the Quebec state-builders of the future, whether radical or moderate in their nationalism. Federal authority to assert a countervailing national will may prove more difficult. Certainly, it will be harder to build that elusive shared national foundation of values that was at the heart of the one-Canada concept.

What, then, are we to make of the effort to combine these two competing versions of French Canadian nationalism in the Canadian constitution in the same decade? And what are we to make of the enormous transfer of political power to the courts to balance off and give authoritative meaning to the ambiguous language in which these two nationalisms are couched? The courts are not to be envied: they will more than ever have to navigate in the most treacherous political waters. The ambiguity of the constitutional language, and the powerful symbolism it contains, will unavoidably generate more controversy and potential division. Whatever its decisions, the Supreme Court will find itself as an actor in the very centre of national politics. If the Quebec government is to nominate the three judges from that province, there can be little doubt that the politics between the competing brands of nationalism will be an increasing factor in the court's own deliberations. Indeed, the court will have more formal responsibility for working through these accommodations between the French- and English-speaking peoples than will Parliament, with the virtual abdication of its role to supervise and if necessary remedy or overturn discriminatory provincial laws.

Yet in law some tolerable *modus vivendi* may be struck, sustained by our culture's confidence in judicial neutrality and objectivity. On the political level, the argument for some compromise (if not fusion) between the two conceptions of francophone nationalism would be stronger if each did not necessarily press on with competing agendas respecting the place of the French people in Canada. However, it is not likely that anything will change in this respect: each nationalism points to different homelands, different readings of history, different language policies and different futures. Already, the facile notion undergirding current federal policy — of backing both nationalisms simultaneously — is being put under increasing strain with developments in Alberta and Saskatchewan. To the extent that the symbolism around distinct societies supports provincially defined language policies, further progress with bilingualism seems doubtful. While the success with immersion programs in English-speaking Canada and the expanded legislation in Bill C-72 at the federal level may provide some counterbalance, building on the 1982 bilingual program will be difficult. Not least of the difficulties facing the strategy are the sharply declining numbers of the linguistic minority not already assimilated.

What may be of equal importance is the reduced prominence of bilingualism as the central federal strategic response to Quebec nationalism and separatism. With the shift toward the Meech Lake agreement, the federal government and many other governments in English-speaking Canada have moved away from a single-prong approach to this question. In fact, they have opened the door to an alternative mode of accommodating French Canadian nationalism, and one likely to be taken up again. Since constitutional conferences must be held annually for the foreseeable future, there will be regular opportunities for pushing forward in that direction. Meech Lake demonstrates how attractive that route is for many premiers anxious to get on with province building. It will not be less so in the future.

A common argument is that this result was to a large extent "forced" upon Canada by virtue of the imposition of the 1982 constitution upon Quebec without its consent. Prime Minister Mulroney indicated as much as he spoke on June 14, 1988, the eve of the second Commons vote on Meech Lake overriding the Senate:

> [The process used to secure the 1982 constitutional changes] was a deep wound on the body politic of our country. By deciding to proceed without Quebec, the federal government of the day ensured that:
>
> 1) any attempt to re-integrate Quebec would take place in isolation, thereby depriving the federal government of the flexibility inherent in a comprehensive negotiation.
>
> 2) Because of this isolation, any formula to bring Quebec into the Constitution could be portrayed as "giving in" to Quebec or "giving up too much" for Quebec.

There is some substance to this charge, though it hardly accounts for the particular choices that were agreed upon at Meech Lake. Certainly, in return for acting upon most of Quebec's demands — in some cases, exceeding them — there was room for pressing for some federal objectives. In that respect, the retrospective argument concerning the inflexible negotiating "box" in which Ottawa was placed is overdone.

A better explanation lies in the deep historical roots for both expressions of French Canadian nationalism and in the continuing ambiguity of Quebecers concerning Quebec or Canada as homeland. The idea of Quebec as the French Canadians' country antedates Confederation and was indeed the dominant conception even in 1867. Confederation did not at first challenge this identification of Quebec as French Canada; only after the bitter struggle to protect francophone rights in the Canadian Northwest did an alternative conception of French Canada arise, with the entire nation seen as the natural homeland of the French- as well as the English-speaking peoples. The great champion of that idea of Canada was Henri Bourassa, the eloquent Quebec nationalist whose patriotism encompassed the whole country. It was in his spirit that former prime minister Trudeau promoted bilingualism and the equality of the two founding peoples; it was in his name that Trudeau subsequently denounced Meech Lake's betrayal of this developing Canadian nationalism.

However much Quebecers appreciated the status given the French language under this bilingual strategy, their attachment to Quebec as the ancestral homeland could not be so easily dislodged. Nor could the politics of bilingualism disguise the fact that bilingualism itself was still being resisted in much of English-speaking Canada as an artificial and unnatural policy. There was therefore reason for Quebecers to return to their earliest nationalist tradition, even without the issue of Quebec's non-consent to the 1982 changes. It is noteworthy that few francophones have followed Trudeau in his firm insistence that they must now *choose* between a fairer Canada or a stronger Quebec; they appear to want both. In that respect, the demand of both Trudeau and the separatists that francophones make a clean choice has been refused. Perhaps this ambivalence is not just a failure of a people to make up its mind, or an unresolved tug of loyalties. It may lie at the heart of the federal dilemma. But whether the country can successfully accommodate the full expression of these two French Canadian dreams remains to be seen.

Regionalism and the Shape of Canada

By the mid-1970s, the politics of regionalism had begun to compete with Quebec nationalism for constitutional attention. To some extent, the agendas were similar: on the one hand, to advance provincial powers and, on the other, to extend provincial influence over national institutions and policies. Quebec had always had, by virtue of its electoral clout, considerable influence over the Commons; only in exceptional circumstances such as the conscription crises of the world wars, which pitted the French against the English, did Quebec find the scales tipped decisively against it. The underpopulated hinterlands of East and West did not enjoy that security in Ottawa, especially since the Senate had long ceased to function as an effective shield against discriminatory measures from the Commons. In that respect, the two agendas were antithetical: Quebec formed part of Central Canada and was thought to enjoy, alongside Ontario, disproportionate benefits from the union. Much of the hostility in the regions toward Quebec reflected both the gulf created by language and history and the resentment of French power. But these differences aside, there was a convergence in tactics and agendas, as revealed for example in the formation of the Gang of Eight. The question is: How did regionalism fare in the constitutional deals of the 1980s? How successful was it in hitching itself to Quebec nationalism and riding this force for its own purposes?

In the view of this author, it has been remarkably successful. While Ottawa received no direct increase in its legislative powers as a result of the bargaining over the 1982 amendments, the provinces strengthened their constitutional authority over their natural resources by virtue of section 92A. As a direct result of Saskatchewan's unsuccessful legal struggles in asserting its power over potash rationing and its royalties tax on oil and gas, the 1982 amendments expressly permit what the Supreme Court had earlier denied the provinces. Provinces may now make laws in relation to interprovincial trade in their natural resources, provided they do not discriminate in pricing and supply; provinces may also apply "any mode or system of taxation" (including indirect taxation) on these same resources, provided they do not discriminate against other provinces. In addition, the provinces were given exclusive power to make laws in relation to the exploration, development, conservation and management of their resources — including the making of laws establishing rates of primary production. These are significant new powers, even if Ottawa's own extensive legal instruments, which are capable of intruding into the domain of natural resources, remain firmly in place.

In 1987 all provinces gained new powers in the field of immigration as a result of the acceptance of Quebec's demands in this respect. Immigration had always been a concurrent jurisdiction under section 95 of the Canada Act, 1867: that is, Ottawa and the provinces could both make law in this area but, in the event of a conflict, the federal law would prevail. If the Quebec model is to be accepted as the norm, the new provisions ensure that, once immigration agreements are signed with provinces, all would enjoy rights to share in the selection of immigrants, refugees and the like intending to settle in their provinces, to provide services for their reception and integration, and to be guaranteed numbers of immigrants within the total permitted by Canada proportionate to the province's share of the Canadian population. The agreement with Quebec provides that province with the right to exceed its proportionate share figure by 5 per cent "for demographic reasons," but it is difficult to see how that principle could be equally extended to other provinces. While Ottawa retains the right to set national standards and objectives, these agreements will certainly give provinces a chance to shape the new Canadians' first expectations for and perceptions of their new country. Of course, agreements of this kind are of most interest to Quebec, as it struggles to maintain its demographic weight and character within the federation, but they are already attracting the interest of other provinces as well.

The Meech Lake agreement in 1987 provides much more protection against any further federal intrusions in provincial jurisdictions through the use of the spending power. Ottawa's earlier liberal use of its superior taxing base to offer money for programs in provincial areas of jurisdiction had always been an irritant to federal-provincial relations. Whether the matter concerned medicare or some other popular area of social policy, Ottawa had been able to offer the provinces strings-attached dollars for shared-cost programs on federal terms, even though the field lay within provincial jurisdiction. Quebec had sought to have future use of these conditional grants depend upon securing the agreement of seven provinces representing 50 per cent of the Canadian population, but that turned out to be unacceptable. The 1987 Constitutional Accord, while affirming the constitutionality of the practice, ensures that provinces that do not like the federal program can create their own compatible program and receive financial compensation from Ottawa. This right to opt out with compensation certainly protects provinces from improper interference, although it also legitimizes the federal use of the spending power itself. Provinces will likely find that this new right to opt out will mean prior consultation in any future federal initiatives in shared-cost programs, with the opportunity to shape the nature of them beforehand. This is a significant victory for the provinces, even if Ottawa's ability to channel its spending directly to individuals and associations within the provinces remains untouched.

The Meech Lake "solution" to the problems of the spending power owes much to the principles of regionalism that had been accepted in 1982. For surely the chief victory for regionalism came in that year with the acceptance of Alberta's amending formula in place of the Victoria formula preferred by Ottawa. Alberta's formula uncompromisingly enshrined the "equality of provinces" principle, permitting dissenting provinces the right to opt out but not to block constitutional change. That meant considerably less power for Ontario and Quebec than they would have enjoyed with outright vetoes under the Victoria formula. Under the Alberta scheme, except for those subjects in section 41 requiring unanimity, constitutional changes could go forward with the consent of seven provinces representing at least 50 per cent of the population of all the provinces. With the current population, the consent of either Ontario *or* Quebec would be essential. The acceptance of Alberta's formula was made possible only because Lévesque, then a member of the Gang of Eight, had departed from Quebec's traditional position of demanding a veto and accepted instead a right to opt out of amendments transferring provincial powers to Ottawa with compensation. His move was doubtless a tactical ploy to preserve the alliance against Ottawa, but when a deal was struck on those terms, a distinctive Quebec (and Ontario) veto disappeared permanently.

Lévesque's own tactical blunders had made possible this victory for regionalism at the expense of Quebec's traditional historic veto. The implications of Quebec's defeat were well recognized by Lévesque's Liberal successors in their 1985 Policy Program:

The renunciation by the Parti Québécois government of a universal veto power in exchange for the opting-out formula proved a dramatic setback for Quebec, which is now left with very limited means to prevent centralizing measures which might occur in the future. Quebec thus became a province like all the others, with no explicit recognition of the distinct nature of its society....

Sadly, the Quebec government carried its blundering and recklessness even further. Devoid of any strategy for defending our rights and interests within the federal system, it neglected to demand a specific right of veto in crucial areas where the opting-out formula obviously does not apply: namely, the powers of the Senate, the principle of proportional representation in the House of Commons, the role and powers of the Supreme Court, the creation of new provinces, and the addition of new territories to existing provinces.... [It therefore conceded] that, on such matters of crucial importance to us, Quebec's future can be decided by a majority from which we might be excluded.

The PQ government thus took the ultimate gamble on an opting-out formula which was deficient from the start, since it applied only to half of the constitutional field. Furthermore, ... it was unable ... to preserve the indispensable element of the opting-out formula: financial compensation. It was only at the very last minute ... that the principle of financial compensation was reinstated but, unfortunately, only for matters involving education and culture.

It was not long before the new Liberal government in Quebec tried to reverse the setback, preferably by winning back Quebec's distinctive veto "as a major partner in the federation" and "homeland of the francophone element of Canada's duality"; alternatively, it would at least seek to win a veto over all the special subjects outlined in section 42 and full financial compensation on all provincial transfers of power under the opting-out formula. At Meech Lake, Quebec was granted the second, and least desired, of its negotiating options.

From the perspective of regionalism, the second round of major constitutional changes at Meech Lake consolidated the 1982 achievement. Not only was Quebec's moral and political consent given to the provincialist amending formula in full knowledge of its limitations for Quebec, but the formula was now accepted by Ottawa in its original form. The principle of financial compensation on transfers of provincial power to Ottawa was accepted not just in matters related to culture and education, but to *all* subjects. More important, the underlying principle of the formula, namely, *equality of all provinces,* was now separately and expressly entrenched for the first time in the constitution. Even with respect to the Senate, Supreme Court and other subjects listed in section 42, first ministers refused to accept a pre-eminent place for more-populated provinces, as proposed in the federal draft on the table at Meech Lake. Therefore, in order to grant Quebec's demand that it be guaranteed a say in changes to federal institutions, the ministers decided that the same right should be extended to all. Hence, unanimity would now extend not only to those matters originally contained in section 41, but also to all the weighty subjects in section 42, including reform of federal institutions. In short, the notion of provincial inequality was thoroughly scotched, and considerable headway was made toward extending the equality principle into future constitutional negotiations.

There were, of course, a number of wrinkles and anomalies. The achievement of formal equality of provinces was to some extent compromised by the simultaneous acceptance of Quebec as a "distinct society." Premier Getty had tried to get around this contradiction by arguing later, in connection with French language rights in his province, that Alberta is a distinct society too. While that rhetorical excess was a powerful signal on how the clause would be politically hitched to the equality principle, it was still true that only Quebec was separately recognized as a "distinct society" in the constitution. On the level of theory, this fact could not be easily squared with a simple notion of provincial equality. How far this special recognition of Quebec might lead to real differences in provincial power and status depended, of course, on the future interpretation of the clause by the Supreme Court. But a gap in provincial equality had been opened up by the acceptance of the clause, a gap whose future dimensions and importance could not be known in 1987.

One of the subjects around which the new principle of equality of all provinces could be expected to be much debated would be representation in a new reformed Senate. This was an item, central to the regionalism agenda and built into all future required constitutional conferences, that might serve as the focal point for carrying forward the principle of equality among provinces. Certainly, the idea was at the heart of Alberta's Triple-E Senate proposal, unveiled in 1985, with equality wedded to the elective principle and to effective powers in a second House. The case for equality was considerably strengthened both by the express provisions of the 1982 and 1987 constitutional amendments and by the negotiating experience that reaffirmed the unlikelihood of acceptance of any other principle. On the other hand, with the 1987 agreement to place section 42 subjects on the list of those requiring unanimity, Senate reform, along the lines desired by Alberta, has become more difficult to achieve. Instead of the requirement of seven provinces representing 50 per cent of the population of all the provinces for such changes, unanimity is the new threshold.

If movement on this part of the regional agenda is to take place, both Quebec and Ontario must entertain and presumably accept changes to the second House that will effectively reduce their own power. The odds are not encouraging, but the constitutional requirement to discuss the subject unfailingly every year may eventually lead to a breakthrough under more fortuitous political circumstances than exist now. In a sense, this split outcome is a normal political consequence of the tenets of regionalism itself: what smaller provinces win from acceptance of the notion of equality is a defensive right not to be written out of important future constitutional amendments; what they lose is the ease and flexibility that would have come from a less stringent definition of the national will. They can't have it both ways.

That conclusion should also serve as a reminder to critics who have complained, in 1982 and even more in 1987, of the inflexibility caused by the new Canadian amending formula. On the one hand, opting out has been criticized for providing so strong a disincentive to Ottawa that virtually no changes that would transfer power from the provinces to Ottawa might be contemplated. The incentives for opting out are undoubtedly stronger after Meech Lake, since financial compensation is now to accompany opting out on all subject matters, but it is unlikely we would see many such changes in any case. Besides, the question of accepting or rejecting opting out would depend on the issues at hand and the actual extent of dissent. After all, the idea of opting out has been a living part of the

Canadian political landscape since the 1960s, and it appeared as an idea in constitutional formulae as early as 1936.

While the flexible general amending formula remains, Meech Lake has added inflexibility by pushing many more subjects into the unanimity column. Yet that said, Canada's system of executive federalism — a reliance on negotiations among first ministers — is, while hardly democratic, remarkably informal and fluid. It has already proved to be a good deal more effective in generating and carrying through complicated blocks of amendments than are the amending systems in place in the United States, Australia or most other federations. Agreements were reached with unanimity or its near equivalent on very important and controversial measures in 1981 and again in 1987. It is quite possible that, in the years ahead, this mode of constitutional procedure will enable us to effect amendments despite the high formal requirements of the Meech Lake formula.

The other goal of regionalism — the desire to increase provincial power over national institutions or at least to make them conform more closely to the federal principle — has been notably advanced, particularly in the 1987 negotiations. As an interim measure, provinces have been given the power to nominate all senators, while Ottawa retains the right to rule on their final acceptability. This was a major concession to the provinces, even though it was never on Quebec's list of demands or formally part of the constitutional agenda of first ministers. When Senate reform does become the central issue in the next required round of constitutional talks, the federal government will have conceded, even before the bargaining begins, the principle that all senators are named or elected by the provinces.

Moreover, this concession has been made without any linkage to the question of reduced Senate powers. The federal government, therefore, will not enter into the next round of talks from a position of strength.

However, even under the existing interim arrangements, the House of Commons may well find itself increasingly challenged by a legally powerful reconstituted second chamber. This will be particularly so if the provinces choose nominees for the Senate who have won election in the province under rules established by the provinces — as is possible under the interim arrangements. The government of Alberta, in fact, is already considering adopting such a procedure. Public pressure for an elected Senate will doubtless make other provinces turn in that direction. The federal government would be hard pressed to reject such popularly elected nominees. If agreement on a new Senate cannot be reached in future annual constitutional conferences, the methods of Senate appointment established at Meech Lake may become permanent. Even as they stand, the interim arrangements will greatly increase provincial influence in Parliament.

Another national institution over which provinces wished to have some influence was the Supreme Court. In this area, they gained the right to nominate justices to the highest court in the land. Three justices must be nominated by the Quebec government alone, while the other six common law justices would be named by other provinces. This change will ensure the desired provincial input into the appointment process that had been sought for almost a quarter century. At the same time, the entrenchment of the Supreme Court in the constitution will preserve its nature, role and independence from any unilateral federal action.

By building into the constitution a required annual First Ministers' Conference on the constitution and the economy, the premiers have also ensured that they will have an ongoing influence on federal law and policy. Interstate federalism is now part of the fundamental law of Canada, not just a recent convention to be departed from at will. The First Ministers' Conference has become a constitutionally recognized forum and may evolve increasingly into a new level of government in its own right.

The Fate of the North

There was, however, one vast region which, because it had not yet any membership in the interprovincial club, was largely left out of the constitutional deal-making. Although the North nursed at least as many grievances as any other region, it could not gain a hearing for these grievances as long as it lacked a voice at the table. While the fiction existed that the Northern lands and peoples could be adequately represented by their federal masters, in fact the first ministers of Canada had bigger fish to fry. At no time did the aspirations of the people of the North play anything but a minor part in the 1982 or 1987 settlements.

Of course, aboriginal peoples, some groups of which are still the predominant residents of the North, were the subject of several separate constitutional conferences between 1982 and 1987. While some progress was made, the conferences failed to bring governments to accept the principle of aboriginal self-government. Moreover, from the perspective of aboriginal peoples in the North, the conferences also failed to protect another element of their long-run political future: their right, together with other Northerners, to evolve toward provincehood on terms similar to those enjoyed by other Canadians in the past.

The old rule said that the granting of provincial status within the federation would come with the consent of Parliament and of the people so affected. The new rule established by Trudeau and the premiers in the 1982 constitutional agreement did not require the consent of the affected peoples for such a change; instead it coupled Parliament's consent to that of seven other provinces representing 50 per cent of the Canadian population. Even more disturbing was the alternative to provincehood set out in the new rule: any extension of existing provincial boundaries into the territories could also come by legislative ratification of the same inter-governmental consensus. These changes could not be taken lightly, nor could they be interpreted as equal justice. The fact that certain premiers in the West were known to harbour ambitions of absorbing the territories and extending their boundaries to the Arctic made Northerners even more uneasy with the arrangement.

Thus, the problem was not simply that Northerners, lacking a seat at the table of first ministers, could not further their own agenda; it was that others could change the rules and make the fulfilling of Northerners' aspirations much more difficult. In effect, executive federalism in Canada rendered Northerners the *objects* of policy rather than its subjects; it perpetuated the spirit of colonialism in an even more disturbing form than in the past. Ironically, it was principally Western provinces, which have historically felt so humiliated by their own treatment as a hinterland, that resisted aboriginal self-government, looked hungrily upon Northern lands and demanded a provincial say over the political evolution of the North.

Matters were made worse with the 1987 Constitutional Accord. Governments, ignoring the complaints of Northerners about the inequities in the 1982 rule, went further: the new rule would require unanimous provincial consent for any such changes. In other words, any single province could block Northerners' evolution toward provincehood, whereas the consent of the people of the territories was not, in some form or other, even formally required. Moreover, Northerners were formally excluded from the process of nomination of senators and Supreme Court justices. Since members of the appropriate provincial bars are nominated for the Supreme Court only by provincial governments, it is most unlikely that Northerners could be considered. In the face of widespread criticism, there were promises to correct these "oversights" in subsequent constitutional discussions, but the flaws were not considered sufficiently "egregious" to require change prior to ratification. Neither vigorous protests from virtually all Northern groups, nor denunciations from the territorial legislatures, nor Senate-backed amendments in their favour, nor even court challenges could prevent the entrenchment of these rules. Nothing quite so strikingly illustrates the anti-democratic implications of executive federalism in Canada.

It can confidently be said that these events have set back national unity and provided a ground for future bitterness and resentment. The politics of the Canadian North will undoubtedly prove more difficult and fractious than they would otherwise have been. In the wake of Meech Lake, and with no required procedure for dealing with their grievances, some Northerners, including aboriginal peoples, were already warning the country of the dangers of Northern separatism and hinting that the use of force might prove necessary to see that their concerns were taken seriously. Although not nearly so visible as disgruntled women's groups in the campaign against Meech Lake, Northerners were by far the most conspicuous victims of the process.

The Charter and Canadian Nationhood

If there was any popular national focus to the constitutional talks throughout the 1980s, it would surely have been the "people's" charter. Support for the idea of a charter of rights had been essential to the success of the federal strategy under Trudeau; it was central to the criticism of the Meech Lake agreement; and it promised to be of even more importance in the future. For better or worse, Canada had added a powerful new element to its constitutional makeup, an element that promised to challenge both parliamentary sovereignty and provincialism.

The political struggle over the charter had, of course, left its mark on the document. At the Trudeau government's insistence, bilingualism and minority language rights form an essential part of it. In addition, as part of the effort to win public support, rights are both broad and specifically defined, and governments are required to justify any limits on them. Only "reasonable limits prescribed by law as can be demonstrably justified in a free and democratic society" would be acceptable. The charter represents a giant step beyond the old inadequate guarantees provided under the Canadian Bill of Rights of 1960. On the other hand, the political trade-offs with the provinces in 1982 also left their mark, chiefly in section 33 where legislatures are permitted to override certain freedoms *notwithstanding* the charter guarantees. There is now a substantial body of commentary on the strengths and weaknesses of the charter, and as the years pass we can see how well the critics' judgements have stood the test of time. Most of all, a growing body of jurisprudence around the charter can serve as a backdrop for assessing the assorted hopes and fears of its supporters and opponents. What can now be said about these arguments pro and con?

The least helpful critics were those who, on the eve of its proclamation, doubted the future significance to Canada of the charter. This judgement, usually based on a dismal experience with conservative court interpretations of the Canadian Bill of Rights, completely underestimated the extent to which the Supreme Court would accept its new responsibility and map a different course for itself. From the earliest cases, the Supreme Court's pronouncements on the charter have, to quote the words of Justice Bertha Wilson in *Singh,* reflected judicial recognition of "a clear message to the courts that the restrictive attitude which at times characterized their approach to the Canadian Bill of Rights ought to be re-examined."

Nor was the Canadian public or legal community at all reluctant to use and test the new instrument. Approximately 500 charter cases a year have appeared in lower courts since 1982, forcing the appeal courts to spend more and more of their time on charter issues. The Supreme Court has as a consequence not been able to handle its usual case load. Lawyers in the normal course of their work have initiated many of the charter challenges, particularly those on legal rights in criminal law cases; corporations, labour organizations and other interest groups have also looked to the charter as an important political resource; even the public has turned to the courts for resolutions to some of the most controversial and intractable problems in Canadian politics. In short, the charter has converted the Canadian courtroom into a much more important theatre of political action.

This result was, of course, not unanticipated. From the first, a principal argument of charter opponents was that the document would foster both the judicialization of politics and the politicization of the judiciary. The extent of this danger depended directly upon how ready the public was to invite the court into policymaking through constitutional interpretation, and how "activist" the court itself decided to be in that role. It was clear that once the charter was entrenched, the court would be called upon to give real expression to its many vague and general clauses and phrases. Ultimately, as the saying went, "the constitution [would mean] what the supreme court says it means." Legislation that fell afoul of the constitution would be struck down by the courts; nine judicial sages in Ottawa would have the power to overturn decisions taken by democratically elected legislatures. While a veil of judicial objectivity and neutrality would deliberately be cast over these court pronouncements, the personal and philosophical preferences of the judges would soon be apparent in their judgements on the work of the legislative branch.

Therefore, despite endless claims to the effect that "courts do not question the wisdom of legislation," the Supreme Court has been forced to do exactly that when interpreting and applying the charter to various legislative enactments. Take, for example, its early decisions on legal rights under section 7 or on the broad limitation clause in section 1 of the charter. When presented with strong arguments by government lawyers that "the principles of fundamental justice" in section 7 were meant to provide only procedural rights and that a substantive reading of it would lead the courts into inappropriate court review of legislative policy, the Supreme Court in

Reference re. BC Motor Vehicle Act (1985) took the opposite tack. It gave little weight to the recorded views of the intent of the drafters of the charter on this section, to American experience with a substantive reading of "due process," or to the warnings of it becoming a "superlegislator." Once this decision was taken, the court had no difficulty in finding that the policy choice of the B.C. legislature (to provide fines, imprisonment or both for driving with a suspended licence, whether or not the driver is aware of the suspension) violated section 7 and was therefore inoperative. That decision served as a logical stepping stone for even more controversial reviews of the policy choices of legislatures under section 7, particularly the striking down of the federal law on abortions in *Morgentaler v. The Queen* (1988). This expansive use of section 7 suggests that an increasing number of important political issues may be decided in the courts.

Similarly, the Supreme Court in *Queen v. Oakes* (1986) developed a very exacting test for governments to pass if they wish to limit any charter rights under section 1. While that result was certainly welcomed by civil libertarians, it necessarily thrust upon the court the role of having to scrutinize the ends and means of legislative policy. In deciding whether a limit to a charter right was both "reasonable" and "demonstrably justified in a free and democratic society," the court set out these conditions:

- the legislative objectives must relate to concerns that are "pressing and substantial"; and
- the means chosen to address these sufficiently important objectives must be "reasonable and demonstrably justified" by meeting a three-pronged "proportionality test": a) the measures must be "carefully designed to achieve the objective in question"

— hence, "rationally connected to the objective"; b) the means, even if rationally connected to the objective in this first sense, should impair "as little as possible" the right or freedom in question; and c) there must be a proportionality between the effects of the measures which are responsible for limiting the charter right or freedom, and the objective which has been identified as of "sufficient importance" — that is, the more severe the effects, the more important must the objective be.

This exercise could not be carried out without "second-guessing" the political judgement of the legislative branch on both the objects and means of policy. To date, the court has done exactly that and often found the choices made by the legislatures unacceptable. Scarcely six years after the charter, many laws or parts of laws have been consequently set aside: the reverse-onus clause (placing the burden of establishing innocence upon the accused) in the Narcotics Act *(Oakes)* and the mandatory imprisonment section of the same act *(Smith)*; the absence of a hearing for refugees under the Immigration Act *(Singh)*; and so on. Apart from police officials, many would regard these decisions as welcome, if marginal, improvements in procedural justice, just as they would the improved protection to a right to counsel and freedom from unreasonable search and seizure. Nevertheless, questions of procedural justice can become highly controversial. Take, for example, lower court charter rulings overturning the publication ban on naming a rape complainant or removing the restrictions on questioning the complainant's prior sexual history. These rulings may or may not stand. But it may well be that the charter's blunt anti-coercive thrust may fail to discriminate sufficiently between coercive measures thought warranted by many Canadians and those that are not.

This issue arises with particular force when the subject concerns sensitive areas of social policy. Many Canadians were shocked when the court in *Queen v. Big M Drug Mart Ltd.* (1985) struck down the Lord's Day Act, together with its restrictions on commercial activities on Sundays, as a violation of freedom of conscience and religion. Although the protection of Sundays, this time veiled as a secular law requiring a common day of rest, was subsequently approved as a provincial matter in *Edwards Books and Art Ltd. v. Queen* (1986), the case illustrated the extent to which the court could use its own discretion in applying the charter either to permit or to remove certain areas of social policy from the competence of the legislature. Another surprise came with the Federal Court of Appeal in *Luscher* (1985), in which a section of a federal law banning the importation of pornography was struck down as a violation of freedom of expression.

But no case could quite match *Morgentaler v. Queen*, whose judgement was delivered on January 28, 1988. This decision struck down in one blow the abortion law of Canada as a violation of section 7, the right to security of the person. Legislative policy on abortion was probably the most sensitive area of Canadian public policy; it was an emotional, divisive and contentious issue around which politicians walked with exceeding care. Yet the legislation under section 251 of the Criminal Code that Parliament had introduced to strike a balance between the antagonists — specifically, to ban abortions except when approved by hospital committees in the name of protecting the "life or health" of the mother — had maintained at best an uneasy truce. Neither the vociferous advocates of right to life nor those of free choice were happy with it. Moreover, because of the deep divisions over the subject, there was ongoing difficulty in applying and administering the policy fairly across the country. When the court struck down Parliament's law, whether to the cheers of free-choice advocates or to the denunciations of right-to-life groups, it left a legal vacuum for a reluctant Parliament to fill.

In drafting any subsequent bill, the government will be deeply conscious of the restrictions placed upon it by the court. Not only will the administration of any element of its policy be subject to strict review according to the court's reading of the principles of fundamental justice, but some of the policy choices may no longer be available to Parliament. For example, a careful reading of the *Morgentaler* decision indicated that *any* law restricting abortions in the first trimester of a woman's pregnancy, however fairly administered, might well fail to pass the court's charter test. There could be no clearer reflection of how politicized the work of the court had become.

It would be easy to take sides on the matter of judicial review and democracy by simply deciding how far the court has conformed in its judgements to one's own political prejudices. An activist liberal bench, for example, will be lauded and supported by activist liberals, a conservative bench sustained in its direction by like-minded citizens. But surely this is a superficial and self-defeating posture. The courts will in the normal course of events go through alternating periods of active liberalism and retrenchment in any case, and the deeper question is whether the scope of democratic life is really enhanced by the pragmatic acceptance of judicial law-making.

It is also worth noting that the Supreme Court is rarely consistent in its ideological approach to different kinds of issues. For example, although the court has adopted a fairly vigorous liberal posture in defence of legal rights and procedural guarantees, it has thus far been much less progressive on labour issues. Critics had earlier warned that the charter could turn out to be a weapon for the rich and powerful, and not so much a helpful instrument for ordinary working Canadians. After all, in earlier days in the United States, entrenched rights in the constitution had been of little benefit to the poor, blacks and the disadvantaged; on the contrary, in the hands of conservative justices, these rights had historically served the interests of the "haves" by blocking minimum wage laws, child labour laws, laws regulating hours of work, and even the income tax. Only after the showdown with President Roosevelt in the 1930s did the U.S. Supreme Court reverse itself and begin to make peace with the beginnings of the welfare state.

Ignorant of that history, leaders of the labour movement in Canada looked naively to the charter as a potential area for the protection of their rights. They were also among the fiercest critics of section 33, the clause granting legislators the right to overrule the courts by expressly declaring that legislation might stand *notwithstanding* a court-recognized violation. It has taken only a few cases in the labour field to have disabused them of their illusions. In *RWDSU v. Dolphin Delivery* (1986), the Supreme Court declared that secondary picketing by members of a trade union in a labour dispute was not a protected area under section 2(b) of the charter. Here the court concluded that restricting freedom of expression in this form was "demonstrably justified in a free and democratic society" because secondary picketing threatened to extend the conflict beyond the principal parties in the collective-bargaining process: "the social cost is great, man-hours and wages are lost, production and services will be disrupted, and general tensions within the community may be heightened." There was no compensating rhetoric advanced to explain the practical fact that picketing, or interrupting a company's business, is often the only effective instrument available to employees when tackling large companies.

Even worse was the court's response to the question whether collective bargaining and the right to strike were protected freedoms under the freedom of association clause (2[d]) of the charter. The majority answered in the negative. Even though the right to strike is the cornerstone of our modern system of collective bargaining, the court did not regard it as a fundamental freedom worthy of the same constitutional protection as the larger political, religious and social freedoms. While Chief Justice Dickson and Justice Wilson strongly dissented, the majority had its way. That result left workers with the protection of existing statutory arrangements only, and with considerable doubt regarding the sanctity of the principles undergirding the collective-bargaining system. It was an undeniable political setback for the labour movement, a denial of principles that had been fought for over generations. Without a recognized right to strike, the meaningfulness of unions must be questioned.

On the constitutional level, the case would make unions less secure than employers, who can marshall other charter freedoms in their own interest. The courts have not hesitated to extend to corporations human rights and freedoms; they have taken the charter's reference to *everyone* to include corporations. Already

Southam's successful use of the charter right of freedom from search and seizure in *Lawson Hunter v. Southam* (1984) has been effective in striking out a section of the Combines Investigation Act empowering officials to enter business premises and examine documents. Other such victories can be confidently expected.

Only after decisions are reached on some pending labour issues will Canadians have a more complete picture of how seriously the charter may affect the current balance of power between management and labour. If lower court rulings barring the use of union monies for broad political purposes are approved, they may well cripple the political work of unions, while leaving business organizations free to pursue their usual lobbying and political work. There have also been mixed signals from the courts on the question of recognizing political rights for public service employees. While the Supreme Court excluded charter arguments and failed to protect the political rights of Ontario public servants in *Ontario Public Service Employees Union v. A.G. for Ontario* (1987), the Federal Court of Appeal awarded federal equivalents a significant victory under the charter in a decision on July 16, 1988. If the latter ruling is appealed, it remains unclear how secure that victory will be. Meanwhile, the right-wing National Citizens' Coalition has been successful in the Alberta Court of Appeal in striking down the federal law limiting private political campaigning outside the limits of the Election Expenses Act. Many of these outcomes indicate the advantages well-heeled special interest groups have over public policy through charter litigation.

The results reinforce earlier warnings about the inequality that would flow from charter litigation. The critics were right to point out that access to the legal system is unequally shared. It costs an enormous amount of money to take a constitutional case to the Supreme Court; only well-financed interests can afford to accept these costs. Moreover, the judicial system itself is filled with middle-class, white males — appointed until age 75 — who cannot possibly reflect in their judgements the true character and complexity of the nation as a whole. Nor can the difficult issues they must handle be best resolved in a legal setting and by minds trained in that narrow and traditionally conservative discipline. For these reasons, Canadians would be wise not to harbour extravagant expectations of the courts, but to continue to look to broader democratic political processes for the advancement of their rights. While the courts may provide some welcome advancements alongside some setbacks, they will be no substitute for an active rights-conscious citizenry.

The Charter and the Defence of Bilingualism

There is one area, however, where it is possible that the courts may even save us from ourselves. This is the working through of the dangerously divisive pattern of French and English rights in the provinces. Our history, certainly, stands as a stark warning against leaving these questions to provincial legislative control, subject only to paternal parliamentary protection. That strategy has not worked. Nor is there yet any sign that Canadians are even now able to protect linguistic minorities from discrimination by legislative majorities in the provinces. Progress has been made, but recent events in Manitoba, Saskatchewan, Alberta and Quebec show that the old divisions remain and the political attractions of unilingualism continue.

While bilingualism is now a more readily accepted feature of Canadian political life, it faces obstacles that perhaps only a Supreme Court can successfully confront. The court seems to be aware of its new responsibility and has self-consciously undertaken to defend linguistic minorities against legislative encroachments wherever the constitution permits. That trend was clear even before the arrival of the charter, with the decision in 1979 to overturn the 1890 provincial statute establishing an English-only regime in Manitoba. Since the charter, the court has forcefully applied the minority language educational rights against Bill 101 in Quebec in *A.G. Quebec v. Quebec Association of Protestant School Boards* and the freedom of expression and of equality sections of the charter to strike down the language-of-signs provisions of the same bill in 1988. It has declared in *Société des Acadiens v. Association of Parents* (1986) that individuals in bilingual New Brunswick have the right to court hearings in either of the official languages. The court has required Manitoba in *Reference re. Manitoba Language Rights* (1985) to translate earlier statutes into French and to make all future acts of the legislature bilingual. It has recognized the continuing legality of the 1886 North-West Territories Act, requiring certain bilingual features in what is now the provinces of Saskatchewan and Alberta, even if these guarantees did not enjoy the same firm constitutional footing as those in Manitoba. In short, the court, in the words of Chief Justice Dickson in *Société,* has shown

> a willingness to give constitutional language guarantees a liberal construction, while retaining an acceptance of certain limits on the scope of protection when required by the text of the provisions.

Linguistic duality has been a longstanding concern in our nation. Canada is a country with both French and English solidly embedded in its history. The constitutional language protections reflect continued and renewed efforts in the direction of bilingualism. In my view, we must take special care to be faithful to the spirit and purpose of language rights enshrined in the Charter.

If the court can continue to provide this strong leadership, even in the face of complications introduced by the "distinct society" clause, then the success of constitutional renewal in the 1980s will truly be enduring. A new French-English partnership will have been etched onto a somewhat resistant country. In the light of our history, the odds on winning such a settlement have never been very high, but they are improved now. Who is to say that the gamble was not worth taking?

Appendix 1
Canada Act, 1982 (U.K.)

An Act to give effect to a request by the Senate and House of Commons of Canada

Whereas Canada has requested and consented to the enactment of an Act of the Parliament of the United Kingdom to give effect to the provisions hereinafter set forth and the House of Commons of Canada in Parliament assembled have submitted an address to Her Majesty requesting that Her Majesty may graciously be pleased to cause a Bill to the laid before the Parliament of the United Kingdom for that purpose.

Be it therefore enacted by the Queen's Most Excellent Majesty, by and with the advice and consent of the Lords Spiritual and Temporal, and Commons, in this present Parliament assembled, and by the authority of the same, as follows:

Constitution Act, 1981 enacted

1. The Constitution Act, 1982 set out in Schedule B to this Act is hereby enacted for and shall have the force of law in Canada and shall come into force as provided in that Act.

Termination of power to legislate for Canada

2. No Act of the Parliament of the United Kingdom passed after the Constitution Act, 1982 comes into force shall extend to Canada as part of its law.

French version   3.So far as it is not contained in Schedule B, the French version of this Act is set out in Schedule A to this Act and has the same authority in Canada as the English version thereof.

Short title   4. This Act may be cited as the *Canada Act, 1982*.

Constitution Act, 1982

Canadian Charter of Rights and Freedoms

Whereas Canada is founded upon principles that recognize the supremacy of God and the rule of law:

Guarantee of Rights and Freedoms

Rights and freedoms in Canada   The *Canadian Charter of Rights and Freedoms* guarantees the rights and freedoms set out in it subject only to such reasonable limits prescribed by law as can be demonstrably justified in a free and democratic society.

Fundamental Freedoms

Fundamental freedoms   2. Everyone has the following freedoms:

(a)freedom of conscience and religion;
(b)freedom of thought, belief, opinion and expression, including freedom of the press and other media of communication;
(c)freedom of peaceful assembly; and
(d)freedom of association

Democratic Rights

Democratic rights of citizens

3. Every citizen of Canada has the right to vote in an election of members of the House of Commons or of a legislative assembly and to be qualified for membership therein.

Maximum duration of legislative bodies

4. (1) No House of Commons and no legislative assembly shall continue for longer than five years from the date fixed for the return of the writs at a general election of its members.

Continuation in special circumstances

(2) In time of real or apprehended war, invasion or insurrection, a House of Commons may be continued by Parliament and a legislative assembly may be continued by the legislature beyond five years if such continuation is not opposed by the votes of more than one-third of the members of the House of Commons or the legislative assembly, as the case may be.

Annual sitting of legislative bodies

5. There shall be a sitting of Parliament and of each legislature at least once every twelve months.

Mobility Rights

Mobility of citizens

6. (1) Every citizen of Canada has the right to enter, remain in and leave Canada.

Rights to move and gain livelihood

(2) Every citizen of Canada and every person who has the status of a permanent resident of Canada has the right

(*a*) to move to and take up residence in any province; and

(*b*) to pursue the gaining of a livelihood in any province.

Limitation

(3) The rights specified in subsection (2) are subject to

(*a*) any laws or practices of general application in force in a province other than those that discriminate among persons primarily on the basis of province of present or previous residence; and (*b*) any laws providing for reasonable residency requirements as a qualification for the receipt of publicly provided social services.

Affirmative action programs

(4) Subsections (2) and (3) do not preclude any law, program or activity that has as its object the amelioration in a province of conditions of individuals in that province who are socially or economically disadvantaged if the rate of employment in that province is below the rate of employment in Canada.

Legal Rights

Life, liberty and security of person

7. Everyone has the right to life, liberty and security of the person and the right not to be deprived thereof except in accordance with the principles of fundamental justice.

Search or seizure

8. Everyone has the right to be secure against unreasonable search or seizure.

Detention or imprisonment

9. Everyone has the right not to be arbitrarily detained or imprisoned.

Arrest or detention

10. Everyone has the right on arrest or detention
(*a*) to be informed promptly of the reasons therefor;
(*b*) to retain and instruct counsel without delay and to be informed of that right; and
(*c*) to have the validity of the detention determined by way of *habeas corpus* and to be released if the detention is not lawful.

Proceedings in criminal and penal matters

11. Any person charged with an offence has the right
(*a*) to be informed without unreasonable delay of the specific offence;
(*b*) to be tried within a reasonable time;
(*c*) not to be compelled to be a witness in proceedings against that person in respect of the offence;
(*d*) to be presumed innocent until proven guilty according to law in a fair and public hearing by an independent and impartial tribunal;
(*e*) not to be denied reasonable bail without just cause;

(*f*) except in the case of an offence under military law tried before a military tribunal, to the benefit of trial by jury where the maximum punishment for the offence is imprisonment for five years or a more severe punishment;

(*g*) not to be found guilty on account of any act or omission unless, at the time of the act or omission, it constituted an offence under Canadian or international law or was criminal according to the general principles of law recognized by the community of nations;

(*h*) if finally acquitted of the offence, not to be tried for it again and, if finally found guilty and punished for the offence, not to be tried or punished for it again; and

(*i*) if found guilty of the offence and if the punishment for the offence has been varied between the time of commission and the time of sentencing, to the benefit of the lesser punishment.

Treatment or punishment

12. Everyone has the right not to be subjected to any cruel and unusual treatment or punishment.

Self-crimination

13. A witness who testifies in any proceedings has the right not to have any incriminating evidence so given used to incriminate that witness in any other proceedings, except in a prosecution for perjury or for the giving of contradictory evidence.

Interpreter

14. A party or witness in any proceedings who does not understand or speak the language in which the proceedings are conducted or who is deaf has the right to the assistance of an interpreter.

Equality Rights

Equality before and under law and equal protection and benefit of law

15. (1) Every individual is equal before and under the law and has the right to the equal protection and equal benefit of the law without discrimination and, in particular, without discrimination based on race, national or ethnic origin, colour, religion, sex, age or mental or physical disability.

Affirmative action programs

(2) Subsection (1) does not preclude any law, program or activity that has as its object the amelioration of

conditions of disadvantaged individuals or groups including those that are disadvantaged because of race, national or ethnic origin, colour, religion, sex, age or mental or physical disability.

Official Languages of Canada

Official languages of Canada

16. (1) English and French are the official languages of Canada and have equality of status and equal rights and privileges as to their use in all institutions of the Parliament and government of Canada.

Official languages of New Brunswick

(2) English and French are the official languages of New Brunswick and have equality of status and equal rights and privileges as to their use in all institutions of the legislature and government of New Brunswick.

Advancement of status and use

(3) Nothing in this Charter limits the authority of Parliament or a legislature to advance the equality of status or use of English and French.

Proceedings of Parliament

17. (1) Everyone has the right to use English or French in any debates and other proceedings of Parliament.

Proceedings of New Brunswick legislature

(2) Everyone has the right to use English or French in any debates and other proceedings of the legislature of New Brunswick.

Parliamentary statutes and records

18. (1) The statutes, records and journals of Parliament shall be printed and published in English and French and both language versions are equally authoritative.

New Brunswick statutes and records

(2) The statutes, records and journals of the legislature of New Brunswick shall be printed and published in English and French and both language versions are equally authoritative.

Proceedings in courts established by Parliament

19. (1) Either English or French may be used by any person in, or in any pleading in or process issuing from, any court established by Parliament.

Proceedings in
New Brunswick
courts

(2) Either English or French may be used by any person in, or in any pleading in or process issuing from, any court of New Brunswick.

Communica-
tions by public
with federal
institutions

20. (1) Any member of the public in Canada has the right to communicate with, and to receive available services from, any head or central office of an institution of the Parliament or government of Canada in English or French, and has the same right with respect to any other office of any such institution where

(*a*) there is a significant demand for communications with and services from that office in such language; or

(*b*) due to the nature of the office, it is reasonable that communications with and services from that office be available in both English and French.

Communica-
tions by public
with New
Brunswick
institutions

(2) Any member of the public in New Brunswick has the right to communicate with, and to receive available services from, any office of an institution of the legislature or government of New Brunswick in English or French.

Continuation of
existing
constitutional
provisions

21. Nothing in sections 16 to 20 abrogates or derogates from any right, privilege or obligation with respect to the English and French languages, or either of them, that exists or is continued by virtue of any other provision of the Constitution of Canada.

Rights and
privileges
preserved

22. Nothing in sections 16 to 20 abrogates or derogates from any legal or customary right or privilege acquired or enjoyed either before or after the coming into force of this Charter with respect to any language that is not English or French.

Minority Language Educational Rights

Language of
instruction

23. (1) Citizens of Canada

(*a*) whose first language learned and still understood is that of the English or French linguistic minority population of the province in which they reside, or

(*b*) who have received their primary school instruction in Canada in English or French and reside in a province where the language in which they received that instruction is the language of the English or French linguistic minority population of the province,

have the right to have their children receive primary and secondary school instruction in that language in that province.

Continuity of language instruction

(2) Citizens of Canada of whom any child has received or is receiving primary or secondary school instruction in English or French in Canada, have the right to have all their children receive primary and secondary school instruction in the same language.

Application where numbers warrant

(3) The right of citizens of Canada under subsections (1) and (2) to have their children receive primary and secondary school instruction in the language of the English or French linguistic minority population of a province

(a) applies wherever in the province the number of children of citizens who have such a right is sufficient to warrant the provision to them out of public funds of minority language instruction; and

(b) includes, where the number of those children so warrants, the right to have them receive that instruction in minority language educational facilities provided out of public funds.

Enforcement

Enforcement of guaranteed rights and freedoms

24. (1) Anyone whose rights or freedoms, as guaranteed by this Charter, have been infringed or denied may apply to a court of competent jurisdiction to obtain such remedy as the court considers appropriate and just in the circumstances.

Exclusion of evidence bringing administration of justice into disrepute

(2) Where, in proceedings under subsection (1), a court concludes that evidence was obtained in a manner that infringed or denied any rights or freedoms guaranteed by this Charter, the evidence shall be excluded if it is established that, having regard to all the circumstances, the admission of it in the proceedings would bring the administration of justice into disrepute.

General

Aboriginal rights and freedoms not affected by Charter

25. The guarantee in this Charter of certain rights and freedoms shall not be construed so as to abrogate or derogate from any aboriginal, treaty or other rights or freedoms that pertain to the aboriginal peoples of Canada including

(*a*) any rights or freedoms that have been recognized by the Royal Proclamation of October 7, 1763; and

(*b*) any rights or freedoms that may be acquired by the aboriginal peoples of Canada by way of land claims settlement.

Other rights and freedoms not affected by Charter

26. The guarantee in this Charter of certain rights and freedoms shall not be construed as denying the existence of any other rights or freedoms that exist in Canada.

Multicultural heritage

27. This Charter shall be interpreted in a manner consistent with the preservation and enhancement of the multicultural heritage of Canadians.

Rights guaranteed equally to both sexes

28. Notwithstanding anything in this Charter, the rights and freedoms referred to in it are guaranteed equally to male and female persons.

Rights respecting certain schools preserved

29. Nothing in this Charter abrogates or derogates from any rights or privileges guaranteed by or under the Constitution of Canada in respect of denominational, separate or dissentient schools.

Application to territories and territorial authorities

30. A reference in this Charter to a province or to the legislative assembly or legislature of a province shall be deemed to include a reference to the Yukon Territory and the Northwest Territories, or to the appropriate legislative authority thereof, as the case may be.

Legislative powers not extended

31. Nothing in this Charter extends the legislative powers of any body or authority.

Application of Charter

Application of Charter

32. (1) This Charter applies

(*a*) to the Parliament and government of Canada in respect of all matters within the authority of Parlia-

ment including all matters relating to the Yukon Territory and Northwest Territories; and
(*b*) to the legislature and government of each province in respect of all matters within the authority of the legislature of each province.

Exception

(2) Notwithstanding subsection (1), section 15 shall not have effect until three years after this section comes into force.

Exception where express declaration

33. (1) Parliament or the legislature of a province may expressly declare in an Act of Parliament or of the legislature, as the case may be, that the Act or a provision thereof shall operate notwithstanding a provision included in section 2 or sections 7 to 15 of this Charter.

Operation of exception

(2) An Act or a provision of an Act in respect of which a declaration made under this section is in effect shall have such operation as it would have but for the provision of this Charter referred to in the declaration.

Five year limitation

(3) A declaration made under subsection (1) shall cease to have effect five years after it comes into force or on such earlier date as may be specified in the declaration.

Re-enactment

(4) Parliament or a legislature of a province may re-enact a declaration made under subsection (1).

Five year limitation

(5) Subsection (3) applies in respect of a re-enactment made under subsection (4).

Citation

Citation

34. This Part may be cited as the *Canadian Charter of Rights and Freedoms*.

PART II

RIGHTS OF THE ABORIGINAL PEOPLES OF CANADA

Recognition of existing aboriginal and treaty rights

35. (1) The existing aboriginal and treaty rights of the aboriginal peoples of Canada are hereby recognized and affirmed.

Definition of "aboriginal peoples of Canada"

(2) In this Act, "aboriginal peoples of Canada" includes the Indian, Inuit and Métis peoples of Canada.

PART III

EQUALIZATION AND REGIONAL DISPARITIES

Commitment to promote equal opportunities

36. (1) Without altering the legislative authority of Parliament or of the provincial legislatures, or the rights of any of them with respect to the exercise of their legislative authority, Parliament and the legislatures, together with the government of Canada and the provincial governments, are committed to
  (*a*) promoting equal opportunities for the well-being of Canadians;
  (*b*) furthering economic development to reduce disparity in opportunities; and
  (*c*) providing essential public services of reasonable quality to all Canadians.

Commitment respecting public services

(2) Parliament and the government of Canada are committed to the principle of making equalization payments to ensure that provincial governments have sufficient revenues to provide reasonably comparable levels of public services at reasonably comparable levels of taxation.

PART IV

CONSTITUTIONAL CONFERENCE

Constitutional
conference

37. (1) A constitutional conference composed of the Prime Minister of Canada and the first ministers of the provinces shall be convened by the Prime Minister of Canada within one year after this Part comes into force.

Participation of
aboriginal
peoples

(2) The conference convened under subsection (1) shall have included in its agenda an item respecting constitutional matters that directly affect the aboriginal peoples of Canada, including the identification and definition of the rights of those peoples to be included in the Constitution of Canada, and the Prime Minister of Canada shall invite representatives of those peoples to participate in the discussions on that item.

Participation of
territories

(3) The Prime Minister of Canada shall invite elected representatives of the governments of the Yukon Territory and the Northwest Territories to participate in the discussions on any item on the agenda of the conference convened under subsection (1) that, in the opinion of the Prime Minister, directly affects the Yukon Territory and the Northwest Territories.

PART V

PROCEDURE FOR AMENDING CONSTITUTION OF CANADA

General
procedure for
amending
Constitution
of Canada

38. (1) An amendment to the Constitution of Canada may be made by proclamation issued by the Governor General under the Great Seal of Canada where so authorized by
    (*a*) resolutions of the Senate and House of Commons; and

(b) resolutions of the legislative assemblies of at least two-thirds of the provinces that have, in the aggregate, according to the then latest general census, at least fifty per cent of the population of all the provinces.

Majority of members

(2) An amendment made under subsection (1) that derogates from the legislative powers, the proprietary rights or any other rights or privileges of the legislature or government of a province shall require a resolution supported by a majority of the members of each of the Senate, the House of Commons and the legislative assemblies required under subsection (1).

Expression of dissent

(3) An amendment referred to in subsection (2) shall not have effect in a province the legislative assembly of which has expressed its dissent thereto by resolution supported by a majority of its members prior to the issue of the proclamation to which the amendment relates unless that legislative assembly, subsequently, by resolution supported by a majority of its members, revokes its dissent and authorizes the amendment.

Revocation of dissent

(4) A resolution of dissent made for the purposes of subsection (3) may be revoked at any time before or after the issue of the proclamation to which it relates.

Restriction on proclamation

39. (1) A proclamation shall not be issued under subsection 38(1) before the expiration of one year from the adoption of the resolution initiating the amendment procedure thereunder, unless the legislative assembly of each province has previously adopted a resolution of assent or dissent.

Idem

(2) A proclamation shall not be issued under subsection 38(1) after the expiration of three years from the adoption of the resolution initiating the amendment procedure thereunder.

Compensation

40. Where an amendment is made under subsection 38(1) that transfers provincial legislative powers relating to education or other cultural matters from provincial legislatures to Parliament, Canada shall provide reasonable compensation to any province to which the amendment does not apply.

Amendment by
unanimous
consent

41. An amendment to the Constitution of Canada in relation to the following matters may be made by proclamation issued by the Governor General under the Great Seal of Canada only where authorized by resolutions of the Senate and House of Commons and of the legislative assembly of each province:

(*a*) the office of the Queen, the Governor General and the Lieutenant Governor of a province;

(*b*) the right of a province to a number of members in the House of Commons not less than the number of Senators by which the province is entitled to be represented at the time this Part comes into force;

(*c*) subject to section 43, the use of the English or the French language;

(*d*) the composition of the Supreme Court of Canada; and

(*e*) an amendment to this Part.

Amendment by
general
procedure

42. (1) An amendment to the Constitution of Canada in relation to the following matters may be made only in accordance with subsection 38(1):

(*a*) the principle of proportionate representation of the provinces in the House of Commons prescribed by the Constitution of Canada;

(*b*) the powers of the Senate and the method of selecting Senators;

(*c*) the number of members by which a province is entitled to be represented in the Senate and the residence qualifications of Senators;

(*d*) subject to paragraph 41(*d*), the Supreme Court of Canada;

(*e*) the extension of existing provinces into the territories; and

(*f*) notwithstanding any other law or practice, the establishment of new provinces.

Exception

(2) Subsections 38(2) to (4) do not apply in respect of amendments in relation to matters referred to in subsection (1).

Amendment of
provisions
relating to some
but not all
provinces

43. An amendment to the Constitution of Canada in relation to any provision that applies to one or more, but not all, provinces, including

(*a*) any alteration to boundaries between provinces, and

(*b*) any amendment to any provision that relates to the use of the English or the French language within a province,

may be made by proclamation issued by the Governor General under the Great Seal of Canada only where so authorized by resolutions of the Senate and House of Commons and of the legislative assembly of each province to which the amendment applies.

Amendments by Parliament

44. Subject to sections 41 and 42, Parliament may exclusively make laws amending the Constitution of Canada in relation to the executive government of Canada or the Senate and House of Commons.

Amendments by provincial legislatures

45. Subject to section 41, the legislature of each province may exclusively make laws amending the constitution of the province.

Initiation of amendment procedures

46. (1) The procedures for amendment under sections 38, 41, 42 and 43 may be initiated either by the Senate or the House of Commons or by the legislative assembly of a province.

Revocation of authorization

(2) A resolution of assent made for the purposes of this Part may be revoked at any time before the issue of a proclamation authorized by it.

Amendments without Senate resolution

47. (1) An amendment to the Constitution of Canada made by proclamation under section 38, 41, 42 or 43 may be made without a resolution of the Senate authorizing the issue of the proclamation if, within one hundred and eighty days after the adoption by the House of Commons of a resolution authorizing its issue, the Senate has not adopted such a resolution and if, at any time after the expiration of that period, the House of Commons again adopts the resolution.

Computation of period

(2) Any period when Parliament is prorogued or dissolved shall not be counted in computing the one hundred and eighty day period referred to in subsection (1).

Advice to issue proclamation

48. The Queen's Privy Council for Canada shall advise the Governor General to issue a proclamation under this Part forthwith on the adoption of the resolutions required for an amendment made by proclamation under this Part.

Constitutional conference

49. A constitutional conference composed of the Prime Minister of Canada and the first ministers of the provinces shall be convened by the Prime Minister of Canada within fifteen years after this Part comes into force to review the provisions of this Part.

PART VI

AMENDMENT TO THE CONSTITUTION ACT, 1867

Amendment to Constitution Act, 1867

50. The *Constitution Act, 1867* (formerly named the *British North America Act, 1867*) is amended by adding thereto, immediately after section 92 thereof, the following heading and section:

"Non-Renewable Natural Resources, Forestry Resources and Electrical Energy

Laws respecting non-renewable natural resources, forestry resources and electrical energy

92A. (1) In each province, the legislature may exclusively make laws in relation to
(*a*) exploration for non-renewable natural resources in the province;
(*b*) development, conservation and management of non-renewable natural resources and forestry resources in the province, including laws in relation to the rate of primary production therefrom; and
(*c*) development, conservation and management of sites and facilities in the province for the generation and production of electrical energy.

Export from provinces of resources

(2) In each province, the legislature may make laws in relation to the export from the province to another part of Canada of the primary production from non-renewable natural resources and forestry resources in the province and the production from facilities in the province for the generation of electrical energy, but such laws may not authorize or provide for discrimination in prices or in supplies exported to another part of Canada.

Authority of Parliament

(3) Nothing in subsection (2) derogates from the authority of Parliament to enact laws in relation to the matters referred to in that subsection and, where such a law of Parliament and a law of a province conflict, the law of Parliament prevails to the extent of the conflict.

Taxation of resources

(4) In each province, the legislature may make laws in relation to the raising of money by any mode or system of taxation in respect of
    (*a*) non-renewable natural resources and forestry resources in the province and the primary production therefrom, and
    (*b*) sites and facilities in the province for the generation of electrical energy and the production therefrom,
whether or not such production is exported in whole or in part from the province, but such laws may not authorize or provide for taxation that differentiates between production exported to another part of Canada and production not exported from the province.

"Primary production"

(5) The expression "primary production" has the meaning assigned by the Sixth Schedule.

Existing powers or rights

(6) Nothing in subsections (1) to (5) derogates from any powers or rights that a legislature or government of a province had immediately before the coming into force of this section."

Idem

51. The said Act is further amended by adding thereto the following Schedule:

"THE SIXTH SCHEDULE

Primary Production from Non-Renewable Natural Resources and Forestry Resources

1. For the purposes of section 92A of this Act,
    (*a*) production from a non-renewable natural resource is primary production therefrom if
        (i) it is in the form in which it exists upon its recovery or severance from its natural state, or
        (ii) it is a product resulting from processing or refining the resource, and is not a manufactured product or a product resulting from refining crude oil, refining upgraded heavy crude oil, refining gases or liquids derived from coal or refining a synthetic equivalent of crude oil; and
    (*b*) production from a forestry resource is primary production therefrom if it consists of sawlogs, poles, lumber, wood chips, sawdust or any other primary wood product, or wood pulp, and is not a product manufactured from wood."

PART VII

GENERAL

Primacy of Constitution of Canada

52. (1) The Constitution of Canada is the supreme law of Canada, and any law that is inconsistent with the provisions of the Constitution is, to the extent of the inconsistency, of no force or effect.

Constitution of Canada

(2) The Constitution of Canada includes
    (*a*) the *Canada Act*, including this Act;
    (*b*) the Acts and orders referred to in Schedule I; and
    (*c*) any amendment to any Act or order referred to in paragraph (*a*) or (*b*).

Amendments to Constitution of Canada

(3) Amendments to the Constitution of Canada shall be made only in accordance with the authority contained in the Constitution of Canada.

Repeals and
new names

53. (1) The enactments referred to in Column I of Schedule I are hereby repealed or amended to the extent indicated in Column II thereof and, unless repealed, shall continue as law in Canada under the names set out in Column III thereof.

Consequential
amendments

(2) Every enactment, except the *Canada Act*, that refers to an enactment referred to in Schedule I by the name in Column I thereof is hereby amended by substituting for that name the corresponding name in Column III thereof, and any British North America Act not referred to in Schedule I may be cited as the *Constitution Act* followed by the year and number, if any, of its enactment.

Repeal and
consequential
amendments

54. Part IV is repealed on the day that is one year after this Part comes into force and this section may be repealed and this Act renumbered, consequential upon the repeal of Part IV and this section, by proclamation issued by the Governor General under the Great Seal of Canada.

French version
of Constitution
of Canada

55. A French version of the portions of the Constitution of Canada referred to in Schedule I shall be prepared by the Minister of Justice of Canada as expeditiously as possible and, when any portion thereof sufficient to warrant action being taken has been so prepared, it shall be put forward for enactment by proclamation issued by the Governor General under the Great Seal of Canada pursuant to the procedure then applicable to an amendment of the same provisions of the Constitution of Canada.

English and
French versions
of certain
constitutional
texts

56. Where any portion of the Constitution of Canada has been or is enacted in English and French or where a French version of any portion of the Constitution is enacted pursuant to section 55, the English and French versions of that portion of the Constitution are equally authoritative.

English and
French versions
of this Act

57. The English and French versions of this Act are equally authoritative.

Commence-
ment

58. Subject to section 59, this Act shall come into force on a day to be fixed by proclamation issued by the

276 The Canadian Constitution

Queen or the Governor General under the Great Seal of Canada.

Commencement of paragraph 23(1)(a) in respect of Quebec

59. (1) Paragraph 23(1)(a) shall come into force in respect of Quebec on a day to be fixed by proclamation issued by the Queen or the Governor General under the Great Seal of Canada.

Authorization of Quebec

(2)A proclamation under subsection (1)shall be issued only where authorized by the legislative assembly or government of Quebec.

Repeal of this section

(3)This section may be repealed on the day paragraph 23(1)(a)comes into force in respect of Quebec and this Act amended and renumbered, consequential upon the repeal of this section, by proclamation issued by the Queen or the Governor General under the Great Seal of Canada.

Short title and citations

60. This Act may may be cited as the *Constitution Act, 1982*, and the Constitution Acts 1867 to 1975 (No.2) and this Act may be cited together as the *Constitution Acts, 1867 to 1982*.

[Author's note: Hereafter follows Schedule I, which modernizes the constitution by updating titles of earlier constitutional acts and by repealing all or part of earlier enactments made redundant by the new constitution.]

Appendix 2
1983 Constitutional Accord on Aboriginal Rights

Whereas pursuant to section 37 of the Constitution Act 1982, a constitutional conference composed of the Prime Minister of Canada and the first ministers of the provinces was held on March 15 and 16, 1983, to which representatives of the aboriginal peoples of Canada and elected representatives of the governments of the Yukon Territory and the Northwest Territories were invited;

And whereas it was agreed at that conference that certain amendments to the Constitution Act, 1982 would be sought in accordance with section 38 of that Act;

And whereas that conference had included in its agenda the following matters that directly affect the aboriginal peoples of Canada:

AGENDA
1. Charter of Rights of the Aboriginal Peoples (expanded Part II) including:
   • Preamble

- Removal of "Existing," and expansion of Section 35 to include recognition of modern treaties, treaties signed outside Canada and before Confederation, and specific mention of "Aboriginal Title" including the rights of aboriginal peoples of Canada to a land and water base (including land base for the Metis)
- Statement of the particular rights of aboriginal peoples
- Statement of principles
- Equality
- Enforcement
- Interpretation

2. Amending formula revisions, including:
- Amendments on aboriginal matters not to be subject to provincial opting out (Section 42)
- Consent clause

3. Self-government

4. Repeal of Section 42(l)(e) and (f)

5. Amendments to Part III, including:
- Equalization   )
- Cost-sharing   ) Resourcing of
- Service delivery   ) aboriginal governments

6. Ongoing process, including further first ministers conferences and the entrenchment of necessary mechanisms to implement rights

And whereas that conference was unable to complete its full consideration of all the agenda items;

And whereas it was agreed at that conference that future conferences be held at which those agenda items and other constitutional matters that directly affect the aboriginal peoples of Canada will be discussed;

NOW THEREFORE the Government of Canada and the provincial governments hereby agree as follows:

1.   A constitutional conference composed of the Prime Minister of Canada and the first ministers of the provinces will be convened by the Prime Minister of Canada within one year after the completion of the constitutional conference held on March 15 and 16, 1983.

2. The conference convened under subsection (1) shall have included in its agenda those items that were not fully considered at the conference held on March 15 and 16, 1983, and the Prime Minister of Canada shall invite representatives of the aboriginal peoples of Canada to participate in the discussions on those items.

3. The Prime Minister of Canada shall invite elected representatives of the governments of the Yukon Territory and the Northwest Territories to participate in the discussions on any item on the agenda of the conference convened under subsection (1) that, in the opinion of the Prime Minister, directly affects the Yukon Territory and the Northwest Territories.

4. The Prime Minister of Canada will lay or cause to be laid before the Senate and House of Commons, and the first ministers of the provinces will lay or cause to be laid before their legislative assemblies prior to December 31, 1983, a resolution in the form set out in the Schedule to authorize a proclamation to be issued

by the Governor General under the Great Seal of Canada to amend the Constitution Act, 1982.

5. In preparation for the constitutional conferences contemplated by this Accord, meetings composed of ministers of the governments of Canada and the provinces, together with representatives of the aboriginal peoples of Canada and elected representatives of governments of the Yukon Territory and the Northwest Territories shall be convened at least annually by the government of Canada.

6. Nothing in this Accord is intended to preclude or substitute for, any bilateral or other discussions or agreements between governments and the various aboriginal peoples and, in particular, having regard to the authority of Parliament under Class 24 of section 91 of the Constitution Act, 1967, and of the special relationship that has existed and continues to exist between the Parliament and government of Canada and the peoples referred to in that Class, this Accord is made without prejudice to any bilateral process that has been or may be established between the government of Canada and those peoples.

7. Nothing in this Accord shall be construed so as to affect the interpretation of the Constitution of Canada.

SCHEDULE
Motion for a Resolution to authorize His Excellency the Governor General to issue a proclamation respecting amendments to the Constitution of Canada

Whereas the Constitution Act, 1982 provides that an amendment to the Constitution of Canada may be made by proclamation issued by the Governor General under the Great Seal of Canada where so authorized by resolutions of the Senate and House of Commons and resolutions of the legislative assemblies as provided for in section 38 thereof;

And Whereas the Constitution of Canada, reflecting the country and Canadian society, continues to develop and strengthen the rights and freedoms that it guarantees;

And Whereas, after a gradual transition of Canada from colonial status to the status of an independent and sovereign state, Canadians have, as of April 17, 1982, full authority to amend their constitution in Canada;

And Whereas historically and equitably it is fitting that the early exercise of that full authority should relate to the rights and freedoms of the first inhabitants of Canada, the aboriginal peoples;

Now Therefore the [Senate] [House of Commons] [legislative assembly] resolves that His Excellency the Governor General be authorized to issue a proclamation under the Great Seal of Canada amending the Constitution of Canada as follows:
PROCLAMATION AMENDING THE CONSTITUTION OF CANADA

1. Paragraph 25(b) of the Constitution Act 1982 is repealed and the following substituted therefor:
(b) "any rights or freedoms that now exist by way of and claims agreements or may be so acquired."

2. Section 35 of the Constitution act, 1982 is amended by adding thereto the following subsections:

"(3) For greater certainty, in subsection (1) 'treaty rights' includes rights that now exist by way of land claims agreements or may be so acquired."

(4) Notwithstanding any other provision of this Act, the aboriginal and treaty rights referred to in subsection (1) are guaranteed equally to male and female persons."

3.The said Act is further amended by adding thereto, immediately after section 35 thereof, the following section:

"35.1 The government of Canada and the provincial governments are committed to the principle that, before any amendment is made to Class 24 of section 91 of the Constitution Act, 1867, to section 25 of this Act or to this Part,

(a) a constitutional conference that includes in its agenda an item relating to the proposed amendment, composed of the Prime Minister of Canada and the first ministers of the provinces, will be convened by the Prime Minister of Canada, and

(b) the Prime Minister of Canada will invite representatives of the aboriginal peoples of Canada to participate in the discussions on that item"

4. The said Act is further amended by adding thereto, immediately after section 37 thereof the following Part Part IV.I

CONSTITUTIONAL CONFERENCES

37.1(1) In addition to the conference convened in March 1983, at least two constitutional conferences composed of the Prime Minister of Canada and the first ministers of the provinces shall be convened by the Prime Minister of Canada, the first within three years after April 17, 1982 and the second within five years after that date.

(2) Each conference convened under subsection (1) shall have included in its agenda constitutional matters that directly affect the aboriginal peoples of Canada, and the Prime Minister of Canada shall invite representatives of those peoples to participate in the discussion on those matters.

(3) The Prime Minister of Canada shall invite elected representatives of the governments of the Yukon and the Northwest Territories to participate in the discussions on any item on the agenda of a conference convened under subsection (1) that, in the opinion of the Prime Minister, directly affects the Yukon Territory and the Northwest Territories."

(4) Nothing in this section shall be construed so as to derogate from subsection 35(1)

5. The said Act is further amended by adding thereto immediately after section 54 thereof, the following section:

"54.1 Part IV.1 and this section are repealed on April 18, 1987."

6. The said Act is further amended by adding thereto the following section

"61. A reference to the Constitution Acts, 1867 to 1982 shall be deemed to include a reference to the Constitution Amendment Proclamation, 1983."

7. This Proclamation may be cited as the Constitution Amendment Proclamation, 1983.

Appendix 3
Meech Lake Communiqué
of April 30, 1987

At their meeting today at Meech Lake, the Prime Minister and the ten Premiers agreed to ask officials to transform into a constitutional text the agreement in principle found in the attached document.

First Ministers also agreed to hold a constitutional conference within weeks to approve a formal text intended to allow Quebec to resume its place as a full participant in Canada's constitutional development.

Quebec's Distinct Society

(1) The Constitution of Canada shall be interpreted in a manner consistent with

    a) the recognition that the existence of French-speaking Canada, centred in but not limited to Quebec, and English-speaking Canada, concentrated outside Quebec but also present in

Quebec, constitutes a fundamental characteristic of Canada; and

b) the recognition that Quebec constitutes within Canada a distinct society.

(2) Parliament and the provincial legislatures, in the exercise of their respective powers, are committed to preserving the fundamental characteristic of Canada referred to in paragraph (1)(a).

(3) The role of the legislature and Government of Quebec to preserve and promote the distinct identity of Quebec referred to in paragraph (1)(b) is affirmed.

Immigration

— Provide under the Constitution that the Government of Canada shall negotiate an immigration agreement appropriate to the needs and circumstances of a province that so requests and that, once concluded, the agreement may be entrenched at the request of the province;

— such agreements must recognize the federal government's power to set national standards and objectives relating to immigration, such as the ability to determine general categories of immigrants, to establish overall levels of immigration and prescribe categories of inadmissible persons;

—under the foregoing provisions, conclude in the first instance an agreement with Quebec that would:

- incorporate the principles of the Cullen-Couture Agreement on the selection abroad and in Canada of independent immigrants, visitors for medical treatment, students and temporary workers, and on the selection of refugees abroad and economic criteria for family reunification and assisted relatives;

- guarantee that Quebec will receive a number of immigrants, including refugees, within the annual total established by the federal government for all of Canada proportionate to its share of the population of Canada, with the right to exceed that figure by 5% for demographic reasons; and

- provide an undertaking by Canada to withdraw services (except citizenship services) for the reception and integration (including linguistic and cultural) of all foreign nations wishing to settle in Quebec where services are to be provided by Quebec, with such withdrawal to be accompanied by reasonable compensation:

—nothing in the foregoing should be construed as preventing the negotiation of similar agreements with other provinces.

Supreme Court of Canada

—Entrench the Supreme Court and the requirement that at least three of the nine justices appointed be from the civil bar;

—provide that, where there is a vacancy on the Supreme Court, the federal government shall appoint a person from a list of candidates proposed by the provinces and who is acceptable to the federal government.

Spending Power

—Stipulate that Canada must provide reasonable compensation to any province that does not participate in a future national shared-cost program in an area of exclusive provincial jurisdiction if that province undertakes its own initiative on programs compatible with national objectives.

Amending Formula

—Maintain the current general amending formula set out in section 38, which requires the consent of Parliament and at least two-thirds of the provinces representing at least fifty percent of the population;

—guarantee reasonable compensation in all cases where a province opts out of an amendment transferring provincial jurisdiction to Parliament;

—because opting out of constitutional amendments to matters set out in section 42 of the Constitution Act, 1982 is not possible, require the consent of Parliament and all the provinces for such amendments.

Second Round

—Require that a First Ministers' Conference on the Constitution be held not less than once per year and that the first be held within twelve months of proclamation of this amendment but not later than the end of 1988;

—entrench in the Constitution the following items on the agenda:

1) Senate reform including:

—the functions and role of the Senate
—the powers of the Senate
—the method of selection of Senators
—the distribution of Senate seats

2) fisheries roles and responsibilities; and

3) other agreed upon matters

—entrench in the Constitution the annual First Ministers' Conference on the Economy now held under the terms of the February 1985 Memorandum of Agreement;

—until constitutional amendments regarding the Senate are accomplished the federal government shall appoint persons from lists of candidates provided by provinces where vacancies occur and who are acceptable to the federal government.

Appendix 4
1987 Constitutional Accord

WHEREAS first ministers, assembled in Ottawa, have arrived at a unanimous accord on constitutional amendments that would bring about the full and active participation of Quebec in Canada's constitutional evolution, would recognize the principle of equality of all the provinces, would provide new arrangements to foster greater harmony and cooperation between the Government of Canada and the governments of the provinces and would require that annual first ministers' conferences on the state of the Canadian economy and such other matters as may be appropriate be convened and that annual constitutional conferences composed of first ministers be convened commencing not later than December 31, 1988;

AND WHEREAS first ministers have also reached unanimous agreement on certain additional commitments in relation to some of those amendments;

NOW THEREFORE the Prime Minister of Canada and the first ministers of the provinces commit themselves and the governments they represent to the following:

1. The Prime Minister of Canada will lay or cause to be laid before the Senate and House of Commons,

and the first ministers of the provinces will lay or cause to be laid before their legislative assemblies, as soon as possible, a resolution, in the form appended hereto, to authorize a proclamation to be issued by the Governor General under the Great Seal of Canada to amend the Constitution of Canada.

2. The Government of Canada will, as soon as possible, conclude an agreement with the Government of Quebec that would
   (a) incorporate the principles of the Cullen-Couture agreement on the selection abroad and in Canada of independent immigrants, visitors for medical treatment, students and temporary workers, and on the selection of refugees abroad and economic criteria for family reunification and assisted relatives,
   (b) guarantee that Quebec will receive a number of immigrants, including refugees, within the annual total established by the federal government for all of Canada proportionate to its share of the population of Canada, with the right to exceed that figure by five per cent for demographic reasons, and
   (c) provide an undertaking by Canada to withdraw services (except citizenship services) for the reception and integration (including linguistic and cultural) of all foreign nationals wishing to settle in Quebec where services are to be provided by Quebec, with such withdrawal to be accompanied by reasonable compensation,

and the Government of Canada and the Government of Quebec will take the necessary steps to give the agreement the force of law under the proposed amendment relating to such agreements.

3. Nothing in this Accord should be construed as preventing the negotiation of similar agreements with other provinces relating to immigration and the temporary admission of aliens.

4. Until the proposed amendment relating to appointments to the Senate comes into force, any person summoned to fill a vacancy in the Senate shall be chosen from among persons whose names have been submitted by the government of the province to which the vacancy relates and must be acceptable to the Queen's Privy Council for Canada.

MOTION FOR A RESOLUTION TO AUTHORIZE AN AMENDMENT TO THE CONSTITUTION OF CANADA

WHEREAS the *Constitution Act, 1982* came into force on April 17, 1982, following an agreement between Canada and all the provinces except Quebec; AND WHEREAS the Government of Quebec has established a set of five proposals for constitutional change and has stated that amendments to give effect to those proposals would enable Quebec to resume a full role in the constitutional councils of Canada;

AND WHEREAS the amendment proposed in the schedule hereto sets out the basis on which Quebec's five constitutional proposals may be met;

AND WHEREAS the amendment proposed in the schedule hereto also recognizes the principle of the equality of all the provinces, provides new arrangements to foster greater harmony and cooperation between the Government of Canada and the governments of the provinces and requires that conferences be convened to consider important constitutional, economic and other issues;

AND WHEREAS certain portions of the amendment proposed in the schedule hereto relate to matters referred to in section 4l of the *Constitution Act, l982*;

AND WHEREAS section 4l of the *Constitution Act, l982* provides that an amendment to the Constitution of Canada may be made by proclamation issued by the Governor General under the Great Seal of Canada where so authorized by resolutions of the Senate and the House of Commons and of the legislative assembly of each province;

NOW THEREFORE the (Senate) (House of Commons) (legislative assembly) resolves that an amendment to the Constitution of Canada be authorized to be made by proclamation issued by Her Excellency the Governor General under the Great Seal of Canada in accordance with the schedule hereto.

SCHEDULE
CONSTITUTION AMENDMENT, 1987

CONSTITUTION ACT, 1867

1. The Constitution Act, 1867 is amended by adding thereto, immediately after section 1 thereof, the following section:

Interpretation

"2. (1) The Constitution of Canada shall be interpreted in a manner consistent with

(a) the recognition that the existence of French-speaking Canadians, centered in Quebec but also present elsewhere in Canada, and English-speaking Canadians, concentrated outside Quebec but also present in Quebec, constitutes a fundamental characteristic of Canada; and

(b) the recognition that Quebec constitutes within Canada a distinct society.

Role of Parliament and legislatures

(2) The role of the Parliament of Canada and the provincial legislatures to preserve the fundamental characteristics of Canada referred to in paragraph (1)(a) is affirmed.

Role of legislature and Government of Quebec

(3) The role of the legislature and Government of Quebec to preserve and promote the distinct identity of Quebec referred to in paragraph (1)(b) is affirmed.

Rights of legislatures and governments preserved

(4) Nothing in this section derogates from the powers, rights or privileges of Parlia-

ment or the Government of Canada, or of the legislatures or governments of the provinces, including any powers, rights or privileges relating to language."

2. The said Act is further amended by adding thereto, immediately after section 24 thereof, the following section:

Names to be submitted

"**25.** (1) Where a vacancy occurs in the Senate, the government of the province to which the vacancy relates may, in relation to that vacancy, submit to the Queen's Privy Council for Canada the names of persons who may be summoned to the Senate.

Choice of Senators from names submitted

(2) Until an amendment to the Constitution of Canada is made in relation to the Senate pursuant to section 41 of the Constitution Act, 1982, the person summoned to fill a vacancy in the Senate shall be chosen from among persons whose names have been submitted under subsection (1) by the government of the province to which the vacancy relates and must be acceptable to the Queen's Privy Council for Canada."

3. The said Act is further amended by adding thereto, immediately after section 95 thereof, the following heading and sections:

"Agreements on Immigration and Aliens

Commitment to negotiate

95A. The Government of Canada shall, at the request of the government of any province, negotiate with the government of that province for the purpose of concluding an agreement relating to immigration or the temporary admission of aliens into that province that is appropriate to the needs and circumstances of that province.

Agreements

95B. (l) Any agreement concluded between Canada and a province in relation to immigration or the temporary admission of aliens into that province has the force of law from the time it is declared to do so in accordance with subsection 95C(l) and shall from that time have effect notwithstanding class 25 of section 9l or section 95.

Limitation

(2) An agreement that has the force of law under subsection (l) shall have effect only so long and so far as it is not repugnant to any provision of an Act of the Parliament of Canada that sets national standards and objectives relating to immigration or aliens, including any provision that establishes general classes of immigrants or relates to levels of immigration for Canada or that prescribes classes of individuals who are inadmissible into Canada.

Application of Charter

(3) The Canadian Charter of Rights and Freedoms applies in respect to any agree-

ment that has the force of law under subsection (1) and in respect of anything done by the Parliament or Government of Canada, or the legislature or government of a province, pursuant to any such agreement.

Proclamation relating to agreements

95C. (1) A declaration that an agreement referred to in subsection 95B(1) has the force of law may be made by proclamation issued by the Governor General under the Great Seal of Canada only where so authorized by resolutions of the Senate and House of Commons and of the legislative assembly of the province that is a party to the agreement.

Amendment of agreements

(2) An amendment to an agreement referred to in subsection 95B(l) may be made by proclamation issued by the Governor General under the Great Seal of Canada only where so authorized

(a) by resolutions of the Senate and House of Commons and of the legislative assembly of the province that is a party to the agreement; or

(b) in such other manner as is set out in the agreement.

Application of sections 46 to 48 of Constitution Act, 1982

95D. Sections 46 to 48 of the Constitution Act, 1982 apply, with such modifications as the circumstances require, in respect of any declaration made pursuant to subsection 95C(1), any amendment to an agreement made pursuant to subsection 95C(2) or any amendment made pursuant to section 95E.

Amendments to sections 95A to the 95D or this section

95E. An amendment to sections 95A to 95D or this section may be made in accordance with the procedure set out in subsection 38(1) of the Constitution Act, 1982, but only if the amendment is authorized by resolutions of the legislative assemblies of all the provinces that are, at the time of the amendment, parties to an agreement that has the force of law under subsection 95B (1)."

4. The said Act is further amended by adding thereto, immediately preceding section 96 thereof, the following heading:

General

5. The said Act is further amended by adding thereto, immediately preceding section 101 thereof, the following heading:

"Courts Established by the Parliament of Canada"

6. The said Act is further amended by adding thereto, immediately after section 101 thereof, the following heading and sections:

"Supreme Court of Canada"

Supreme Court continued

101A (1) The court existing under the name of the Supreme Court of Canada is hereby continued as the general court of appeal for

Canada, and as an additional court for the better administration of the laws of Canada, and shall continue to be a superior court of record.

Constitution of
Court

(2) The Supreme Court of Canada shall consist of a chief justice to be called the Chief Justice of Canada and eight other judges, who shall be appointed by the Governor General in Council by letters patent under the Great Seal.

Who may be appointed judges

101B. (1) Any person may be appointed a judge of the Supreme Court of Canada who, after having been admitted to the bar of any province or territory, has, for a total of at least ten years, been a judge of any court in Canada or a member of the bar of any province or territory.

Three judges
from Quebec

(2) At least three judges of the Supreme Court of Canada shall be appointed from among persons who, after having been admitted to the bar of Quebec, have, for a total of at least ten years, been judges of any court of Quebec or of any court established by the Parliament of Canada, or members of the bar of Quebec.

Names may be submitted

101C. (1) Where a vacancy occurs in the Supreme Court of Canada, the government of each province may, in relation to that vacancy, submit to the Minister of Justice of Canada the names of any of the persons who have been admitted to the bar of that province and are qualified under section 101B for appointment to that court.

Appointment from names submitted

(2) Where an appointment is made to the Supreme Court of Canada, the Governor General in Council shall, except where the Chief Justice is appointed from among members of the Court, appoint a person whose name has been submitted under subsection (1) and who is acceptable to the Queen's Privy Council for Canada.

Appointment from Quebec

(3) Where an appointment is made in accordance with subsection (2) of any of the three judges necessary to meet the requirement set out in subsection 101B(2), the Governor General in Council shall appoint a person whose name has been submitted by the Government of Quebec.

Appointment from other provinces

(4) Where an appointment is made in accordance with subsection (2) otherwise than as required under subsection (3), the Governor General in Council shall appoint a person whose name has been submitted by the government of a province other than Quebec.

Tenure, salaries, etc., of judges

101D. Sections 99 and 100 apply in respect of the judges of the Supreme Court of Canada.

Relationship to section 101

101E. (1) Sections 101A to 101D shall not be construed as abrogating or derogating from the powers of the Parliament of Canada to make laws under section 101 except to the extent that such laws are inconsistent with those sections.

Reference to the
Supreme Court of
Canada

(2) For greater certainty, section 101A shall not be construed as abrogating or derogating from the powers of the Parliament of Canada to make laws relating to the reference of questions of law or fact, or any other matters, to the Supreme Court of Canada.

7. The said Act is further amended by adding thereto, immediately after section 106 thereof, the following section:

Shared-cost pro-
gram

"**106**A. (1) The Government of Canada shall provide reasonable compensation to the government of a province that chooses not to participate in a national shared-cost program that is established by the Government of Canada after the coming into force of this section in an area of exclusive provincial jurisdiction, if the province carries on a program or initiative that is compatible with the national objectives.

Legislative power
not extended

(2) Nothing in this section extends the legislative powers of the Parliament of Canada or of the legislatures of the provinces."

8. The said Act is further amended by adding thereto the following heading and sections:

"XII— Conferences on The Economy and Other Matters

Conferences on the economy and other matters

148. A conference composed of the Prime Minister of Canada and the first ministers of the provinces shall be convened by the Prime Minister of Canada at least once each year to discuss the state of the Canadian economy and such other matters as may be appropriate.

XIII—References

Reference includes amendments

149. A reference to this Act shall be deemed to include a reference to any amendments thereto."

CONSTITUTION ACT, 1982

9. Sections 40 to 42 of the Constitution Act, 1982 are repealed and the following substituted therefor:

Compensation

40. Where an amendment is made under subsection 38(1) that transfers legislative powers from provincial legislatures to Parliament, Canada shall provide reasonable compensation to any province to which the amendment does not apply.

Amendment by u-nanimous consent

41. An amendment to the Constitution of Canada in relation to the following matters may be made by proclamation issued by the Governor General under the Great Seal of Canada only where authorized by resolutions of the Senate and House of Commons and of the legislative assembly of each province.

(a) the office of the Queen, the Governor General and the Lieutenant Governor of a province;

(b) the powers of the Senate and the method of selecting Senators;

(c) the number of members by which a province is entitled to be represented in the Senate and the residence qualifications of Senators;

(d) the right of a province to a number of members in the House of Commons not less than the number of Senators by which the province was entitled to be represented on April 17, 1982;

(e) the principle of proportionate representation of the provinces in the House of Commons prescribed by the Constitution of Canada;

(f) subject to section 43, the use of the English or the French language;

(g) the Supreme Court of Canada;

(h) the extension of existing provinces into the territories;

(i) notwithstanding any other law or practice, the establishment of new provinces; and

(j) an amendment to this Part.

10. Section 44 of the said Act is repealed and the following substituted therefor;

Amendments by Parliament

"**44.** Subject to section 41, Parliament may exclusively make laws amending the Constitution of Canada in relation to the executive government of Canada or the Senate and House of Commons."

11. Subsection 46(1) of the said Act is repealed and the following substituted therefor:

Initiation of amendment procedures

"**46.** (1) The procedures for amendment under sections 38, 41 and 43 may be initiated either by the Senate or the House of Commons or by the legislative assembly of a province."

12. Subsection 47(1) of the said Act is repealed and the following substituted therefor:

Amendments without Senate resolution

47. (1) An amendment to the Constitution of Canada made by proclamation under section 38, 41 or 43 may be made without a resolution of the Senate authorizing the issue of the proclamation if, within one hundred and eighty days after the adoption by the House of Commons of a resolution authorizing its issue, the Senate has not adopted such a resolution and if, at any time after the expiration of that period, the House of Commons again adopts the resolution.

13. Part VI of the said Act is repealed and the following substituted therefor:

"PART VI
Constitutional Conferences

Constitutional conference

50. (1) A constitutional conference composed of the Prime Minister of Canada and the first ministers of the provinces shall be convened by the Prime Minister of Canada at least once each year, commencing in 1988.

Agenda

(2) The conferences convened under subsection (1) shall have included on their agenda the following matters:

(a) Senate reform, including the role and functions of the Senate, its powers, the method of selecting Senators and representation in the Senate;

(b) roles and responsibilities in relation to fisheries; and

(c) such other matters as are agreed upon."

14. Subsection 52(2) of the said Act is amended by striking out the word "and" at the end of paragraph (b) thereof, by adding

the word "and" at the end of paragraph (c) thereof and by adding thereto the following paragraph:

"(d) any other amendment to the Constitution of Canada."

15. Section 61 of the said Act is repealed and the following substituted therefor:

References

"**61.** A reference to the Constitution Act, 1982, or a reference to the Constitution Acts 1867 to 1982, shall be deemed to include a reference to any amendments thereto.

General

Multicultural heritage and aboriginal peoples

16. Nothing in section 2 of the Constitution Act, 1867 affects section 25 to 27 of the Canadian Charter of Rights and Freedoms, section 35 of the Constitution Act, 1982 or class 24 of section 91 of the Constitution Act, 1982.

CITATION

Citation

17. This amendment may be cited as the Constitution Amendment, 1987.

Notes on Sources

Chapter 1

The Trudeau quote comes from a letter to Premier Blakeney, September 13, 1978, in *Proposals on the Constitution, 1971-1978* (Canadian Intergovernmental Conference Secretariat, 1978), p. 26.

Chapter 2

Quotes from the Kirby memorandum are from "Report to Cabinet on Constitutional Discussions, Summer, 1980, and the Outlook for the First Ministers Conference and Beyond," August 30, 1980, pp. 32, 59, 33, 60. Quotations from the first ministers are drawn from transcripts of the proceedings of the First Ministers' Conference, September 1980 (Canadian Intergovernmental Conference Secretariat, September 1980).

Chapter 3

Quotes from the Kirby memorandum are from "Report to Cabinet," pp. 39, 40, 46, 49-50, 51. The Trudeau quote is from the "Statement of the Prime Minister," Office of the Prime Minister, October 2, 1980, p. 2. The

evidence of the debate over unilateral action and the
quote thereon are from Paul Gérin-Lajoie, *Constitutional Amendment in Canada* (Toronto: University of
Toronto Press, 1950), p. 254. Joe Clark's remarks are
taken from the "Statement by Rt. Hon. Joe Clark on the
Proposed Resolution Respecting the Constitution of
Canada," P.C. News Release, October 2, 1980, pp. 1-2.
Those by Premier Davis are from "News Release, Statement on the Constitution in the Legislature, " October
6, 1980. The quotations from the Kershaw report are
from Great Britain, House of Commons, First Report
from the Foreign Affairs Committee, 1980-1981 Session, *British North America Acts: The Role of Parliament*, p. xii. Justice Minister Chrétien is cited from
Canada, House of Commons, Debates, February 17,
1981, p. 7373.

Chapter 4

All quotations in this chapter are taken directly from the
factums of the respective attorneys general or the September 28, 1981, judgement of the Supreme Court on
the Reference regarding the Amendment of the Constitution of Canada.

Chapter 5

Quotations from first ministers are taken either from
transcripts of press conferences, from direct interviews,
or as reported by the *Globe and Mail* on the dates
indicated. Those taken at the conference are from the
"Transcript of the Federal-Provincial Conference of
First Ministers," November 2 and 5, 1981 (Canadian
Intergovernmental Conference Secretariat). The post-
conference rhetoric is as quoted in the *Globe and Mail*,
November 16, 1981.

Chapter 6

The story of the conferences on aboriginal rights can be followed in David Hawkes, "Negotiating Aboriginal Self-Government," in Peter Leslie, ed., *Canada: The State of the Federation, 1985* (Kingston: Queen's University, 1985), pp.151-72, and more fully in Bryan Schwartz, *First Principles, Second Thoughts* (Montreal: Institute for Research on Public Policy, 1986). Premier Pawley's statement appears in the *Winnipeg Free Press,* May 1. The extensive quotations of Pierre Elliott Trudeau are taken directly from the proceedings of the Joint Senate-House of Commons Committee, August 27, 1987, 14:132-33, 144. The remarks of Gil Rémillard appear in the *Montreal Gazette,* June 8 and 16. The entry from Bryan Schwartz is from *Fathoming Meech Lake* (Winnipeg: Legal Research Institute of the University of Manitoba, 1987), p. 4. Frances Russell's piece appears in the *Winnipeg Free Press,* April 20, 1988. Premier McKenna is quoted in the *Winnipeg Free Press* on April 26, and Senator Lowell Murray in the *Montreal Gazette* on April 2.

Chapter 7

The argument concerning the entrenchment of these two competing models of French Canadian nationalism was first broadly sketched in my earlier essay "The French, the English and the 1980 Constitutional Agreements," *Bridges* magazine, vol. 5, no. 4 (May/June 1988), pp. 5-7. A more extended analysis of my views of Meech Lake in substance and process can be found in "Much Ado about Meech," in Peter M. Leslie and Ronald Watts, eds., *The State of the Federation: 1987-88* (Kingston: Institute of Intergovernmental Relations,

Queen's University, 1988), pp. 97-115. All citations in this chapter are drawn directly from public documents and the sources are indicated in the text.